WOODSMITH CUSTOM WOODWORKING

Home Entertainment

D1530478

WOODSMITH CUSTOM WOODWORKING

Home Entertainment

By the editors of Woodsmith magazine

CONTENTS

WOODSMITH CUSTOM WOODWORKING

Home Entertainment

Lap Desk

Magazine Rack

TV & CD CABINETS 78

Roll-Around TV Stand

FUN & GAMES

Many of us go home after a hard day at work with a single goal in mind — to relax. So it's always great when a little quality time spent in the workshop helps to achieve this goal.

The chess board is easy to build thanks to an interesting technique we used to make the checkerboard top. And what better way is there to relax than with a game of chess? But, if card-playing is more your style, the playing card holder has great-looking finger joints, and the carving design in the top offers a unique challenge.

And for the kids — help stimulate their creativity by building a lap desk with storage for a large roll of drawing paper. Finally, the toy chest features a storage compartment on one end with a sliding top and a couple of drawers for games at the other end.

Playing Card Holder

Stacked like the cards in a deck, the finger joints at each corner of this project are both attractive and strong. To really get this box "decked out," you can add the carved accents to the lid .

Held together by a rubber band, my decks of playing cards just filled some space in my "junk" drawer when they weren't being used. The edges and corners were getting ragged from being jostled by everything else in the drawer.

So when I bought some new cards, I decided to build a holder that would keep them in good shape and also look nice enough to leave out on display.

JOINERY. Part of the visual appeal of this project is the joinery. Call them finger joints or box joints, but either way, this card holder uses them to their best advantage. By reducing the scale of the joint so

the pins (or fingers) are the width of a single blade cut, the joint adds a decorative touch to the corners of the box, yet still remains quite strong.

PRECISE FIT. In addition to making these small box (or finger) joints, the challenge on this card holder is to build a box within a box (actually a tray within a lid) to within very small tolerances.

And since the fit between the two parts should be close, that's where box joints offer another advantage. With this joint, there's not a lot of math needed to figure out the lengths of the workpieces. The pieces are simply cut to length to match the outside dimensions of the lid or tray.

CARD SIZE. That leads me to one other item you should note. The case, as shown here, is built to hold standard-size playing cards. If you plan on using the holder for bridge cards (or some other size of cards), the lengths of the pieces may have to be changed.

CARVED ACCENTS. I decided to add a carving to the lid of my box to give it another visual highlight. Nothing fancy. Just a design to dress up the box a bit. I settled on the four suits in a deck. (A full-size pattern is included on page 11.) Of course, you can easily substitute another pattern of your choosing, or leave this detail off altogether.

EXPLODED VIEW

OVERALL DIMENSIONS:
$6\frac{3}{8}$W x $4\frac{9}{16}$D x $1\frac{7}{8}$H

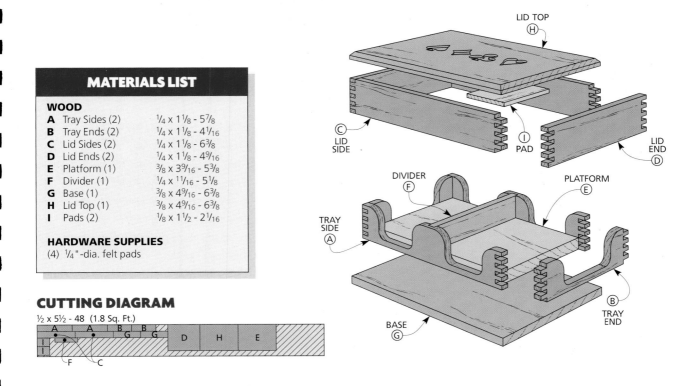

MATERIALS LIST

WOOD

A	Tray Sides (2)	$\frac{1}{4}$ x $1\frac{1}{8}$ - $5\frac{7}{8}$
B	Tray Ends (2)	$\frac{1}{4}$ x $1\frac{1}{8}$ - $4\frac{1}{16}$
C	Lid Sides (2)	$\frac{1}{4}$ x $1\frac{1}{8}$ - $6\frac{3}{8}$
D	Lid Ends (2)	$\frac{1}{4}$ x $1\frac{1}{8}$ - $4\frac{9}{16}$
E	Platform (1)	$\frac{3}{8}$ x $3\frac{9}{16}$ - $5\frac{3}{8}$
F	Divider (1)	$\frac{1}{4}$ x $1\frac{1}{16}$ - $5\frac{1}{8}$
G	Base (1)	$\frac{3}{8}$ x $4\frac{9}{16}$ - $6\frac{3}{8}$
H	Lid Top (1)	$\frac{3}{8}$ x $4\frac{9}{16}$ - $6\frac{3}{8}$
I	Pads (2)	$\frac{1}{8}$ x $1\frac{1}{2}$ - $2\frac{1}{16}$

HARDWARE SUPPLIES

(4) $\frac{1}{4}$"-dia. felt pads

CUTTING DIAGRAM

$\frac{1}{2}$ x $5\frac{1}{2}$ - 48 (1.8 Sq. Ft.)

TRAY & LID

To build the card holder, begin by planing two pieces of stock $\frac{1}{4}$" thick. These strips should be $1\frac{1}{2}$" wide by 35" long, which will yield enough stock for the four sides of the tray, the tray divider, and the four sides of the lid.

Note: All the dimensions given here are based on stock that's exactly $\frac{1}{4}$" thick.

After planing the stock, I started work on the four pieces for the tray. The first pieces to cut to length are the two tray sides (A) and the ends (B) *(Fig. 1)*.

LID PARTS. After the pieces for the tray have been cut to size, they're used to determine the lengths of the lid sides (C) and the lid ends (D).

That is, the length of the lid side (C) is equal to the length of the tray side plus the thickness of the two lid ends. Likewise, the length of the lid end (D) is equal to the length of the tray end plus the thickness of the two lid sides.

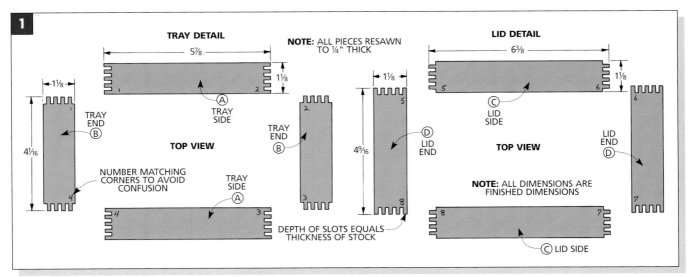

FINGER JOINTS

Once the pieces for the tray and lid are cut to size, the finger joints can be cut. I used my box joint jig to do this.

Normally, when cutting finger joints, I would set up the jig and adjust the depth of cut so it's a little deeper than the thickness of the stock ($\frac{1}{4}$" in this case). But on this card holder, the pieces are so small, I decided to cut the joints for an exact fit.

JOINTS FOR TRAY. When the jig is set up, start the joints on the tray sides so there's a finger on the top edge *(Fig. 2)*. Then cut the joints on the tray ends, so there's a slot on the top edge.

LID FRAME JOINTS. The joints on the lid pieces are the reverse of the joints on the tray. That is, start with a slot on the top edge of the lid sides, and with a finger on the top edge of the lid ends *(Fig. 3)*.

CUT TO WIDTH. Now these pieces can be trimmed to final width. But rather than measuring this cut, just trim the bottom edge off the tray sides to leave five full fingers (and four slots between them) *(Fig. 2)*. Then trim the tray ends to leave five full slots (with four fingers).

DIVIDER DADO & CUTOUTS

Before assembling the frames, a dado must be cut on the inside face of each tray side. This is for a divider that's added later. To make these cuts, attach a fence to the miter gauge to give full support to these small pieces *(Fig. 4)*.

Then set the rip fence as a stop so the saw blade cuts a dado just slightly off the center line of the tray side. Adjust the depth of cut to $\frac{1}{8}$" and make a pass. Without changing the rip fence setting, turn the piece end for end and make another pass *(Fig. 5)*.

This procedure automatically centers the dado on the length of the piece. If the dado isn't quite wide enough, tap the rip fence away from the blade and make two more passes until the dado fits the thickness of the divider.

CURVED CUTOUTS. Once the dadoes are cut, the curved cutouts can be marked on all four pieces of the tray. Locate the center points of the holes *(Fig. 6)*, and drill them with a Forstner bit.

CUT OUT RADIUS. After the holes are drilled, lay out the radius on the top edge of each corner using a nickel as a pattern *(Fig. 6)*. Then cut the pieces to shape on a band saw, and sand the edges smooth with a small drum sander.

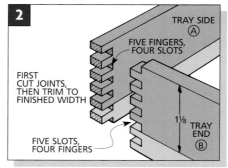

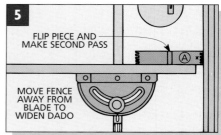

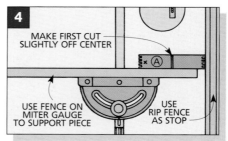

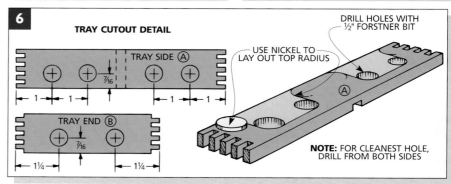

TRAY & LID FRAMES

Now that the box joints, dadoes, and cutouts have been added, the tray frame can be assembled. Just apply some glue with a small artist's brush, and push the joints tightly together by hand. (You won't need to clamp them.) Make sure the joints are square, and let this assembly dry.

PLATFORM. To complete the tray, make a platform (E) to raise the deck of cards above the bottom of the cutouts, so even the last card is easy to pick up.

Cut the platform from $\frac{3}{8}$"-thick stock to fit inside the tray frame tightly *(Fig. 7)*. Take note of where the actual gluing surfaces are and use the glue sparingly to secure the platform inside the frame.

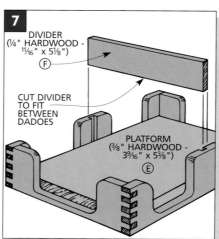

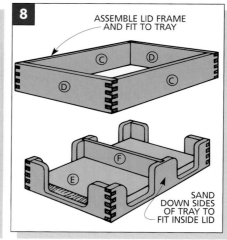

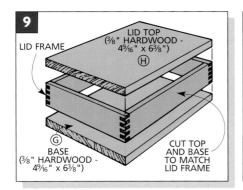

9

LID FRAME

LID TOP
(³⁄₈" HARDWOOD -
4⁹⁄₁₆" x 6³⁄₈")
(H)

(G)

BASE
(³⁄₈" HARDWOOD -
4⁹⁄₁₆" x 6³⁄₈")

CUT TOP
AND BASE
TO MATCH
LID FRAME

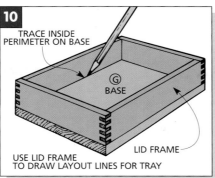

10

TRACE INSIDE
PERIMETER ON BASE

(G)
BASE

LID FRAME

USE LID FRAME
TO DRAW LAYOUT LINES FOR TRAY

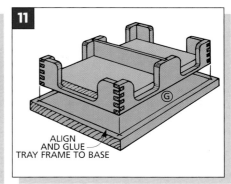

11

(G)

ALIGN
AND GLUE
TRAY FRAME TO BASE

DIVIDER. Now to complete the tray, cut the divider (F) to width so the top edge is flush with the top edge of the tray *(Figs. 7 and 8)*. Then glue it in place.

ASSEMBLE LID FRAME. Next, the lid frame can be assembled to fit over the tray *(Fig. 8)*. First, dry-assemble the sides and ends of the lid and test the fit.

It will probably be a smidgen too tight. That's okay. Go ahead and glue up the lid and then sand down the sides of the tray until the lid fits easily over the tray.

ADD BASE. After the lid and tray are sanded to a good fit, the base (G) can be added to the bottom of the tray. Since this piece is exactly the same size as the lid top (H) for the lid frame, I cut both pieces at the same time.

CUT TO SIZE. First, resaw and plane enough stock ³⁄₈" thick for both pieces. Then use the lid frame as a guide to cut both pieces to final size *(Fig. 9)*.

Next, the base is mounted to the tray so there's an even overhang on all four edges (refer to *Fig. 11*). To align the tray, use the lid frame as a guide. Place the lid frame over the base and mark the inside circumference *(Fig. 10)*.

ASSEMBLY. Now the tray is glued to the base *(Fig. 11)*. This is an awkward clamping job at best. The easiest way to even out the pressure of the C-clamps was to make a "sandwich" by placing a board on the top edges of the tray.

LID

At this point the tray is complete. Now the lid frame can be completed by mounting the lid top (H). But before gluing it on, I thought I'd try my hand at a little carving by adding the symbols for the four suits on the lid top. Refer to *Fig. 14* for a full-size pattern of the carving I made.

HOLD-DOWN PADS. After the top was carved, I cut two ¹⁄₈"-thick hold-down pads (I) and glued them to the underside of the top so they're centered over

each tray *(Fig. 12)*. (As the decks are used, they tend to "puff up." These pads help keep the cards in the trays and prevent them from sliding over the divider.)

GLUE TOP TO LID. Finally, the lid top can be glued to the lid frame. After the glue has set up, it may be necessary to do some additional sanding for a better fit. Now place the lid over the tray and sand the outside perimeter of the box until the surfaces of the top, the lid frame, and the base are flush with each other.

ROUT CHAMFERS. After sanding the two frames, I used the router table to rout a ¹⁄₈" chamfer all the way around the top outside edge of the lid *(Step 1 in Fig. 13a)*. Then there's one more thing to do. To make the lid slide over the tray a little easier, rout a chamfer on the bottom inside edge of the lid *(Step 2)*. Since the router bit won't quite fit into the corners, I had to clean them up with a chisel.

FINISHING STEPS

Only a couple of items remain to complete the card holder. The first is to sand all the surfaces smooth and apply a finish. (I used three coats of tung oil.)

Then, after the finish had dried completely, I mounted self-adhesive felt pads to the bottom of the tray. Locate the pads ³⁄₄" from each corner of the base. ∎

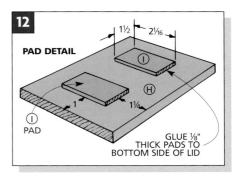

12

PAD DETAIL

1½
2¹⁄₁₆

(I)

(H)

1

1¼

(I)
PAD

GLUE ¹⁄₈"
THICK PADS TO
BOTTOM SIDE OF LID

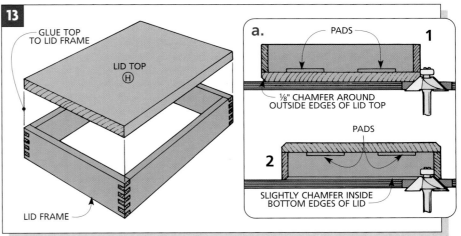

13

GLUE TOP
TO LID FRAME

LID TOP
(H)

LID FRAME

a.

PADS

1

¹⁄₈" CHAMFER AROUND
OUTSIDE EDGES OF LID TOP

PADS

2

SLIGHTLY CHAMFER INSIDE
BOTTOM EDGES OF LID

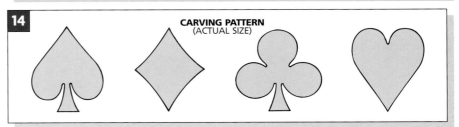

14

CARVING PATTERN
(ACTUAL SIZE)

Lap Desk

This project has everything a budding artist needs. A special compartment holds a roll of paper, there's plenty of storage for markers and crayons, and it's easily carried to wherever inspiration may strike.

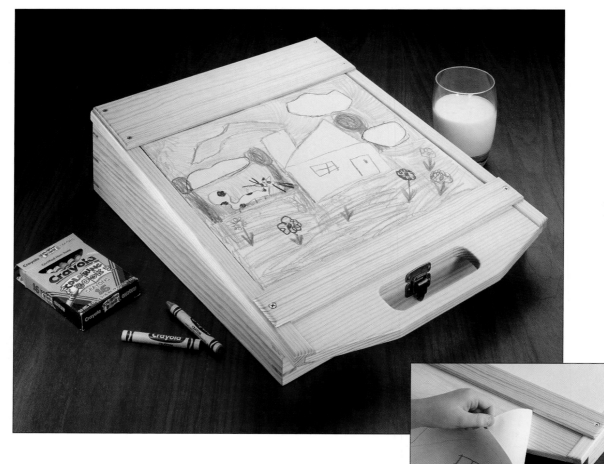

With laptop computers every-where you look, who needs a lap desk? Well, kids for one. At least that's what a friend with two young daughters tells me. He says his girls go through crayons and paper faster than I go through sandpaper and glue. And this desk is sized just right for them.

After talking over some ideas, I started sketching designs. That's when I realized that a lap desk is handy to have in the shop too. There's never enough bench space to sketch up an idea for a jig or write a materials list. (And if there is space on the bench, it usually has a layer or two of dust anyway.)

MATERIALS. I wanted to keep the desk inexpensive and simple. So it's built with pine, ¼" plywood, and a small piece of plastic laminate.

SPLINED MITERS. The corners of the case are joined with miters. And I added splines across the joint. These do more than add strength — they also add a decorative touch. And when it comes to making the slots for the splines, you can be creative. For some ideas, check out the Designer's Notebook on page 17 and the Technique article on page 20.

While I was working out the design, my friend suggested an intriguing feature: a compartment that would hold a roll

of paper. The paper would feed out the back and be held down by a couple of guides. This way, you never have to worry about running out of paper. And you don't have to hold the paper in place when drawing. Plus, there's still plenty of room inside for pencils, triangles, and a compass — or crayons and coloring books.

EXPLODED VIEW

OVERALL DIMENSIONS:
13⅝"W x 17¾"D x 4³⁄₁₆"H

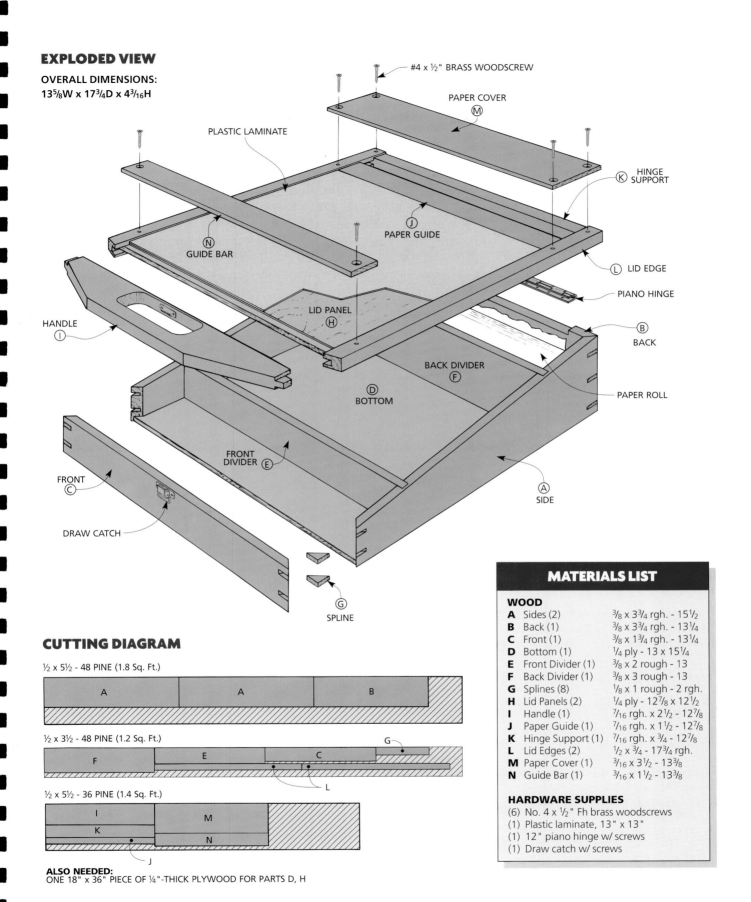

#4 x ½" BRASS WOODSCREW

PAPER COVER ⓂM

PLASTIC LAMINATE

HINGE SUPPORT Ⓚ

ⓃN GUIDE BAR

Ⓙ PAPER GUIDE

Ⓛ LID EDGE

PIANO HINGE

HANDLE ⒾI

LID PANEL Ⓗ

ⒷB BACK

BACK DIVIDER Ⓕ

Ⓓ BOTTOM

PAPER ROLL

FRONT DIVIDER ⒺE

FRONT ⒸC

ⒶA SIDE

DRAW CATCH

ⒼG SPLINE

CUTTING DIAGRAM

½ x 5½ - 48 PINE (1.8 Sq. Ft.)

| A | A | B |

½ x 3½ - 48 PINE (1.2 Sq. Ft.)

G

| F | E | C | |

L

½ x 5½ - 36 PINE (1.4 Sq. Ft.)

| I | M |
| K | N |

J

ALSO NEEDED:
ONE 18" x 36" PIECE OF ¼"-THICK PLYWOOD FOR PARTS D, H

MATERIALS LIST

WOOD
A	Sides (2)	⅜ x 3¾ rgh. - 15½
B	Back (1)	⅜ x 3¾ rgh. - 13¼
C	Front (1)	⅜ x 1¾ rgh. - 13¼
D	Bottom (1)	¼ ply - 13 x 15¼
E	Front Divider (1)	⅜ x 2 rough - 13
F	Back Divider (1)	⅜ x 3 rough - 13
G	Splines (8)	⅛ x 1 rough - 2 rgh.
H	Lid Panels (2)	¼ ply - 12⅞ x 12½
I	Handle (1)	⁷⁄₁₆ rgh. x 2½ - 12⅞
J	Paper Guide (1)	⁷⁄₁₆ rgh. x 1½ - 12⅞
K	Hinge Support (1)	⁷⁄₁₆ rgh. x ¾ - 12⅞
L	Lid Edges (2)	½ x ¾ - 17¾ rgh.
M	Paper Cover (1)	³⁄₁₆ x 3½ - 13⅜
N	Guide Bar (1)	³⁄₁₆ x 1½ - 13⅜

HARDWARE SUPPLIES
(6) No. 4 x ½" Fh brass woodscrews
(1) Plastic laminate, 13" x 13"
(1) 12" piano hinge w/ screws
(1) Draw catch w/ screws

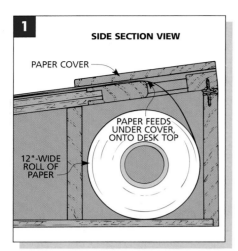

1

SIDE SECTION VIEW

PAPER COVER

PAPER FEEDS UNDER COVER, ONTO DESK TOP

12"-WIDE ROLL OF PAPER

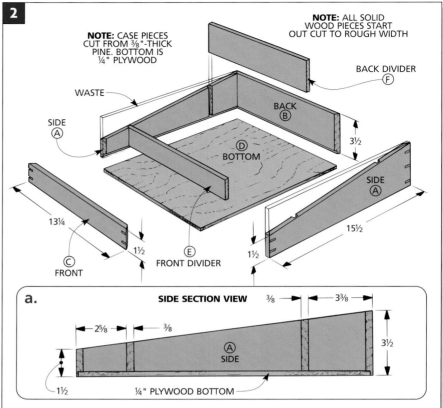

2

NOTE: CASE PIECES CUT FROM ³⁄₈"-THICK PINE. BOTTOM IS ¼" PLYWOOD

NOTE: ALL SOLID WOOD PIECES START OUT CUT TO ROUGH WIDTH

WASTE

BACK DIVIDER Ⓕ

SIDE Ⓐ

BACK Ⓑ

3½

Ⓓ BOTTOM

SIDE Ⓐ

13¼

1½

15½

Ⓒ FRONT

Ⓔ FRONT DIVIDER

1½

a. SIDE SECTION VIEW

³⁄₈   3³⁄₈

2⁵⁄₈   ³⁄₈

Ⓐ SIDE

3½

1½   ¼" PLYWOOD BOTTOM

CASE

When designing the Lap Desk, about the only criteria I had to work around was the size of the paper. (12"-wide rolls of paper are commonly available at art supply stores.) The 12" roll was about 2³⁄₄" in diameter. So the inside of the case needed to be 12¹⁄₄" wide and 3" deep at the back where the roll is stored *(Fig. 1)*.

Other than size, the only other thing to keep in mind was weight. I didn't want the case to get too heavy, so I planed some stock down to ³⁄₈" thick for the case pieces and the dividers inside.

CUT TO SIZE. Because the case slopes from front to back, it's easier if the sides (A), back (B), and front (C) all start out ripped to rough width. (I ripped the front 1³⁄₄" wide and the sides and back 3³⁄₄" wide.) Then the four pieces are mitered to final length *(Fig. 2)*.

CUT DADOES. The inside of the desk is divided into three compartments. The rear compartment holds the roll of paper. The other two are for drawing supplies.

To hold the dividers that are added later, two ³⁄₈"-wide dadoes are cut in each side piece *(Figs. 3 and 3a)*. I wanted to make sure the dadoes aligned between both pieces, so I attached a stop block to an auxiliary miter gauge fence. And don't worry too much about any chipout. It will be cleaned up when a rabbet is cut along the bottom edge in the next step or when the pieces are tapered later.

CUT RABBET. For the bottom of the case, I used a piece of ¼"-thick plywood *(Fig. 2a)*. It fits into a rabbet cut on the bottom of each case piece. So I attached an auxiliary fence to my rip fence and buried the dado blade in it, leaving ¼" exposed *(Fig. 4a)*. Then I cut a ¼" x ¼" rabbet on each piece *(Fig. 4)*.

3

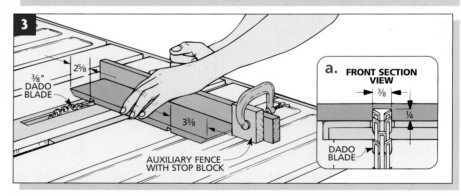

2⁵⁄₈

³⁄₈" DADO BLADE

3³⁄₈

AUXILIARY FENCE WITH STOP BLOCK

a. FRONT SECTION VIEW

³⁄₈

¼

DADO BLADE

4

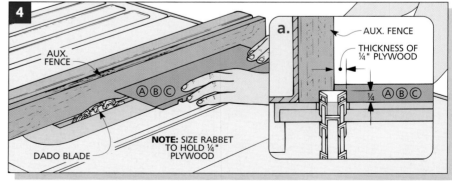

AUX. FENCE

Ⓐ Ⓑ Ⓒ

DADO BLADE

NOTE: SIZE RABBET TO HOLD ¼" PLYWOOD

a.

AUX. FENCE

THICKNESS OF ¼" PLYWOOD

¼   Ⓐ Ⓑ Ⓒ

TAPER PIECES. The next step is to taper the sides of the case. To do this, start by drawing the taper on one of the pieces *(Fig. 2a)*. Then to make sure the sides end up identical, you can fasten them together with carpet tape. (The dadoes should face each other and the ends should be flush.) I cut the taper on the band saw and sanded the edges smooth with a sanding block *(Fig. 5)*.

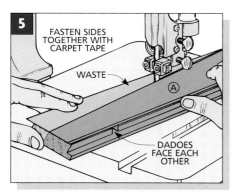

5 FASTEN SIDES TOGETHER WITH CARPET TAPE

WASTE

Ⓐ

DADOES FACE EACH OTHER

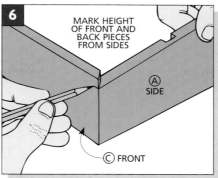

6 MARK HEIGHT OF FRONT AND BACK PIECES FROM SIDES

Ⓐ SIDE

Ⓒ FRONT

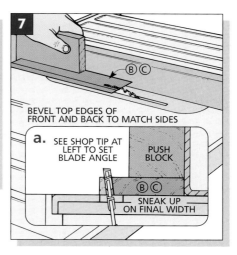

7

Ⓑ Ⓒ

BEVEL TOP EDGES OF FRONT AND BACK TO MATCH SIDES

a. SEE SHOP TIP AT LEFT TO SET BLADE ANGLE

PUSH BLOCK

Ⓑ Ⓒ

SNEAK UP ON FINAL WIDTH

SHOP TIP . . . *Matching an Angle*

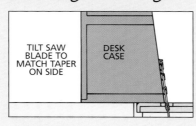

When you're ready to bevel the front and back of the Lap Desk, don't rely on a bevel gauge (or trial and error) to set the angle of the saw blade. You can get a perfect match the first time by using the side of the desk itself as an angle gauge (see drawing).

TILT SAW BLADE TO MATCH TAPER ON SIDE

DESK CASE

Now the top edges of the front and back pieces can be beveled to match the taper of the sides. I dry-assembled the pieces and marked the final height directly from the sides *(Fig. 6)*. But you don't want to simply cut to the lines in one pass. You'll get a better fit if you sneak up on the final height *(Figs. 7 and 7a)*.

Note: When tilting the saw blade for cutting the bevels, I didn't rely on the markings on the saw. Instead, I set one of the sides on the saw and tilted the blade to match it (see the Shop Tip above).

CASE BOTTOM. After the top edges of the front and back pieces have been

beveled, I dry-assembled the case one more time so I could measure for the bottom panel (D). The panel is cut from a piece of 1/4"-thick plywood to fit in the rabbeted opening *(Fig. 8)*. (My bottom panel ended up 13" x 151/4".)

ASSEMBLE CASE. Now the case can be glued together. I used band clamps for this, and to make things easier, I assembled the case in two steps. First, I glued the four case pieces together, using the bottom panel simply to keep the assembly square. Then after the glue was dry, I went ahead and glued the bottom panel into the rabbets *(Fig. 8)*.

DIVIDERS. The only case pieces left to add now are the front (E) and back dividers (F). These 3/8"-thick pieces are cut to length to fit between the sides in the dadoes *(Fig. 8)*. (Mine were 13" long.)

Like the front and back of the case, the dividers start out oversize in width (height) and then are trimmed to match the sides. Again, I marked the height right from the side pieces *(Fig. 8a)*. Then tilt the blade and sneak up on the final height. Finally, glue the dividers in place.

SHOP TIP
Sanding Flush

No matter how carefully you work, it's likely that the top edges of the case aren't going to be perfectly flush. If things are just a little out of alignment, that's okay. There's a quick way to get them flush. Lay down some adhesive-backed sandpaper on a flat surface (like the top of a table saw). Then sand the top edges in a circular manner until the edges are all flush (see photo).

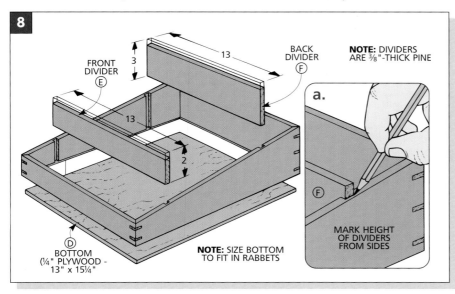

8

FRONT DIVIDER Ⓔ

3

13

BACK DIVIDER Ⓕ

NOTE: DIVIDERS ARE 3/8"-THICK PINE

13

2

a.

Ⓕ

MARK HEIGHT OF DIVIDERS FROM SIDES

Ⓓ BOTTOM (1/4" PLYWOOD - 13" x 151/4"

NOTE: SIZE BOTTOM TO FIT IN RABBETS

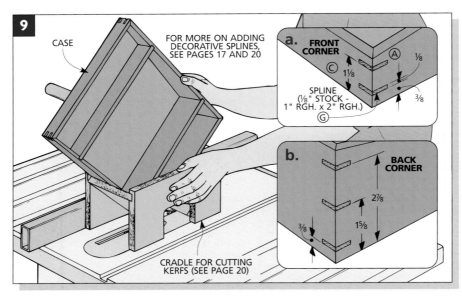

9

CASE

FOR MORE ON ADDING DECORATIVE SPLINES, SEE PAGES 17 AND 20

a. FRONT CORNER

Ⓐ 1/8

Ⓒ 1 1/8

SPLINE (1/8" STOCK - 1" RGH. x 2" RGH.)

Ⓖ 3/8

b. BACK CORNER

2 7/8

1 5/8

3/8

CRADLE FOR CUTTING KERFS (SEE PAGE 20)

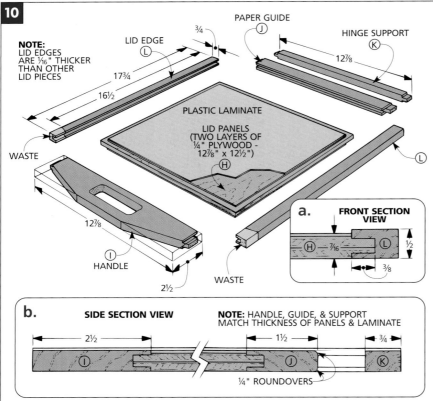

10

NOTE: LID EDGES ARE 1/16" THICKER THAN OTHER LID PIECES

LID EDGE Ⓛ

3/4

PAPER GUIDE Ⓙ

HINGE SUPPORT Ⓚ

12 7/8

17 3/4

16 1/2

PLASTIC LAMINATE

LID PANELS (TWO LAYERS OF 1/4" PLYWOOD - 12 7/8" x 12 1/2")

Ⓗ

WASTE

12 7/8

Ⓘ HANDLE

2 1/2

WASTE

Ⓛ

a. FRONT SECTION VIEW

Ⓗ 7/16 Ⓛ 1/2

3/8

b. SIDE SECTION VIEW

NOTE: HANDLE, GUIDE, & SUPPORT MATCH THICKNESS OF PANELS & LAMINATE

2 1/2 Ⓘ

1 1/2 Ⓙ

3/4 Ⓚ

1/4" ROUNDOVERS

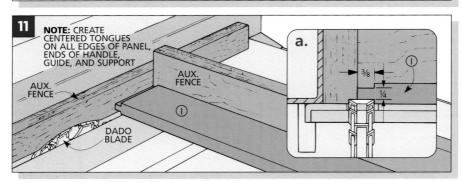

11

NOTE: CREATE CENTERED TONGUES ON ALL EDGES OF PANEL, ENDS OF HANDLE, GUIDE, AND SUPPORT

AUX. FENCE

AUX. FENCE

Ⓘ

DADO BLADE

a.

Ⓘ

3/8

1/4

DECORATIVE SPLINES. Before beginning work on the lid, I strengthened the miters by adding decorative cross splines (G). (This also offers you a chance to customize the look of the desk. The Designer's Notebook on the opposite page shows a few ideas.)

To do this, kerfs are cut across the corners with the case held in a simple cradle *(Fig. 9).* When laying out these kerfs, note that the bottom kerfs on the front and back corners are all the same. But the remaining ones are different *(Figs. 9a and 9b).* (For more on this jig and the procedure, see page 20.)

After the kerfs were cut, I glued a spline in each. (I used pine.) Again, see the article on page 20 for details.

LID

With the case of the desk complete, I worked on the lid *(Fig. 10).* This is basically just a frame and panel assembly, but I did make a few modifications.

First, to end up with a durable writing surface, I made the lid panel out of two layers of 1/4"-thick plywood and a piece of plastic laminate.

Also, I created an opening in the back for the paper to feed through. This is easy to do. Instead of one rail piece in the back, there are two rails with a 1"-wide opening between them.

And finally, on the edges of the lid, I used stock that was thicker than the panel. When the paper covers are added later, this creates a tiny gap for the paper to feed through. The extra thickness also helps guide the paper.

LID PANEL. To make the lid, I wanted to end up with a panel that was 12 7/8" x 12 1/2". To do this, I glued two oversized 1/4" plywood lid panels (H) together with contact cement *(Fig. 10).* While I had the contact cement out, I added a layer of plastic laminate on top, then trimmed the assembly to final size.

HANDLE, GUIDE, AND SUPPORT. With the lid panel glued up, I worked on the rail pieces next. The handle (I) in front and the paper guide (J) and hinge support (K) in back are cut from stock that's planed to match the thickness of the panel *(Fig. 10).* (Mine was 7/16" thick.) Then they're all cut to length and width.

The next thing to do is create a centered tongue on each of the lid pieces. The panel gets a tongue on all four edges *(Fig. 10).* The handle, guide, and support have tongues cut only on their ends.

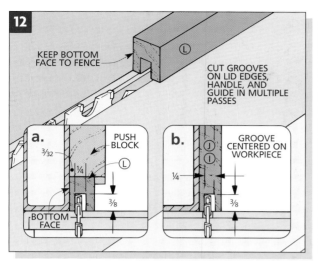

12
KEEP BOTTOM FACE TO FENCE
(L)
CUT GROOVES ON LID EDGES, HANDLE, AND GUIDE IN MULTIPLE PASSES

a.
3/32
PUSH BLOCK
(L)
1/4
3/8
BOTTOM FACE

b.
(J)
(I)
1/4
GROOVE CENTERED ON WORKPIECE
3/8

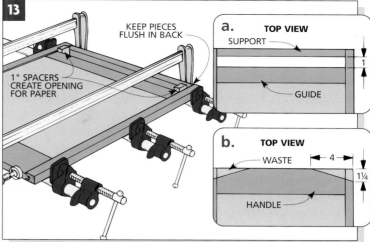

13
KEEP PIECES FLUSH IN BACK
1" SPACERS CREATE OPENING FOR PAPER

a. TOP VIEW
SUPPORT
1
GUIDE

b. TOP VIEW
WASTE
4
1 1/4
HANDLE

I created these 1/4"-thick tongues by cutting two 3/8"-wide rabbets *(Fig. 11)*.

LID EDGES. To hold all these lid pieces together, I made two lid edges (L). These pieces are also cut from stock that's 1/16" thicker than the panel so there's room to feed the paper through later *(Fig. 10a)*.

After the lid edges are cut to size, I cut grooves in their inside edges for holding the other lid pieces *(Fig. 12)*. Since the edges are thicker than the other pieces, the grooves aren't centered. The goal is to make all the pieces flush along the bottom, so when cutting the grooves, keep the bottom face of the pieces against the fence *(Fig. 12a)*.

While you're cutting the grooves on the lid edges, you can cut this same groove on the inside edges of the handle and paper guide too. This allows these pieces to fit tight against the lid panel *(Figs. 10, 10b, and 12b)*.

Before gluing the lid together, I did something to make feeding the paper through a little easier. I routed a 1/4" roundover on the outside edges of the paper guide (J) *(Fig. 10b)*.

LID ASSEMBLY. Now all the pieces of the lid can be glued together *(Fig. 13)*. The hinge support and lid edges should be flush in back, and there should be a 1"-wide space between the paper guide and the hinge support *(Fig. 13a)*.

Then at the front of the lid, lay out and cut the shape of the handle *(Fig. 13b)*. (But don't cut the handle opening yet.)

DESIGNER'S NOTEBOOK

With a simple jig and a little imagination, you can customize splined miter joints in a variety of ways.

DECORATIVE SPLINE VARIATIONS

■ Miter joints are attractive because they hide the end grain in a joint. However, the big drawback to the joint is that you're gluing end grain to end grain. This isn't a very strong bond.

■ By using a special cradle (see page 20), you can cut slots to accept splines that dress up and reinforce the joint.

■ You can liven up the appearance of the joint by tilting or varying the height of the blade, cutting wider slots, or by using the cradle on a router table with profile router bits. Splines and case pieces made from contrasting woods add even more visual interest as shown below.

Varying Lengths. *The kerfs for these walnut splines were routed in a maple box. To rout the shorter kerfs, simply lower the 1/4" straight bit.*

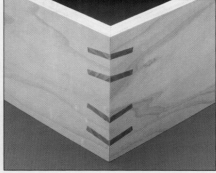

Angled. *To cut the kerfs for these cherry splines, I tilted the blade 7°. And I made two passes with each setting, flipping the box between passes.*

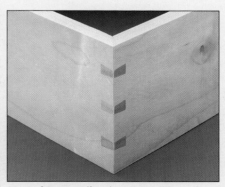

Keyed Dovetails. *These aren't true dovetails. The kerfs are routed with a dovetail bit after the box is assembled. Then the "key" is added. See page 21 for details.*

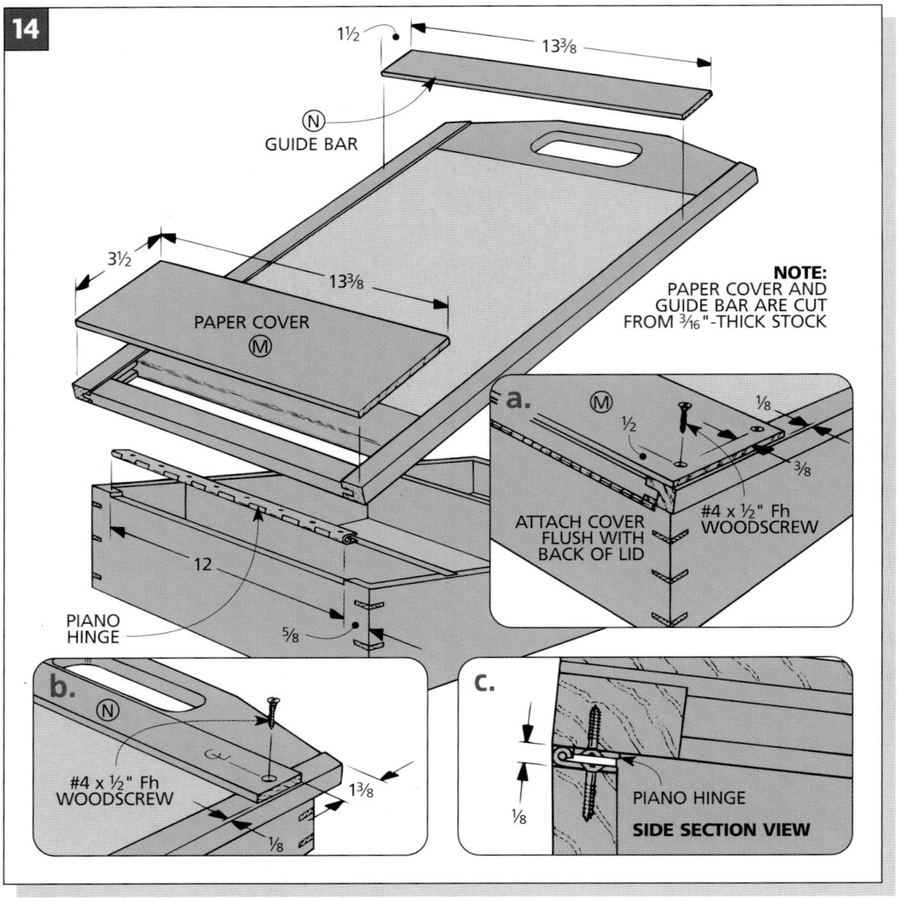
14
1½
13⅜
Ⓝ
GUIDE BAR
3½
13⅜
PAPER COVER
Ⓜ
NOTE:
PAPER COVER AND
GUIDE BAR ARE CUT
FROM 3/16"-THICK STOCK
12
PIANO
HINGE
⅝
a.
Ⓜ
½
⅛
⅜
ATTACH COVER
FLUSH WITH
BACK OF LID
#4 x ½" Fh
WOODSCREW
b.
Ⓝ
#4 x ½" Fh
WOODSCREW
1⅜
⅛
c.
⅛
PIANO HINGE
SIDE SECTION VIEW

PAPER COVER AND GUIDE BAR. To hold the paper flat against the lid, I added a $3/16$"-thick paper cover (M) and guide bar (N) *(Fig. 14)*. They're cut $1/4$" shorter than the width of the lid and simply screwed in place *(Figs. 14a and 14b)*.

PIANO HINGE. Now the lid can be attached to the case. To do this, I used a piano hinge, routing the mortise in the case only *(Fig. 14c)*. (Details about how this was done are in the Shop Tip below.)

HANDLE OPENING. Now that the lid is attached, the opening in the handle can

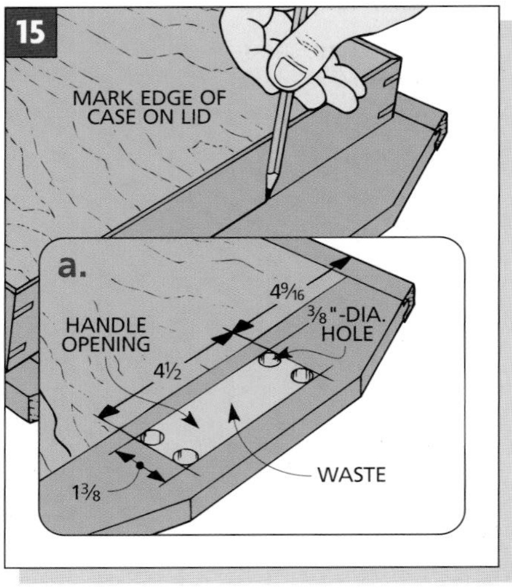
15
MARK EDGE OF
CASE ON LID
a.
HANDLE
OPENING
4⁹⁄₁₆
⅜"-DIA.
HOLE
4½
1⅜
WASTE

SHOP TIP . . . . *Piano Hinge Mortise*

When making a mortise for a piano hinge, I typically use a straight bit in a hand-held router. But the back edge of the Lap Desk poses a challenge since it's beveled *(Fig. 1)*. So rather than try to hold the router at an angle, I decided the router table was a better choice.

However, this introduces another problem. Since the hinge doesn't run the full width of the desk, the mortise is stopped at both ends.

And with the desk face down on the router table, you can't see the ends of the mortise as you're routing.

So instead of routing the mortise in one long continuous pass, I "nibbled" away the waste in a series of short passes by moving the desk back and forth over the bit *(Fig. 2)*.

The key here is to start and stop the mortise about $1/8$" away from the ends *(Fig. 2a)*. (I drew layout lines on the back of the desk to mark the end-points.) Then the ends of the mortise can be squared up with a sharp chisel *(Fig. 2a)*.

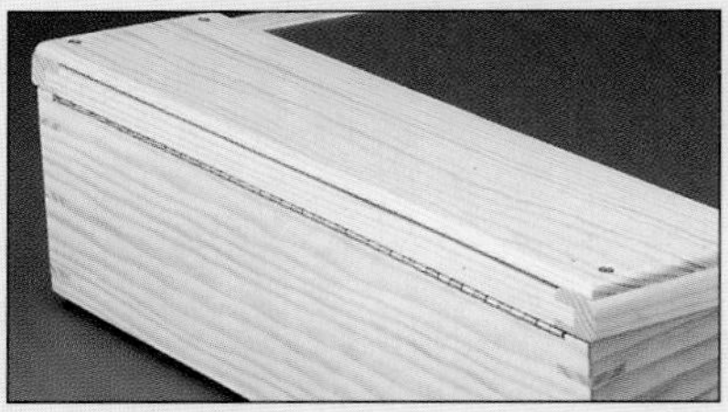

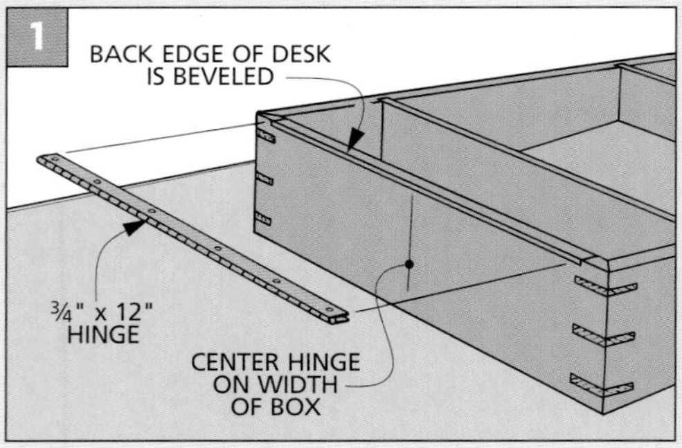
1
BACK EDGE OF DESK
IS BEVELED
¾" x 12"
HINGE
CENTER HINGE
ON WIDTH
OF BOX

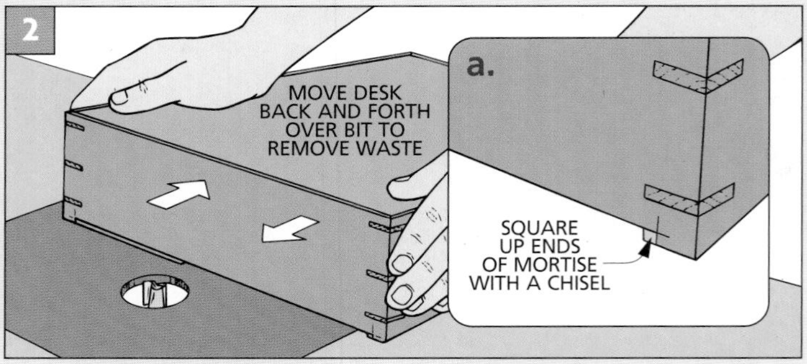
2
MOVE DESK
BACK AND FORTH
OVER BIT TO
REMOVE WASTE
a.
SQUARE
UP ENDS
OF MORTISE
WITH A CHISEL

be created. I laid out the handle so it was flush with the case *(Figs. 15 and 15a)*. Then I drilled holes in the corners and cleaned out the waste with a jig saw.

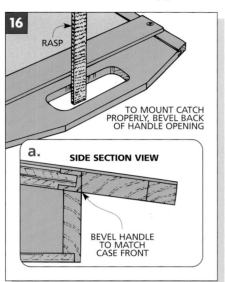

16

RASP

TO MOUNT CATCH PROPERLY, BEVEL BACK OF HANDLE OPENING

a. SIDE SECTION VIEW

BEVEL HANDLE TO MATCH CASE FRONT

But the handle's not quite done yet. The inside edge of the handle needs to be flush with the case so you can add the catch *(Fig. 16a)*. I did this with a rasp and some sandpaper *(Fig. 16)*.

Finally before attaching the catch, I softened all the sharp edges with sandpaper. To prevent scratching the laminate, I applied masking tape around its edges. Leave the tape on when applying the finish too. (I applied a couple of coats of a wipe-on finish.) Then I screwed the catch to the lid and case *(Fig. 17)*. ■

17

DRAW CATCH

#2 x ¼" BRASS WOODSCREW

To make the Lap Desk light enough for even a child to carry, I chose a lightweight wood (pine) and planed it to 3/8" thick. A large handle at the top makes it easy to carry the desk anywhere.

DESIGNER'S NOTEBOOK

Don't want a roll of paper? Try this version of the desk.

CONSTRUCTION NOTES:

■ The only modifications in this design are made to the lid.

First off, this version of the desk is meant to be used with sheets of paper, not a roll. So there's no need to feed paper through the lid. That's why the paper guide (J) and hinge support (K) are replaced with a pencil trough (O) that consists of a single piece of solid wood (see drawing below). And you won't need the paper cover (M) or guide bar (N).

Note: The compartment used for the paper roll can now be used as storage.

■ To make the trough, rout a cove 1" from each edge of the workpiece. Then clean out the waste between the coves with a straight bit (detail 'a').

■ Now cut a stub tenon on each end of the pencil trough (O).

■ To provide a smoother edge between the writing surface and the lid edge (L), the edging is planed to match the combined thickness of the plywood and the laminate used for the top (7/16" in my case).

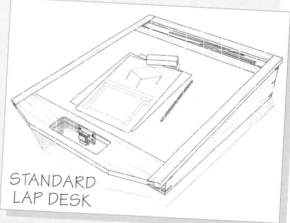

STANDARD LAP DESK

■ Since the edging pieces are thinner, the groove in each one is centered on the thickness of the workpiece.

■ Next, the handle, lid edges, and pencil trough can be glued around the lid panel.

■ Finally, the hinge can be fastened to the pencil trough and case using the same technique as before.

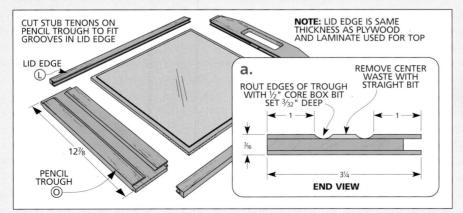

CUT STUB TENONS ON PENCIL TROUGH TO FIT GROOVES IN LID EDGE

LID EDGE (L)

12⅞

PENCIL TROUGH (O)

NOTE: LID EDGE IS SAME THICKNESS AS PLYWOOD AND LAMINATE USED FOR TOP

a.

ROUT EDGES OF TROUGH WITH ½" CORE BOX BIT SET 3/32" DEEP

REMOVE CENTER WASTE WITH STRAIGHT BIT

7/16

1 1

3¼

END VIEW

MATERIALS LIST

CHANGED PART
L Lid Edges (2) 7/16 x ¾ - 17¾ rgh.
NEW PART
O Pencil Trough (1) 7/16 x 3¼ - 12⅞

Note: Do not need parts J, K, M, N. Also, No. 4 x ½" brass woodscrews not required.

TECHNIQUE .... *Splined Miters*

Anytime I join a box with miters, I have to decide whether or not the joint should be reinforced. I like the clean look of miters, but they don't put up with a lot of abuse. So if the box is going to be handled much, like the Lap Desk on page 12, I'll come up with a way to strengthen the corners.

Typically, I create a stronger miter by adding splines. They cross the joint line, creating a lot more glue surface to hold the pieces together. And the splines can be designed to be hidden or exposed depending on how they're oriented. For the Lap Desk, I decided to use exposed, decorative splines to add subtle accents to the corners of the desk (see photo at right).

LAYING OUT THE SPLINES. There are just about any number of decorative spline styles and combinations you can use on a mitered corner. So the first thing to do is come up with a design.

When adding decorative splines, you can use contrasting woods or vary the lengths, thicknesses, and spacing of the splines. (See the box on page 17 for three examples.) You can even add dovetail-shaped splines, called "keyed dovetails."

When deciding what kind of decorative splines to use (and how many), I try to make the splines an interesting accent but not the "main attraction." The thing to keep in mind is that too many splines or too much contrast between the woods can be distracting.

KERFS. Once you decide on the spline layout and the box has been assembled, you can begin work on adding the splines. The process is pretty simple. First, kerfs are cut across the corners of the box. Then thin strips of wood (the splines) are cut to fit snug in the kerfs.

One thing to note about the kerfs. If you cut them on the table saw, choose a blade that cuts a flat-bottomed groove (*Fig. 1*). The kerfs can also be cut on the router table, using a straight bit.

Note: If you use a dovetail bit to create the kerfs, you'll need to use this same bit to make the "key" that fits the opening. See the bottom of the next page for more details.

CRADLE. The trickiest part of creating the kerfs is holding the project at a 45° angle to the table. So to do this safely, I use a simple cradle (*Fig. 2*).

Note: This cradle works on the router table as well (see the photo on the next page).

To build the cradle, start with two side pieces cut from ³/₄"-thick plywood. Then cut two ¹/₄"-deep dadoes at a 45° angle (*Fig. 3*). These hold two support pieces that form a 90° corner. But before screwing the support pieces between the sides, I cut a "window" on one of the side pieces (*Fig. 2*). This makes it easier to set the height of the blade (or bit) and to position the fence.

CUTTING KERFS. When the cradle has been screwed together, you're ready to cut the kerfs for the splines. What you want is the deepest kerf you can cut without cutting through the inside corner of the box. So to set the height of the blade (or router bit), I set the box in the cradle and position it next to the blade (*Fig. 4a*). Then I raise the blade until it's about ¹/₁₆" below the inside corner.

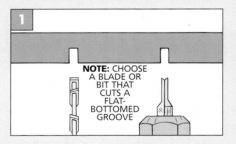

NOTE: CHOOSE A BLADE OR BIT THAT CUTS A FLAT-BOTTOMED GROOVE

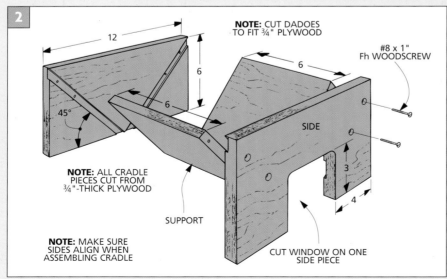

NOTE: CUT DADOES TO FIT ³/₄" PLYWOOD

12

6

6

6

45°

#8 x 1" Fh WOODSCREW

SIDE

3

4

SIDE

SUPPORT

NOTE: ALL CRADLE PIECES CUT FROM ³/₄"-THICK PLYWOOD

NOTE: MAKE SURE SIDES ALIGN WHEN ASSEMBLING CRADLE

CUT WINDOW ON ONE SIDE PIECE

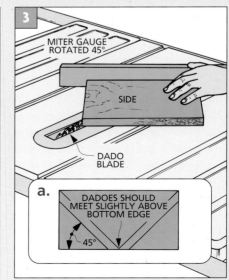

MITER GAUGE ROTATED 45°

SIDE

DADO BLADE

a. DADOES SHOULD MEET SLIGHTLY ABOVE BOTTOM EDGE

45°

Now I can remove the box and position the fence. Here, the "window" in the cradle comes in handy again. I simply slide a ruler into the window against the inside face of the cradle and measure over to the blade *(Fig. 4b)*.

Cutting the kerfs is just a matter of pushing the cradle over the blade. Just make sure the box stays tight against the inside edge of the cradle.

CUTTING THE SPLINES. With the kerfs cut, the splines are next. You can cut the thin strips on either the table saw or band saw and sand them to final thickness. They should slide into the kerfs easily, but there shouldn't be any gaps.

Once you've placed the spline in the kerf, mark its length with a pencil. Then remove it from the slot and cut it to rough size with a hand saw.

When gluing in the splines, there's only one thing to watch out for. If you're not careful, you can end up with a tiny gap along one edge. They have a tendency to "rock" when you tap them in place — when tapping in one side, the other side often pulls away from the kerf. And sometimes, excess glue will hide this gap.

After the glue dries, all that's left is to trim the splines flush. I use a hand saw to do most of this work *(Fig. 5)*. But to avoid scratching the box, I leave a little "stub" and then sand the spline smooth, using sandpaper on a flat surface (like the top of my table saw) *(Fig. 6)*. This gives you a perfectly flush spline.

Cradle. *A shop-made cradle holds the project at the correct angle to cut kerfs across the mitered corners. The cradle can be used on either the table saw or the router table (see photo above).*

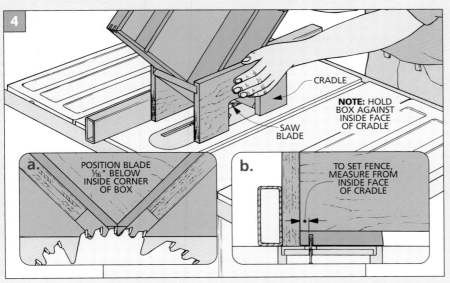

4

CRADLE

SAW BLADE

NOTE: HOLD BOX AGAINST INSIDE FACE OF CRADLE

a. POSITION BLADE ⅟₁₆" BELOW INSIDE CORNER OF BOX

b. TO SET FENCE, MEASURE FROM INSIDE FACE OF CRADLE

5

SECOND: TRIM EXCESS WITH HAND SAW

FIRST: MAKE SPLINE TO FIT KERF WITH NO GAPS

G

SPLINE (⅛" HARDWOOD - 1" RGH. x 2" RGH.)

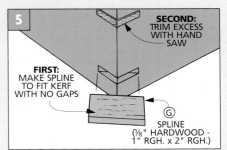

6

SAND SPLINES FLUSH

ADHESIVE-BACKED SANDPAPER ON FLAT SURFACE

DOVETAIL SPLINES

Saw blades and straight bits offer plenty of ways to dress up a splined miter joint (see the Designer's Notebook on page 17 for some ideas). For an even fancier look, try a dovetail bit.

SPLINES. Using the cradle shown above, the box is run through a dovetail bit in the router table to cut the slots in each joint. Once the slots are cut, keys can be made to fill them. I started with a thick blank and adjusted the height of the bit to equal the depth of the slots *(Fig. 1a)*.

Make a pass with each edge of the blank against the router table fence to form the dovetail-shaped key *(Fig. 1)*. (To save stock and setup time, I routed a key on both edges of the blank.)

Now nudge the fence slightly and sneak up on the thickness of the key for a snug fit in the slot.

When the keys fit, they can be ripped free *(Fig. 2)*. Don't worry about cutting them to an exact height. In fact, a small "cap" left on top makes it easier to handle them. Then cut lengths of the keys and glue them into the slots.

Once the glue dries, the keys need a little trimming. I used a small back saw to remove most of the waste. Finally, sand the keys flush with the side of the box.

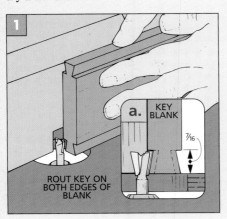

1

KEY BLANK

a. ⁷⁄₁₆

ROUT KEY ON BOTH EDGES OF BLANK

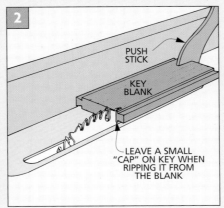

2

PUSH STICK

KEY BLANK

LEAVE A SMALL "CAP" ON KEY WHEN RIPPING IT FROM THE BLANK

Chess Board

You don't have to cut sixty-four little squares to build this Chess Board. Just four strips of maple and four of walnut. The board is actually the lid for a case that provides a storage place for chess pieces.

The biggest problem in building a chess board is figuring out how to deal with all those little squares. The solution is simple — you don't.

THE BOARD. The squares in this Chess Board aren't a problem because they don't start out as squares at all. They start out as straight strips of wood that are glued together in a parallel pattern. Then they're cut apart and glued together again in a "checkered" pattern.

I used maple for the light squares, and walnut for the dark squares and the case. (Of course you'll need to supply the chess pieces or checkers. See page 126 for sources of each.)

CASE. Although this Chess Board is ready for use after the top is built, I added a mitered case around the board to store the chess pieces in. See the Designer's Notebook on page 29 for an idea on how to keep them from rolling around.

DESIGN. The lid of the Chess Board is hinged to the case, but it doesn't open from the front as you might expect. Instead, the lid opens from the side. This way, players sitting across from each other can both reach inside to take out their game pieces.

ORIENTATION. There's another reason for paying attention to how the board is oriented. In the game of chess, each player (as they face one another) should have a white square in the lower right-hand corner. This is always where the king's rook starts out.

If you build the box with the board installed the other way, it will still work. You'll just have to open it from front to back instead of side to side.

HARDWARE. To add a bit of accent to the case, I cut a pair of shallow kerfs around the outside. Then I installed a solid brass spring catch and neat little square-knuckle hinges that fit between the grooves. A hardware kit is available from *Woodsmith Project Supplies*. For more information see page 126.

EXPLODED VIEW

OVERALL DIMENSIONS:
17³⁄₈W x 17³⁄₈D x 3H

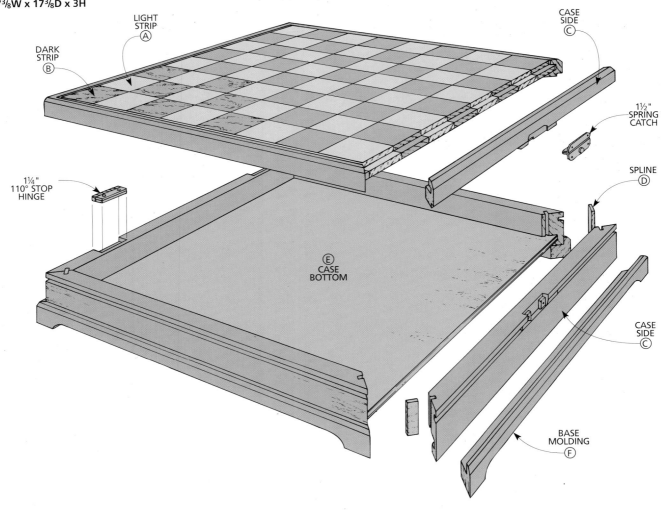

LIGHT STRIP Ⓐ

DARK STRIP Ⓑ

CASE SIDE Ⓒ

1½" SPRING CATCH

1¼" 110° STOP HINGE

Ⓔ CASE BOTTOM

SPLINE Ⓓ

CASE SIDE Ⓒ

BASE MOLDING Ⓕ

MATERIALS LIST

WOOD
A	Light Strips (4)	¾ x 3 - 18½ rough
B	Dark Strips (4)	¾ x 3 - 18½ rough
C	Case Sides (4)	¾ x 2⅝ - 16⅞
D	Splines (4)	⅛ x 1⅝ - ½
E	Case Bottom (1)	¼ ply - 16⅜ x 16⅜
F	Base Molding (4)	¾ x ⅞ - 17½ rough

HARDWARE SUPPLIES
(2) 1¼" 110° stop hinges
(1) 1½" spring catch
(1) Spray-on flocking

CUTTING DIAGRAM

¾ x 6 - 96 WALNUT (4 Bd. Ft.)

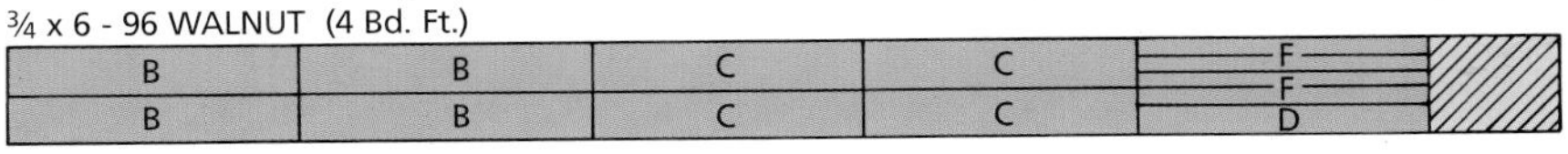

B	B	C	C	F
B	B	C	C	D

¾ x 6 - 48 MAPLE (2 Bd. Ft.)

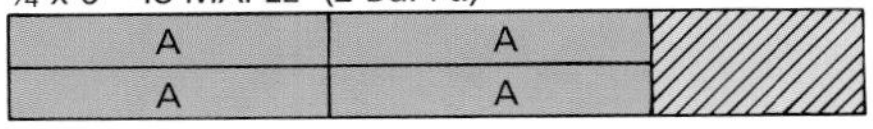

A	A	
A	A	

¼" PLYWOOD - 18 x 18

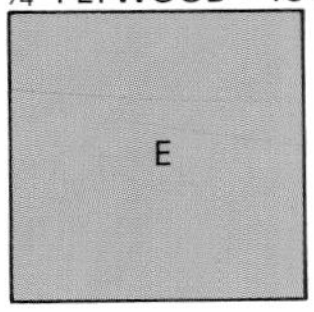

E

PLAYING SURFACE

The playing surface (or top) of the Chess Board starts out like a small table top — it's made up of strips of wood edge-glued together. But the strips are alternating light and dark-colored woods. (This is how you start creating the checkered effect for the top.)

OVERSIZE STRIPS. There are two other things to take into consideration when gluing up the panel. First, start with longer light and dark strips (A, B) than needed. This length (18½" rough) allows for trimming to finished size later.

Second, to end up with uniform-size (2") squares, the *inside* strips must start out 2" wide. The two *outside* strips — one of each color — start out wider (2½") *(Fig. 1)*. This way, there's room to trim the outside strips later, and still allow room for a tongue (to fit in the sides of the case) (refer to *Fig. 5*).

TRIM AND PLANE. When the glue has had time to set up on the edge-glued panel, square up the uneven ends of the board. Then you can plane (or you could also sand) each side perfectly smooth and flat (to ⅝" thick).

"BARBER POLE" STRIPS. Now the panel can be crosscut into eight "barber pole"

strips *(Fig. 2)*. Again, the two outside strips should be cut wider than the rest.

Note: I kept the best-looking side of the playing surface face *up* while I was cutting the strips. And I also placed each strip back together in the same order as it came off the panel.

CHESS BOARD PATTERN. Now the strips can be glued back together to form a chess board. But first, you need to turn every other strip end for end *(Fig. 3)*.

The idea is to end up with 2½"-wide squares around all sides of the board. And different colors at adjacent corners.

Note: To help keep the ends — and faces — of each strip flush, I made an assembly platform *(Fig. 3)*. (It's a good idea to wax the platform to keep glue from sticking.) Then, to keep the corners of all the squares aligned, I glued the strips together one at a time.

Once all the strips are glued together, clamp across the panel to pull the joints

tight. After the glue has had time to set up completely, plane or sand the panel to finished thickness (½").

TRIM TO SIZE. Now the panel can be trimmed to finished size. To allow for a ³⁄₁₆"-wide tongue all around, I cut the panel 16⅜" square. (This equals eight 2" squares across, plus two tongues.)

To do this, first make a mark near each corner the same distance (8³⁄₁₆") out from the center of the panel *(Fig. 4)*. Then cut off each edge at the mark.

FOUR RABBETS. Next cut a rabbet along all four edges of the board *(Fig. 5)*. These rabbets create tongues that fit into a groove all around the inside of the

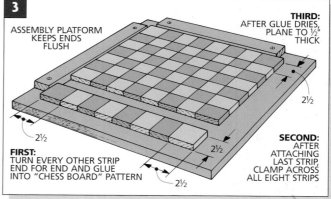

1 LIGHT STRIP Ⓐ Ⓑ DARK STRIP 18½ ROUGH 2½ 2 2½
NOTE: BOARD BLANK STARTS OUT ¾" THICK

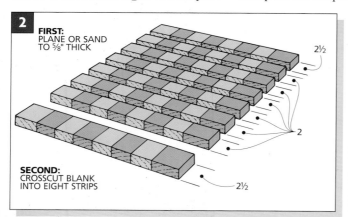

2 **FIRST:** PLANE OR SAND TO ⅝" THICK 2½ 2 **SECOND:** CROSSCUT BLANK INTO EIGHT STRIPS 2½

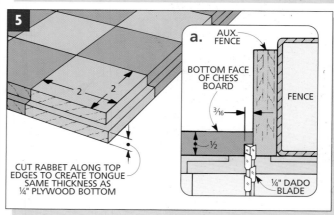

3 ASSEMBLY PLATFORM KEEPS ENDS FLUSH **THIRD:** AFTER GLUE DRIES, PLANE TO ½" THICK 2½ **FIRST:** TURN EVERY OTHER STRIP END FOR END AND GLUE INTO "CHESS BOARD" PATTERN 2½ 2½ 2½ **SECOND:** AFTER ATTACHING LAST STRIP, CLAMP ACROSS ALL EIGHT STRIPS

4 CUT BOARD TO FINISHED SIZE (16⅜" SQUARE) 8³⁄₁₆ 16⅜ 8³⁄₁₆ TRIM ALL FOUR SIDES TO PENCIL MARKS

5 2 2 **a.** AUX. FENCE BOTTOM FACE OF CHESS BOARD FENCE ³⁄₁₆ ½ ¼" DADO BLADE CUT RABBET ALONG TOP EDGES TO CREATE TONGUE SAME THICKNESS AS ¼" PLYWOOD BOTTOM assembled case. The rabbets also produce outside squares identical in size to the inside squares (2" by 2").

Note: Cut the rabbets along the *top* edge of the board *(Fig. 5a)*. Also, sneak up on the depth of the rabbet so the tongues match the thickness of a piece of 1/4" plywood. This way, the playing surface top and the plywood bottom fit into the case the same way later on.

CASE

To provide space for holding the game pieces, I built a walnut case that uses the playing surface as a lid.

The case is built from four identically-sized pieces of stock which are all machined the same way.

CUT TO SIZE. Begin the case by cutting four equally-sized blanks for the case sides (C). Cut them to finished width and rough length *(Fig. 6)*.

INSIDE GROOVES. Now grooves can be cut along the inside face of each piece to hold the chess board top and plywood bottom. I cut each groove in two passes on the table saw *(Fig. 6)*. Cut the grooves to width to match the thickness of the

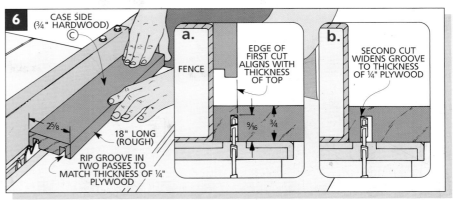

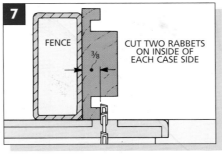

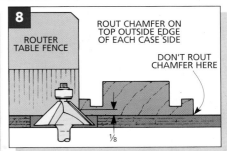

1/4" plywood to be used for the case bottom *(Figs. 6a and 6b)*.

RABBET AND CHAMFER. To allow room for the playing surface to "float" in the

case, next cut a rabbet along each inside edge of each piece *(Fig. 7)*. Then rout a chamfer along the top outside edge only of each piece *(Fig. 8)*.

SHOP TIP .... Cutting a Case in Two

When making a box with a lid, you want the sides of the box and lid to align perfectly. To do this, first assemble all the pieces of the box: the top, bottom and four sides. Then cut off the lid using the table saw.

Set the saw blade slightly higher than the thickness of the box sides and position the rip fence so the lid is cut off right where you want it *(Fig. 1)*.

Now, place the bottom of the box against the

fence and begin cutting off the lid *(Fig. 1)*. First, cut through the two opposite ends of the box.

To keep the lid from pinching the blade on the last two cuts, slide two pieces of 1/8" hardboard

through the box from one kerf to the other, putting strips of tape above and below the pieces of hardboard to keep them from slipping *(Fig. 2)*.

Now complete cutting off the lid using two passes.

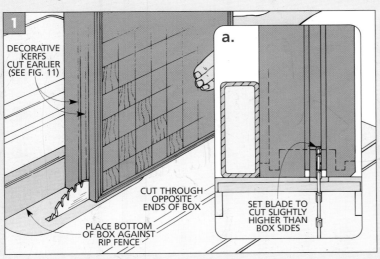

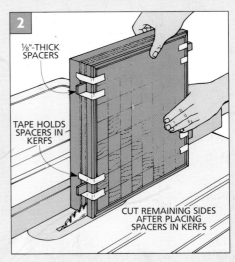

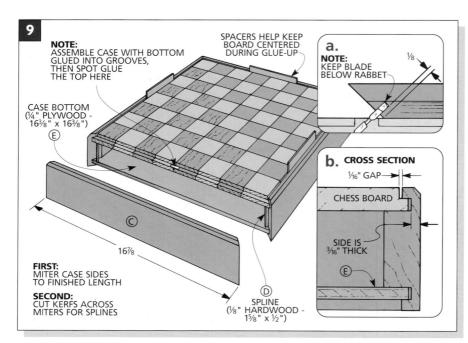

9

NOTE: ASSEMBLE CASE WITH BOTTOM GLUED INTO GROOVES, THEN SPOT GLUE THE TOP HERE

SPACERS HELP KEEP BOARD CENTERED DURING GLUE-UP

CASE BOTTOM (¼" PLYWOOD - 16⅜" x 16⅜") Ⓔ

Ⓒ

16⅞

FIRST: MITER CASE SIDES TO FINISHED LENGTH

SECOND: CUT KERFS ACROSS MITERS FOR SPLINES

a. NOTE: KEEP BLADE BELOW RABBET
⅛

b. CROSS SECTION
1/16" GAP
CHESS BOARD
SIDE IS 3/16" THICK
Ⓔ

Ⓓ SPLINE (⅛" HARDWOOD - 1⅝" x ½")

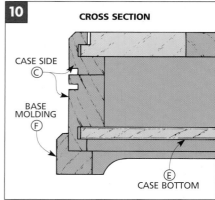

10 CROSS SECTION
CASE SIDE Ⓒ
BASE MOLDING Ⓕ
CASE BOTTOM Ⓔ

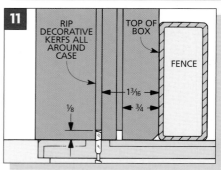

11 RIP DECORATIVE KERFS ALL AROUND CASE
TOP OF BOX
FENCE
1 3/16
¾
⅛

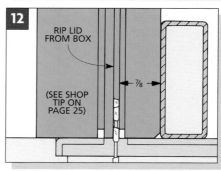

12 RIP LID FROM BOX
(SEE SHOP TIP ON PAGE 25)
⅞
FENCE

MITERS AND SPLINES. The case sides are joined with miters cut across the ends *(Fig. 9)*. All four pieces are mitered to the exact same length.

To determine this length, first measure the chess board (16⅜" square). Then add ⅛" to allow for a 1/16" gap all around *(Fig. 9b)*. Finally, add ⅜" to account for the thickness of the two sides.

I mitered all four case sides to length. This was 16⅞" when measured from long point to long point *(Fig. 9)*.

The mitered ends of the sides are held together with splines that fit into kerfs. I cut the kerfs on the table saw with the blade set to 45° *(Fig. 9a)*.

Then cut four splines (D) to length to fit the kerfs. Note the grain direction of the splines (see Exploded View on page 23). You want the grain to run perpendicular to the joint line.

PLYWOOD BOTTOM. Before assembling the case, cut a piece of ¼" plywood for the case bottom (E) *(Figs. 9 and 10)*. The bottom should be the same size as the chess board *(Fig. 9b)*.

The mitered case can now be glued together with the top and bottom in place. This is an all-at-one-time process, so it helps to use a slow-set (white) in all the joints and mating pieces.

Note: The plywood bottom is glued into the grooves, but so the top can "float" in its grooves, I added just a spot of glue before assembly *(Fig. 9)*.

DECORATIVE KERFS. To give the flat sides of the case a more interesting look, I cut a pair of decorative kerfs around

the box *(Fig. 11* and the photo below). (To get a flat bottom, I used a rip blade.)

CUT OFF LID. Now the lid can be cut away from the case *(Fig. 12)*. (Refer to the Shop Tip box on page 25 to learn more on how I did this.)

BASE MOLDING

In order to give the case a more finished appearance, I added a strip of decorative molding around the base.

This base molding also lifts the game board up so you can get your fingers under it to pick up the box.

TWO BLANKS. The molding strips start out as two oversize blanks *(Fig. 13)*. This makes them easier to work with when routing the pieces.

Note: The rough length of these blanks should be approximately ⅝" longer than the case side.

After cutting the blanks to length, two holes can be drilled near the end of each blank. These holes are later part of an arch that creates "feet" on the ends of each piece of molding.

CHAMFERS AND RABBETS. Once the holes are drilled in each blank, I cut decorative chamfers along the two edges of each blank *(Figs. 14 and 14a)*.

Next, to create a ledge for the case to sit on, rout a rabbet on the remaining two edges *(Figs. 15 and 15a)*.

RIP AND ROUT. The next step is to rip each molding blank to produce two strips of base molding (F) *(Fig. 16)*. Then, clean out the waste between the holes to create

a foot at each end. To do this, I made a rough cut with the band saw first. Then I cleaned up the edge with a straight bit in a series of light passes on the router table. (Refer to the Shop Tip on the next page.)

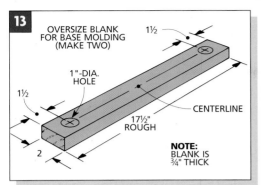

13

OVERSIZE BLANK
FOR BASE MOLDING
(MAKE TWO)

1½

1"-DIA.
HOLE

1½

CENTERLINE

17½"
ROUGH

2

NOTE:
BLANK IS
¾" THICK

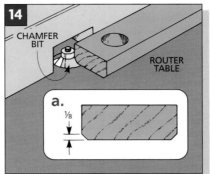

14

CHAMFER
BIT

ROUTER
TABLE

a.

⅛

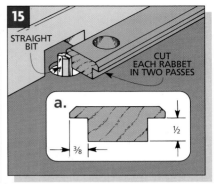

15

STRAIGHT
BIT

CUT
EACH RABBET
IN TWO PASSES

a.

⅜

½

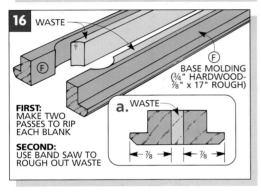

16

WASTE

F

F

BASE MOLDING
(¾" HARDWOOD-
⅞" x 17" ROUGH)

FIRST:
MAKE TWO
PASSES TO RIP
EACH BLANK

SECOND:
USE BAND SAW TO
ROUGH OUT WASTE

a. WASTE

⅞   ⅞

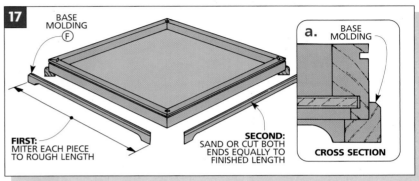

17

BASE
MOLDING
F

FIRST:
MITER EACH PIECE
TO ROUGH LENGTH

SECOND:
SAND OR CUT BOTH
ENDS EQUALLY TO
FINISHED LENGTH

a.

BASE
MOLDING

CROSS SECTION

MITER AND ATTACH. Now the strips of molding can be mitered to finished length. But first, there are a couple of considerations when cutting these miters. To get started, I like to keep the "feet" on each end of the strips the same size. So a uniform amount needs to be cut off both ends of the strips.

And second, the molding has to be mitered to fit around the case. To do this, sneak up on the final lengths (alternately cutting or sanding from both ends) until they just fit.

Finally, the molding is glued around the base of the case *(Figs. 17 and 17a)*.

SHOP TIP . . . . *Routing a Straight Edge*

To create the look of feet on the corners of the Chess Board, I cut out an area on the bottom edge of the base molding pieces.

To do this, I drilled the holes first, then I roughed out the waste on the band saw, cutting about ⅛" on the waste side of the line *(Fig. 1)*. There's only one problem — when making this cut the band saw leaves a ragged edge between the holes.

Solving this problem isn't too difficult. All that's needed to smooth and straighten this edge, and clean up to the final line, is a router table.

To do this, start by mounting a straight bit in the router table *(Fig. 2)*. Set the fence so the outside of the bit just trims the stock *(Fig. 2a)*.

Safety Note: Never trap a workpiece between the bit and the fence. It can grab and kick back.

Now, carefully hold the "feet" of the workpiece firmly against the router table fence, and slide the workpiece from right to left.

Note: The fence has to be twice the length of the workpiece to provide a surface for the feet to run on.

To avoid chatter and produce a smooth edge, rout out the waste in a series of light passes, sneaking up on the final line.

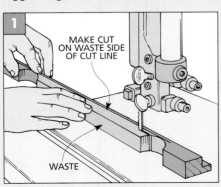

1

MAKE CUT
ON WASTE SIDE
OF CUT LINE

WASTE

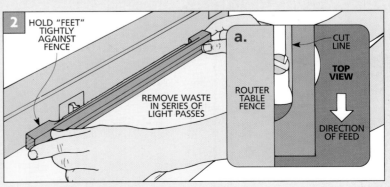

2

HOLD "FEET"
TIGHTLY
AGAINST
FENCE

REMOVE WASTE
IN SERIES OF
LIGHT PASSES

a.

CUT
LINE

**TOP
VIEW**

ROUTER
TABLE
FENCE

DIRECTION
OF FEED

Next, the lid can be attached to the case. The first thing to do is to determine which side will be the "front" of the box. (A front has a white square in the lower right corner.) I attached the hinges so the lid opens to the *side*.

HINGES. Lay out the positions of the hinge mortises along the top edge of the case side (*Fig. 18*).

Cut the mortises to the same depth as the thickness of the hinge knuckle. At the same time, this should also equal the width of the "ridge" between the decorative kerfs (*Fig. 18a*).

Note: To make it easier, I mortised the hinge into the case *only*, not the lid.

Each hinge can now be screwed to the lid and the case.

FILLER STRIPS. Install a spring catch on the opposite side of the case from the hinges. Because the catch will span the two decorative kerfs, I filled the kerfs with short filler strips first (*Fig. 19*).

CATCH MORTISES. Now, shallow mortises have to be cut for both halves of the catch (*Fig. 20*). Then both parts of the catch can be attached to the case.

FLOCKING. Finally, I used flocking to line the inside bottom of the Chess Board, but you could also line the case with felt. See Sources on page 126. ■

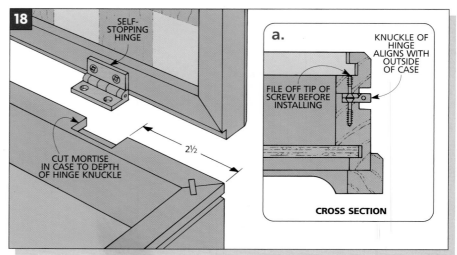

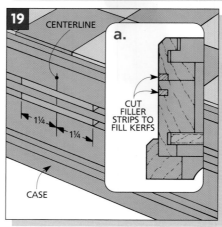

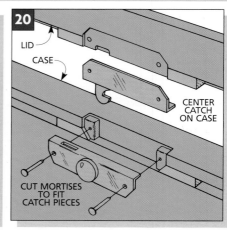

SHOP TIP . . . . *Mitered Sanding Block*

After cutting the lid off the Chess Board, you'll want to sand the saw blade marks off the edges. But sanding edges of mitered corners can be tricky.

Rubbing sandpaper all the way from one end of the box to the other would result in sanding across the grain of the adjoining mitered ends.

So I made a sanding block with mitered ends. This way I can sand right up to the miter line without sanding across the grain of the mitered piece.

To make a mitered sanding block, cut a rabbet in a piece of scrap (*Fig. 1*). One "wall" of the rabbet provides a flat surface to attach the sandpaper. The other wall (at 90° to the first) serves as a fence to guide the sanding

block along the inside face of the workpiece (*Fig. 2*).

After the rabbet is cut in the sanding block, you can miter the ends to 45° (*Fig. 1*). Finally, attach a piece of self-adhesive sandpaper to the wide face of the rabbet.

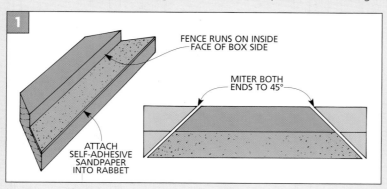

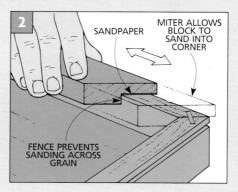

DESIGNER'S NOTEBOOK

With the addition of these optional dividers, the Chess Board becomes even more useful. The thirty-two compartments hold all your chess pieces and keep them from rattling around inside the case.

CONSTRUCTION NOTES:

■ The dividers (G) are just fourteen strips of thin stock that fit together with interlocking notches *(Fig. 1)*.

■ Start by resawing all the strips from maple *(Step 1)*. Then rip them all to a width of 1³/₈" *(Step 2)*.

■ Now cut the strips to length to match the inside dimensions of the box *(Step 3)*.

Note: To prevent chipout here, I attached an extension to the miter gauge and added a stop block to it.

■ Notch the strips on the table saw. Set the blade to a height a little more than half the

width of the strips (³/₄") *(Step 4)*.

■ Now separate the strips into two piles: one for the five front-to-back strips (labeled 1 and 2 in *Fig. 1*) and one for the nine left-to-right strips (3 and 4).

■ Cut notches on the five strips and set them aside.

■ Finally, cut notches on the remaining nine.

■ Then rip strips 2 and 4 to 1" wide *(Fig. 1a)*.

MATERIALS LIST

NEW PART
G Dividers (14)   ¹/₈ x 1³/₈ - 15³/₈

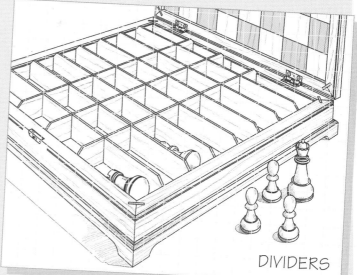

DIVIDERS

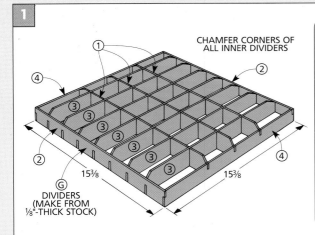

1

CHAMFER CORNERS OF ALL INNER DIVIDERS

DIVIDERS (MAKE FROM ¹/₈"-THICK STOCK)

15³/₈

15³/₈

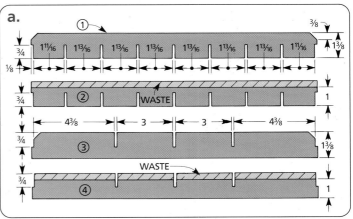

a.

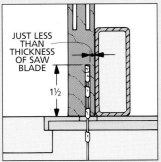

1 Resaw enough ³/₄"-thick maple to produce fourteen strips all the same thickness.

JUST LESS THAN THICKNESS OF SAW BLADE

1½

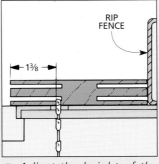

2 Adjust the height of the blade to rip the strips one at a time to a width of 1³/₈".

RIP FENCE

1³/₈

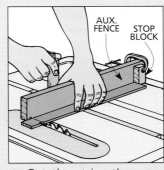

3 Cut the strips the same length with an auxiliary fence and stop block.

AUX. FENCE   STOP BLOCK

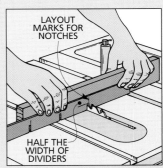

4 Lay out all of the notches, then cut them one at a time on all the divider pieces.

LAYOUT MARKS FOR NOTCHES

HALF THE WIDTH OF DIVIDERS

Toy Chest

Store your children's favorite toys and stuffed animals in this sturdy frame and panel Toy Chest. It's heavy-duty design features a sliding top on one end and easy-to-access drawer storage at the other.

There's one question I get a lot from fellow woodworkers, who also happen to be parents or grandparents: "I'm looking for a design for a nice toy box, can you help?" It's an innocent enough question. The problem is the answer isn't so easy. No matter how good my design is, I always seem to get lots of "suggestions" to make it better.

"No, the lid can't be hinged, it'll fall on their heads." "No, you can't put the handle there, it'll pinch their fingers." "Put it on wheels." "Add drawers." "It needs to be sturdy enough for kids to stand on."

SLIDING LID. Now I feel like I've finally come up with the perfect design. I tried

to incorporate all of these great suggestions into this frame and panel Toy Chest. The key element to this design was to make sure it had a sliding lid (rather than a hinged lid that could slam down and bump a young head). I also tried to make it sturdy enough to stand up to the most rambunctious kids.

When I got down to the practical side of how this box would be constructed, I was once again at no loss for suggestions. It had to be more than a simple box — it had to "look nice" and at the same time be "easy to build." With this in mind, I decided to build the Toy Chest using frame and panel construction.

CONSTRUCTION. The side and end frames are really easy to build using stub tenons and grooves that can be cut on a table saw. To learn more about cutting stub tenons and grooves see the Joinery article on page 32. The attractive panels are made from oak plywood and the frame pieces are made from solid oak with a natural finish, but you could make it from a less expensive wood, like pine, and paint it if you like.

COUNTRY-STYLE CHEST. After I built the chest, I realized it could be changed just a bit to make it a great-looking Country-Style Chest. See the Designer's Notebook on page 37 for details.

EXPLODED VIEW

OVERALL DIMENSIONS:
18W x 44D x 16⅛H

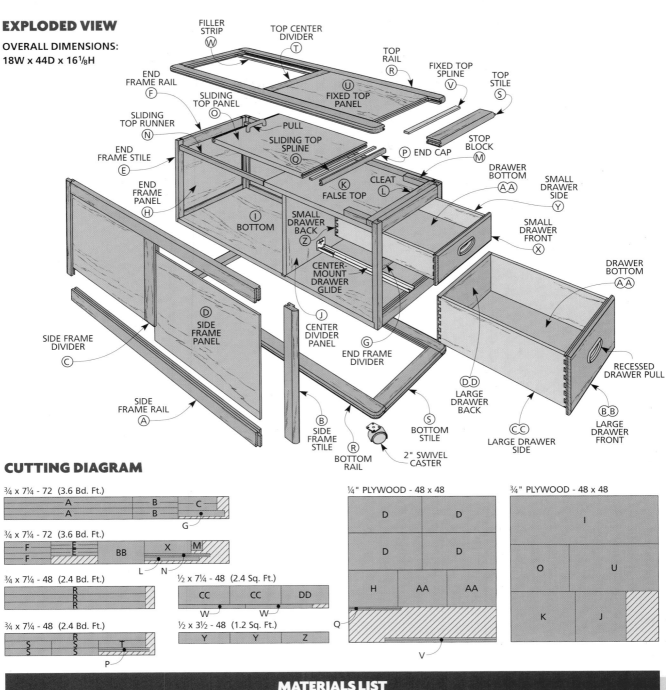

CUTTING DIAGRAM

¾ x 7¼ - 72 (3.6 Bd. Ft.)

¾ x 7¼ - 72 (3.6 Bd. Ft.)

¾ x 7¼ - 48 (2.4 Bd. Ft.)

¾ x 7¼ - 48 (2.4 Bd. Ft.)

½ x 7¼ - 48 (2.4 Sq. Ft.)

½ x 3½ - 48 (1.2 Sq. Ft.)

¼" PLYWOOD - 48 x 48

¾" PLYWOOD - 48 x 48

MATERIALS LIST

WOOD

A Side Frame Rails (4) ¾ x 1⅝ - 40½
B Side Frame Stiles (4) ¾ x 1⅝ - 14½
C Side Frame Dvdrs. (2) ¾ x 2⅛ - 12
D Side Frm. Panels (4) ¼ ply - 12 x 19⅝
E End Frame Stiles (4) ¾ x 1⅛ - 14½
F End Frame Rails (4) ¾ x 1⅝ - 14½
G End Frame Dvdr. (1) ¾ x 1⅝ - 14½
H End Frame Panel (1) ¼ ply - 12 x 14½
I Bottom (1) ¾ ply - 16 x 42
J Center Dvdr. Pnl. (1) ¾ ply - 15½ x 12⅜
K False Top (1) ¾ ply - 15½ x 20⅝
L Cleat (1) ¾ x 1⅛ - 15½
M Stop Blocks (2) ¾ x 1½ - 3⅞

N Sldg. Top Runners (2) ½ x ¾ - 20⅝
O Sliding Top Panel (1) ¾ ply - 15⅜ x 19⅝
P End Caps (2) ½ x ¾ - 15⅜
Q Sldg. Top Splines (2) ¼ ply - ½ x 15⅜
R Top/Bottom Rails (4) ¾ x 2⅛ - 44
S Top/Bottom Stiles (4) ¾ x 2⅛ - 14½
T Top Center Dvdr. (1) ¾ x 2⅛ - 14½
U Fixed Top Panel (1) ¾ ply - 13¾ x 18¾
V Fixed Top Spline (1) ¼ ply - ¾ x 70
W Filler Strips (2) ¼ x ⅜ - 20⅞
X Small Dwr. Front (1) ¾ x 4 - 14¼
Y Small Dwr. Sides (2) ½ x 3¼ - 16
Z Small Dwr. Back (1) ½ x 3¼ - 13½

AA Drawer Bottoms (2) ¼ ply - 13 x 15⅛
BB Lg. Dwr. Front (1) ¾ x 6⅝ - 14¼
CC Lg. Dwr. Sides (2) ½ x 5⅞ - 16
DD Lg. Dwr. Back (1) ½ x 5⅞ - 13½

HARDWARE SUPPLIES

(12) No. 8 x 1¼" Fh woodscrews
(8) No. 8 x 1" Fh woodscrews
(1) 3" door pull (oak)
(2) ¾" x 1" felt pads
(2) Recessed drawer pulls (oak)
(2) 17"-long center-mount drawer glides
(4) 2" swivel casters w/ screws

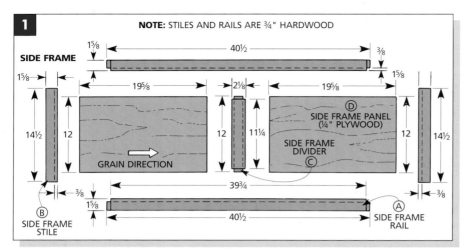

1

NOTE: STILES AND RAILS ARE ¾" HARDWOOD

SIDE FRAME

1⅝ | 40½ | ⅜

1⅝ | 19⅝ | 2⅛ | 19⅝ | 1⅝

14½ | 12 | | SIDE FRAME PANEL (¼" PLYWOOD) | | 14½

GRAIN DIRECTION | 12 | 11¼ | SIDE FRAME DIVIDER (C) | 12

39¾

⅜ | ⅜

1⅝

B SIDE FRAME STILE | 40½ | A SIDE FRAME RAIL

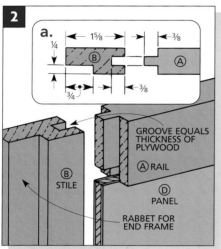

2

a.

1⅝ | ⅜

¼

B | A

¾ | ⅜

GROOVE EQUALS THICKNESS OF PLYWOOD

B STILE

A RAIL

D PANEL

RABBET FOR END FRAME

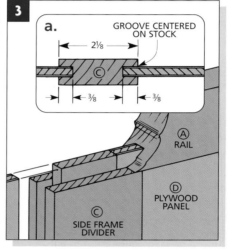

3

a.

GROOVE CENTERED ON STOCK

2⅛

C

⅜ | ⅜

A RAIL

D PLYWOOD PANEL

C SIDE FRAME DIVIDER

SIDE FRAMES

The first step in building the Toy Chest is to construct the two long side frames. Each of these frames consists of two side frame rails (A), two side frame stiles (B), a side frame divider (C), and two side frame panels (D). I used stub tenon and grooves to join the pieces. (Find out more about how to make this joint in the Joinery box below.)

CUT RAILS AND STILES. First, rip enough stock for the two rails and two stiles to a final width of 1⅝" *(Fig. 1)*. Then the rails are trimmed to their final length of 40½". (This includes an extra ¾" for the two ⅜"-long stub tenons on the rails.) Next, the stiles are trimmed to a final length of 14½".

SIDE FRAME DIVIDER. The side frame divider (C) is an extra stile that holds the plywood panels in place and adds strength to support the top of the Toy Chest. I felt that this stile would look a little better if it was wider than the stiles at the ends of the side frame. So I ripped it to 2⅛" wide *(Fig. 3)*.

Then I trimmed the dividers to a final length of 12" *(Fig. 1)*. (This includes ¾" for the two ⅜"-long stub tenons.)

CUT GROOVES. Once the rails, stiles, and dividers for the side frames are cut to size, the next step is to cut grooves on their inside edges.

JOINERY .... *Stub Tenons & Grooves*

The sides and ends of the Toy Chest are made from solid wood frames and plywood panels. But instead of traditional joinery, I've used stub tenons and grooves. What's nice about this joinery is its simplicity and its strength.

CUT GROOVES. Before I start cutting any of the joinery, I've found it's helpful to mark the face sides of all the pieces with an "X." This helps me keep things straight later on (see drawing).

The length for the tenons (⅜") is determined by the depth of the grooves cut in the frame members. These grooves serve two purposes: they serve as "open" mortises for the stub tenons, and they hold the plywood panels in the frames (see drawing at right).

Be sure to center the grooves on the thickness of the frame pieces. The easiest way to do this is to adjust the fence so the

saw blade is centered on the workpiece. Then make a single pass with each face set against the fence. Then it's easier to cut centered tenons to match.

STUB TENONS. To complete the joinery, a "stub" tenon is cut on the ends of each rail (see drawing).

Make the initial cuts so the tenon is too thick for the groove, again flipping the workpiece after each pass to center the tenon. Then gradually raise the blade, sneaking up on the final fit.

PLYWOOD PANELS. To size the panels, dry-assemble the frame and measure the opening. Then add ¾" to both dimensions (for the ⅜"-deep grooves on both sides) and cut the panels to size.

FINAL ASSEMBLY. Before I start the assembly, I've found it's best to do all final sanding first. It's difficult to do after the frames are assembled.

Then line up the pieces with the "X" facing up. Add glue to the grooves of one rail and stile and add the plywood panel.

Finally, spread glue in the grooves of the other stile and rail, and fit them over the panel. Then clamp the frame together and make sure the assembly is square.

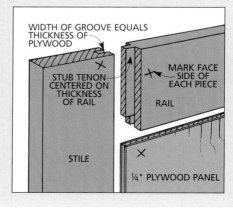

WIDTH OF GROOVE EQUALS THICKNESS OF PLYWOOD

STUB TENON CENTERED ON THICKNESS OF RAIL

MARK FACE SIDE OF EACH PIECE

RAIL

STILE

¼" PLYWOOD PANEL

These grooves not only hold the plywood panels in the frames, they also accept the stub tenons cut later on the rails *(Fig. 2)*. Lay out the pieces for the frames and mark the face side of each piece, and then mark the inside edge (where the grooves will be cut).

Note: On the divider, be sure to cut grooves on both edges *(Fig. 3a)*.

All of the grooves are centered on the thickness of the stock and are $^3/_8$" deep, and they should equal the actual thickness of the plywood you're using for the panels. (For more information on why the groove is centered, and on cutting the entire stub tenon and groove joint, see the Joinery box on the previous page.)

STUB TENONS. Next, cut the stub tenons on the ends of the rails and center dividers. These tenons are sized to fit the grooves and are $^3/_8$" long.

PANELS. Now that the frame pieces are complete, all that's needed are the plywood panels. To find the dimensions for the side frame panels (D), first dry-clamp the frames together (with the center dividers in place) and measure the inside dimensions of both openings. Then add $^3/_4$" to both dimensions to allow for the depth of the grooves. (Mine ended up being 12" x 19$^5/_8$".)

Note: When cutting the oak plywood panels to size, I cut them so the grain was running with the long dimension *(Fig. 1)*. Also, one nice touch you can add to this project is to cut and mark the panels so when they're installed in the frames, the grain pattern continues from one panel to the next on each frame.

CUT RABBETS. The last step before gluing up the frames is to cut rabbets on the stiles *(Fig. 2)*. These rabbets are used later to join the side frames to the end frames. The rabbets are cut so they're $^1/_4$" deep, and as wide as the thickness of the stock used for the end frames.

ASSEMBLE FRAME. Finally, dry-clamp the side frames together to make sure everything fits. When they check out, glue the frames together (gluing the panels into the grooves). After both side frames were complete, I went to work on the end frames.

END FRAMES

One of the end frames is similar in construction to the side frames — a basic frame with a plywood panel. But the other end frame has two drawer openings, so there's no panel. Instead, there's an end

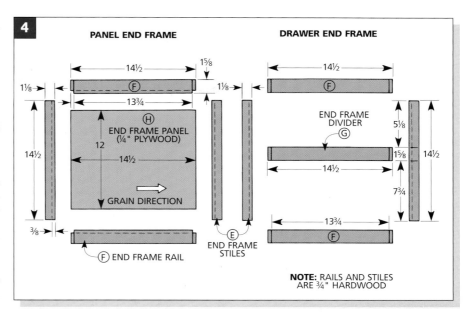

4 | PANEL END FRAME | DRAWER END FRAME

14½ 1⅝ 1⅛
1⅛ 13¾
(F)
(H)
END FRAME PANEL (¼" PLYWOOD)
14½ 12 14½
GRAIN DIRECTION
3/8
(F) END FRAME RAIL
END FRAME STILES
(E)

DRAWER END FRAME
14½
(F)
END FRAME DIVIDER (G)
5⅛ 1⅝ 14½
14½ 7¾
13¾
(F)

NOTE: RAILS AND STILES ARE ¾" HARDWOOD

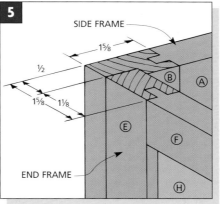

5
SIDE FRAME
1⅝
½
1⅝ 1⅛
(B) (A)
(E)
(F)
END FRAME
(H)

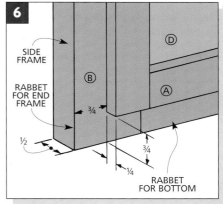

6
SIDE FRAME
RABBET FOR END FRAME
(D)
(B) (A)
¾
½ ¾
¼
RABBET FOR BOTTOM

frame divider (G) between the drawers *(Fig. 4)*. (It's a good idea to cut the pieces and joinery for both frames at the same time to save set-up time and to ensure that the frames end up identical.)

The end frame rails (F) and the end frame divider (G) are cut 1$^5/_8$" wide, but here the end frame stiles are only 1$^1/_8$" wide *(Fig. 4)*. But thanks to the rabbet in the side frame, when you look at the corner where these two frames meet, you'll see the same width stile (1$^5/_8$") on each side *(Fig. 5)*.

JOINERY. After the stiles, rails, and divider are cut to size, work can begin on the joinery. This is the same stub tenon and groove joinery used on the side frames. I cut the grooves in all the stiles first, then cut the tenons on all the rails and the divider to fit the grooves.

PANEL. Next, you'll need to cut the end frame panel (H). To determine its size, dry-clamp the frame together and measure the distance between the inside edges of the rails and stiles. Then add

$^3/_4$" to both dimensions (to allow for the two $^3/_8$"-deep grooves), and cut the plywood panel to size *(Fig. 4)*.

ASSEMBLY. After the panel is cut to size, you're ready to start assembling the end panels. As with the other frames, you should dry-clamp the two end frames first and check their fit before gluing them up. Then two rails and two stiles can be glued up around the panel *(Fig. 4)*.

When you're ready to assemble the drawer end frame, you'll need to position the end frame divider (G) so there's an opening of 3$^1/_2$" between it and the top rail. This leaves a 6$^1/_8$" opening for the bottom drawer (refer to *Fig. 7* on page 34). (The drawer hardware is added later.)

RABBET FOR BOTTOM PANEL. After the two side frames and both end frames are assembled, there's one final step. A rabbet is cut on the inside bottom edge of all four frames. These rabbets are used to join the $^3/_4$" plywood base to the bottom edges of the frames in the next step (see *Fig. 6* above and *Fig. 7* on page 34).

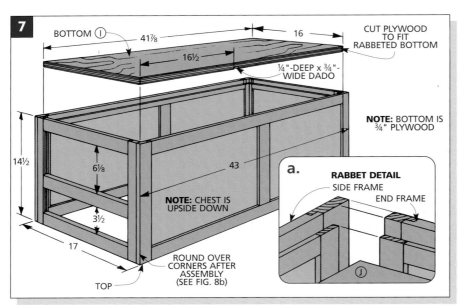

7

BOTTOM ⓘ — 41⅞ — 16

CUT PLYWOOD TO FIT RABBETED BOTTOM

16½

¼"-DEEP x ¾"-WIDE DADO

NOTE: BOTTOM IS ¾" PLYWOOD

14½

6⅛

43

3½

17

NOTE: CHEST IS UPSIDE DOWN

ROUND OVER CORNERS AFTER ASSEMBLY (SEE FIG. 8b)

TOP

a. **RABBET DETAIL**
SIDE FRAME
END FRAME
ⓙ

JOINING THE FRAMES

Now assemble the frames to form the basic chest. To keep this assembly square, place (don't glue) the plywood bottom (I) in the frames as they're being clamped.

CUT BOTTOM. To size the bottom, first dry-clamp the frames together, then measure and cut the bottom to fit the rabbeted bottom frame *(Fig. 7)*.

CUT DADO. Once the glue has set up, remove the bottom and cut a dado for the center divider, 16½" from the "drawer"

end *(Fig. 7)*. After the dado is cut, glue and clamp the bottom in place.

ROUT EDGES. Finally, round off the four corners of the chest *(Figs. 7 and 8b)*.

DIVIDER & FALSE TOP

A center divider panel separates the chest into two halves. To support the divider, I added a false top over the drawer end of the chest *(Fig. 8)*.

DIVIDER PANEL. The divider (J) is cut to width so it fits between the two side

frames. Trim it so its top edge is 1⅝" below the top edge of the side frame *(Fig. 8)*. (This makes room for the false and sliding tops, plus ⅛" for clearance.)

FALSE TOP. Next, cut the false top (K) to width so it fits between the two side frames, and to length so it extends 3⅝" beyond the divider *(Fig. 8)*.

ASSEMBLY. Before placing these two pieces in the chest, screw them together. Next, glue and clamp a cleat (L) to the end of the false top *(Fig. 8)*. And finally, install this assembly inside the chest by gluing the bottom edge of the divider in the dado, and screwing the cleat to the drawer end frame *(Figs. 8 and 8a)*.

SLIDING TOP

The next step is to add the sliding top and a pair of runners to the chest.

STOP BLOCKS. But first, I glued two stop blocks (M) to the false top *(Fig. 9)*. The blocks keep the top from opening too far and felt tabs on the ends of the blocks reduce banging as the lid is opened.

RUNNERS. Then to support the sliding top, install two sliding top runners (N) *(Figs. 9 and 9a)*. To cut these small strips, first round over two edges of a 2"-wide piece of stock. Then trim a ½"-wide strip off each edge to form the runners. Finally, screw them (no glue) into place so they're level with the top of the false top *(Fig. 9)*.

TOP PANEL. The sliding top panel (O) is a piece of ¾" plywood with caps on both ends to hide the edges. To make it, first cut the plywood to size *(Fig. 9)*.

END CAPS. To mount the end caps (P), I used groove and spline joinery. Once again, to make it safer to work with these small pieces, I cut a groove on both edges of a 2"-wide piece of oak first. Then with the same setup on the saw, I cut grooves on both ends of the plywood. Now cut the end caps from each edge of the piece, and trim them to fit the width of the top.

Next, I joined the caps to the panel with two sliding top splines (Q) cut to fit the grooves, gluing and clamping them to the panel *(Fig. 9b)*. Finally, rout ¼" roundovers on the edges of the end caps.

DRAWER PULL. The last step is to add a handle to the sliding lid. There are two ways to do this. If your kids are older you can use the recessed drawer pulls (see the Technique article on page 36). But to give younger kids something to grab onto, you may want to use a D-shaped handle, centering it 2⅛" from the front edge *(Fig. 9)*. (See Sources, page 126.)

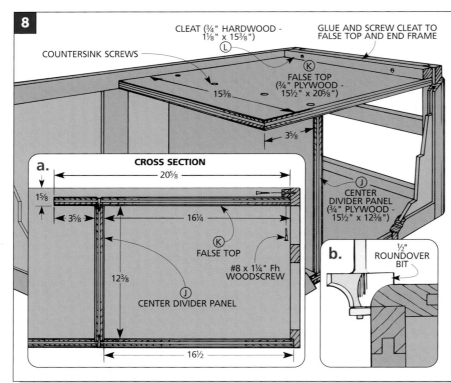

8

COUNTERSINK SCREWS

CLEAT (¾" HARDWOOD - 1⅛" x 15⅜")
ⓛ

GLUE AND SCREW CLEAT TO FALSE TOP AND END FRAME

ⓚ
FALSE TOP (¾" PLYWOOD - 15½" x 20⅝")

15⅜

3⅝

CENTER DIVIDER PANEL (¾" PLYWOOD - 15½" x 12⅜")
ⓙ

a. **CROSS SECTION**
20⅝
1⅝
3⅝
16¼
ⓚ
FALSE TOP
#8 x 1¼" Fh WOODSCREW
12⅜
ⓙ
CENTER DIVIDER PANEL
16½

b. ½" ROUNDOVER BIT

There are two more frames to build to complete this chest: one for the top and one for the bottom.

RAILS. The top and bottom rails (R) are exactly the same. So they can be ripped to width and cut 1" longer than the length of the assembled chest *(Fig. 10)*.

STILES. There are four identical stiles (S) for each frame, and a top center divider (T) for the top frame only. They're ripped to width and then cut to length so that the completed frames will overhang the case on the front and back by 1/2".

BOTTOM FRAME. Now the bottom frame can be assembled. Cut 1/4"-wide by 3/8"-deep grooves in all the rails. Then cut stub tenons on the ends of all four stiles (and the center divider) to fit the grooves, and glue and clamp the two rails and stiles for the bottom frame together.

FIXED PANEL. The top frame still needs a plywood panel (to cover the false top) before it can be assembled.

To size the fixed top panel (U), center the divider in the top frame and dry-clamp it together. Then measure the opening and cut the panel to this size *(Fig. 10)*.

GROOVES. Again, I used groove and spline joinery to mount the panel into the top frame. So you'll need to cut grooves on the edge of one stile, and one edge of the center divider, and on all four edges of the fixed top panel *(Fig. 10)*.

Note: Since plywood and hardwood are not always the same thickness, I always placed the face sides of the pieces against the fence when cutting the grooves. This way I could compensate for any variation in their thicknesses.

When all the grooves are complete, cut the 1/4" plywood to length for the fixed top splines (V) and glue and clamp the top frame and panel together *(Fig. 11b)*.

FILL GROOVE. Finally, fill the grooves on the inside edges of the rails with a filler strip (W) *(Fig. 11)*. When the inside edges of the top panel are rounded over and sanded, this filler strip disappears.

ROUND CORNERS. To finish both frames, add a 1" radius to the four corners on each frame *(Fig. 11a)*. Then rout 1/4" roundovers on the top and bottom edges.

ATTACH FRAMES. Finally, mount the two frames with a 1/2" overhang all around (refer to *Fig. 12* on page 36). First, glue and clamp the bottom frame in place. Then, apply a couple of coats of finish to the sliding top, put it in place and glue the top frame to the case assembly.

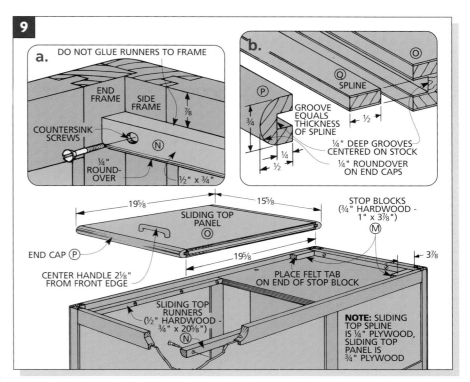

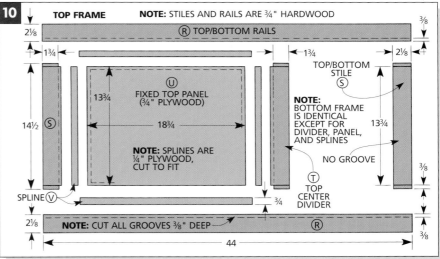

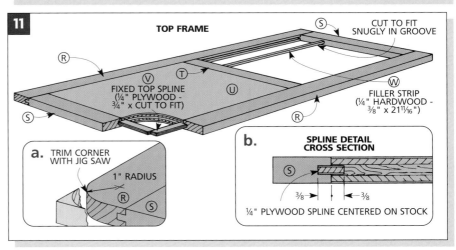

The drawers are joined with machine-cut half-blind dovetails. And I used a rabbeted drawer front for both the top and bottom drawers *(Fig. 13a)*.

DRAWER FRONTS. To size these drawer fronts, first measure the openings and add $\frac{1}{2}$" to each dimension (to allow for a $\frac{1}{4}$" lip on all four edges).

After the small (X) and large (BB) drawer fronts are cut to final size, rout a $\frac{3}{8}$" x $\frac{3}{8}$" rabbet on the back sides to produce the rabbeted drawer front *(Fig. 13a)*.

SIDES AND BACKS. Now cut the small (Y) and large (CC) drawer sides to length. Their height matches the distance between rabbets on the drawer fronts. The small (Z) and large (DD) drawer backs are cut to the same height as the sides, and to length to match the distance between the rabbets on the drawer front.

DOVETAILS. After all the drawer pieces are cut to size, the next step is to rout the half-blind dovetails that join the drawer sides to the drawer fronts and backs.

BOTTOM. When the dovetails are complete, cut the grooves in the drawer's front, sides, and back to hold the plywood bottom in place. These grooves are cut $\frac{3}{8}$" from the bottom edge. Then a pair of drawer bottoms (AA) are cut to fit the grooves. (Mine were 13" x $15\frac{3}{4}$".)

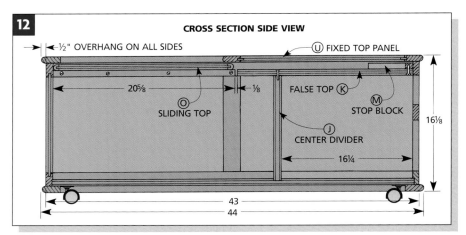

12 CROSS SECTION SIDE VIEW

$\frac{1}{2}$" OVERHANG ON ALL SIDES — (U) FIXED TOP PANEL — $20\frac{5}{8}$ — $\frac{1}{8}$ — FALSE TOP (K) — (M) — (O) SLIDING TOP — STOP BLOCK — (J) CENTER DIVIDER — $16\frac{1}{8}$ — $16\frac{1}{4}$ — 43 — 44

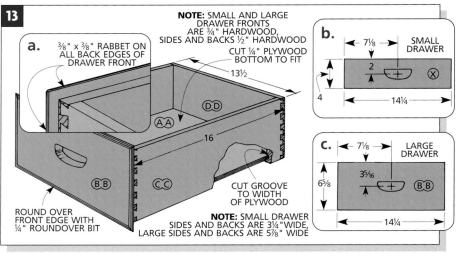

13

a. $\frac{3}{8}$" x $\frac{3}{8}$" RABBET ON ALL BACK EDGES OF DRAWER FRONT

NOTE: SMALL AND LARGE DRAWER FRONTS ARE $\frac{3}{4}$" HARDWOOD, SIDES AND BACKS $\frac{1}{2}$" HARDWOOD

CUT $\frac{1}{4}$" PLYWOOD BOTTOM TO FIT

$13\frac{1}{2}$ — (DD) — (AA) — 16 — (BB) — (CC)

ROUND OVER FRONT EDGE WITH $\frac{1}{4}$" ROUNDOVER BIT

CUT GROOVE TO WIDTH OF PLYWOOD

NOTE: SMALL DRAWER SIDES AND BACKS ARE $3\frac{1}{4}$" WIDE, LARGE SIDES AND BACKS ARE $5\frac{7}{8}$" WIDE

b. $7\frac{1}{8}$ — SMALL DRAWER — 2 — 4 — $14\frac{1}{4}$ — (X)

c. $7\frac{1}{8}$ — LARGE DRAWER — $3\frac{5}{16}$ — $6\frac{5}{8}$ — $14\frac{1}{4}$ — (BB)

TECHNIQUE .... *Routing Recesses*

Before the Toy Chest can be assembled you'll need to make recesses for the drawer pulls.

To rout the recess for these pulls you need a template and a $\frac{7}{16}$" guide bushing mounted to the base of a router.

TEMPLATE. The template is made by flipping one of the oak drawer pulls upside down and tracing the outline of its flange on a piece of $\frac{1}{4}$" hardboard *(Figs. 1 and 1a)*. (The outside profile of the pull will compensate for the slightly narrower cut made when the bushing and $\frac{1}{4}$" bit are combined to cut the recess.)

Now drill two holes inside the lines *(Fig. 2)*, and use a jig saw and file to cut and smooth the opening *(Fig. 3)*.

ROUT RECESS. Try a test cut on scrap and make adjustments to the template if necessary. Then it's just a matter of clamping the template to the drawer front and routing the recess *(Fig. 4)*.

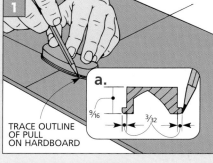

1

a. $\frac{9}{16}$ — $\frac{3}{32}$

TRACE OUTLINE OF PULL ON HARDBOARD

2

DRILL HOLES INSIDE LINES OF OUTLINE

OUTLINE OF DRAWER PULL

3

CUT OUT OPENING WITH JIG SAW

SHAPE AND SMOOTH WITH FILE

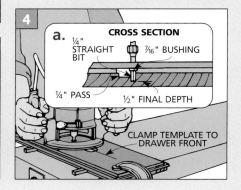

4

a. CROSS SECTION

$\frac{1}{4}$" STRAIGHT BIT — $\frac{7}{16}$" BUSHING

$\frac{1}{4}$" PASS — $\frac{1}{2}$" FINAL DEPTH

CLAMP TEMPLATE TO DRAWER FRONT

DRAWER PULLS. Before assembly, I added the recessed drawer pulls. These pulls are designed to be mounted flush with the fronts of the drawers. So to add them, you'll need to rout a recess for each of the drawer pulls. (See the Technique on the preceding page.) Or for younger kids, install a 3" D-shaped pull centered on each drawer front.

ROUND DRAWER FRONTS. To complete the drawer fronts, use a ¼" roundover bit on the outside edges *(Fig. 13)*. Finally, I glued the drawers together, and glued the pulls in place.

DRAWER GLIDES. To mount the drawers in the chest, I installed center-mounted drawer glides (see Sources on page 126). This hardware requires that notches be cut in the drawer front and back for the channel piece *(Fig. 14)*. Then the other half of the slide hardware is mounted to the rails of the frame and the cabinet divider *(Fig. 14)*. Now, mount 2" plate-style casters to the bottom of the chest.

The top will get lots of use. So to provide maximum protection, I finished it with two coats of clear satin polyurethane. ▪

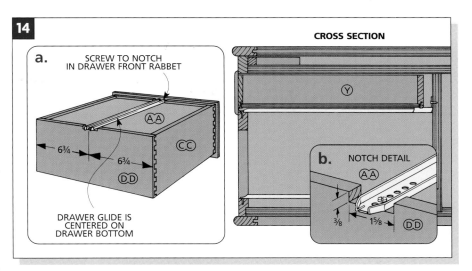

DESIGNER'S NOTEBOOK

Dress up the Toy Chest with just a few simple changes.

CONSTRUCTION NOTES:

▪ A few upgrades and some paint will change this chest into a Country-Style Chest. First, make the side frames and the panel end frames, except this time use ¼"-thick beaded plywood for the side frame (D) and end frame (H) panels.

Note: I aligned the panels with the beads running vertically.

▪ To complete construction of this chest, I added a decorative apron to the bottom frame. The apron dresses up the chest, giving it a more finished look. But there's just one problem. The apron raises the bottom of the chest up enough so that the casters won't reach the floor. To solve this problem, I added spacer blocks to the bottom to provide extra clearance *(Fig. 2)*. The spacers (EE) are made from ¾"-thick hardwood and they're attached to the bottom with glue.

▪ Finally, rip the apron sides (FF) and ends (GG) to width and cut them to length *(Figs. 1 and 2)*.

▪ Add the curved cutout and rabbet to the side aprons. An easy way to cut the curves once they're laid out is to gang all four pieces together (use double-sided tape). Then cut and sand them at the same time.

▪ To attach the aprons, first drill the shank holes *(Fig. 1)*, then place the aprons so there's clearance for the casters and glue and screw them to the frame *(Fig. 2)*.

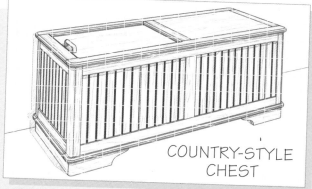

COUNTRY-STYLE CHEST

MATERIALS LIST

NEW PARTS

EE	Spacer Blocks (4)	¾ x 2⅛ - 2⅛
FF	Apron Sides (4)	¾ x 2¼ - 10
GG	Apron Ends (2)	¾ x 2¼ - 15⅞

Note: Beaded plywood used for frame panels.

HARDWARE SUPPLIES

(12) No. 8 x 1½" Fh woodscrews

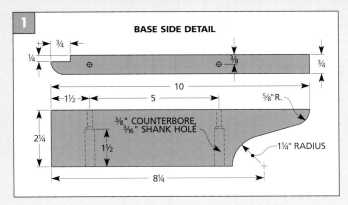

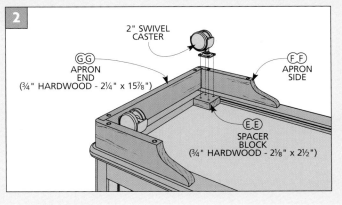

Furniture & Accessories

Y ou know why we call it "home" entertainment? Because home is where you feel most comfortable. The snack tray, the TV trays, and the folding table are easy to build and each adds significantly to the comfort level of your home. The magazine rack and the plant stand provide challenging techniques, with results that enhance your surroundings, but are fun to build.

Routed Snack Tray

You'll want to build lots of snack trays to give away as gifts. That's because they're so much fun to make. From the insides of the tray to the outside circle — everything is done with a router and a routing jig.

Every year I spend at least a couple of weekends during the holiday season building gifts for friends and family. And there are times when I spend *several* weekends working on them. But that wasn't the case with this Routed Snack Tray. Building one is so quick and easy, and so much fun, that I decided to make several of them.

When I was in the middle of routing out the snack trays, it occurred to me that there aren't many projects that can be made entirely with a router. In fact, it was a first for me. Every step in the process — from routing the insides of the tray compartments, to cutting the tray into a circle, to shaping the cove molding on the outside edge of the tray is done with the router.

Granted, some other shop tools are needed to get set up, but once the project blank is ready, the only tool these trays require from start to finish is a router.

PIN ROUTER. The key to routing the clean lines is a shop-built pin router. It's easy to build and use. And because you'll need to build the pin router before you can rout the trays, you might just want to read the Shop Jig article on page 44 before starting in on the trays. You'll not only learn how to build the jig, you'll also get some tips on how to set it up.

ALTERNATE PATTERN. If you're making extra trays as gifts, you may not want all of them to be exactly the same, so there is an alternate pattern for a rectangular-shaped tray described in the Designer's Notebook on page 42.

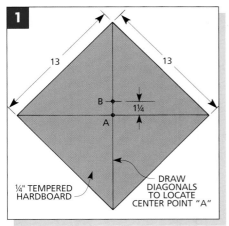

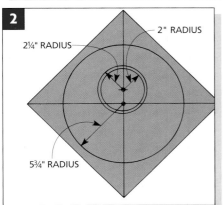

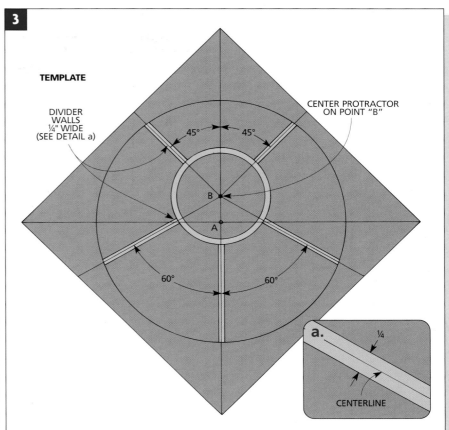

TEMPLATE

Before I could start routing the snack tray, I had to construct a template to use with the pin router (see the Shop Jig on page 44). The template starts out as a 13"-square piece of ¼" tempered hardboard.

The template design has a small circle that's off-centered inside a large circle. To achieve the wedge shaped compartments, I added five dividing walls to connect the circles (refer to *Fig. 3*).

LOCATE CENTERS. The center of the large outside circle (point "A") is located by drawing two diagonal lines connecting the corners of the square *(Fig. 1)*. (The center point is where these diagonal lines intersect.) The center of the smaller, offset circle (point "B") is located on one of the diagonal lines, 1¼" from point "A."

DRAW CIRCLES

After the center points are marked, use a compass to draw three circles *(Fig. 2)*. The largest circle (which represents the inside edge of the outside wall) uses point "A" as its center, and has a radius of 5¾".

The two small circles represent the inside and outside edges of the center compartment walls. Both use point "B" as their center. For the outside edge of the center compartment wall, draw a circle with a radius of 2¼", and for the inside edge, a circle with a 2" radius *(Fig. 2)*.

DIVIDER WALLS. Next, draw lines to separate the large circle into five wedge-shaped compartments. All five lines start at point "B" and use the line on which points "A" and "B" lie as a reference.

First, two divider walls are angled up 45° from point "B." Then two are angled down 60° from point "B." And finally, the fifth wall is right on the line *(Fig. 3)*. Use a protractor, or drafting triangle to determine the angle for each line.

THICKEN WALLS. After the centerlines for the walls are marked, thicken each wall by drawing two more lines ⅛" to each side of the centerline (making each wall ¼" wide) *(Fig. 3a)*. Note that all of these lines start at the outside circle and stop where they intersect the largest of the two offset circles *(Fig. 3)*.

CUT OUT THE PATTERN

After the pattern has been marked on the hardboard, the next step is to cut the template to shape. To cut the curved edges as smoothly and accurately as possible, I decided to use a router with a trammel point attachment. (See page 74 for shop-made router trammel plans.)

STARTER HOLES. Before you do any routing you'll need to drill holes for starting the cuts. The five wedge-shaped compartments each receive two starter holes, one adjacent to the outside wall, and another next to the outside edge of the center compartment wall (refer to *Fig. 5* on page 42). Also drill one starter hole next to the inside edge of the center compartment wall. All of these holes should be drilled so their edges just touch the inside of the line.

TACK DOWN TEMPLATE. After the starter holes are drilled, attach the template to a piece of plywood to keep it steady while routing out the compartments (refer to *Fig. 4* on page 42). (The plywood should be large enough so it can be clamped to a work surface without the clamps getting in the way of the router.)

When tacking the template to the base, drive a brad in each corner of the template. Drive at least two brads in the off-set center circle to keep it (and the router and trammel point attached to this piece) in place as it's cut free by the router.

ROUTING. Now position the trammel point on point "A." Then adjust the trammel so the *outside* edge of the bit cuts exactly on the marked line of the outside circle. (Use a ¼" straight bit set deep enough to cut through the hardboard template in one pass.)

As you rout the compartments, take it easy near the lines for the divider walls. It's better to stop short of these lines than to take the chance of cutting into them.

After the outside is cut, shift the trammel attachment to point "B" and adjust it so the *inside* edge of the bit cuts right on the outside edge of the center compartment wall *(Fig. 5)*. Again, be sure to stop short of the divider walls.

Finally, with the trammel point still set in point "B," adjust its length to cut the inside wall of the center compartment. Be sure to move the router in a clockwise rotation, making a single cut around the entire circumference of this circle.

CUT THE WALLS. When the routing is completed *(Fig. 5)*, carefully remove the template from the plywood holder, and cut out the divider walls.

I used a scroll saw to do this. I cut close to the lines, then I filed and sanded

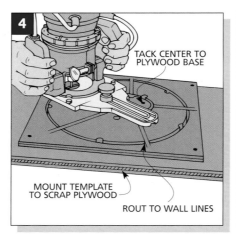

MOUNT TEMPLATE TO SCRAP PLYWOOD

TACK CENTER TO PLYWOOD BASE

ROUT TO WALL LINES

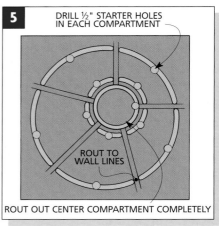

DRILL ½" STARTER HOLES IN EACH COMPARTMENT

ROUT TO WALL LINES

ROUT OUT CENTER COMPARTMENT COMPLETELY

the edges of each compartment as smooth as possible.

TRAY BLANK HOLDER

Before using the template, you'll need to glue it to a base to hold the walls steady as the pin hits them while routing *(Fig. 6)*. I used a scrap piece of ½" medium density fiberboard (MDF). Then I added keeper strips to the sides of the base. The strips form a "holder" box to trap the workpiece *(Fig. 6)*.

TRAY BLANKS. Now the tray blank can be made by edge-gluing enough stock to form a square. I planed and sanded both surfaces of this blank smooth, and then I trimmed it to fit snugly in the tray blank holder box.

Note: Small brads in the corners of the box hold the blank in place *(Fig. 6)*.

TRAY COMPARTMENTS

I wanted each compartment to have a flat bottom which gently curved at the

---

DESIGNER'S NOTEBOOK

The shape has changed — the way it's built stays the same.

CONSTRUCTION NOTES:

■ The only change for this snack tray is the shape — it's rectangular. Just like you did for the round tray, you'll need to start by making a template for the pin router. (See the Shop Jig box on page 44.) Begin by laying out the template on a piece of ¼" tempered hardboard *(Fig. 1)*.

■ Now drill a ½" starter hole in each corner of all six compartments *(Fig. 1)*. Since all the divider walls on this template are straight, I used a jig saw to cut out the waste areas for each template compartment.

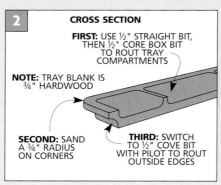

RECTANGULAR TRAY

Note: The holes serve a dual purpose: they give you an easy way to remove the waste areas on the template. Plus they leave each tray compartment with nice rounded corners for the pin router pin to follow.

■ Finally, nail the template to a base and secure the blank with keeper strips. Then rout the tray compartments, sand the radius on the corners, and use a cove bit to rout the edge profile *(Fig. 2)*.

1 TEMPLATE

½" STARTER HOLE

11¼

10¼

5

¼

2½   5   5   2½

½   ¼   ¼   ½

16¾   ½

2 CROSS SECTION

FIRST: USE ½" STRAIGHT BIT, THEN ½" CORE BOX BIT TO ROUT TRAY COMPARTMENTS

NOTE: TRAY BLANK IS ¾" HARDWOOD

SECOND: SAND A ¾" RADIUS ON CORNERS

THIRD: SWITCH TO ½" COVE BIT WITH PILOT TO ROUT OUTSIDE EDGES "corners" (where the bottom meets the divider walls). It took a while to come up with the right combination of bits and pins to achieve the curved-wall effect.

To get a flat bottom, I had to use a straight bit. But that meant the corners would be square. After some experimenting, I found that a combination of a large guide pin in the pin router jig and a small bit in the router would cut each compartment so the edge of the straight bit stopped right where the radius of the corner would start.

This means each compartment is routed in two stages — with two different combinations of bits and pins. In the first stage, I used a $1/2$" straight bit with a 1" guide pin to rout the flat bottoms *(Fig. 7)*.

For the first pass, adjust the straight bit so it cuts about $1/8$" deep. Then turn on the router, plunge the center of one of the compartments down on the bit, and move the pin arm into position *(Fig. 6)*.

ROUT COMPARTMENTS. To rout a compartment, I've found it's best to move the template so the pin is against a wall, and then follow a counter-clockwise path around the perimeter of the compartment. To clean out the waste in the center of the compartment, simply move the template back and forth under the pin until the entire area in the compartment has been passed over with the pin. Then repeat the procedure for each compartment on the template.

Finally, reset the router and make two more passes (in $1/8$" increments) to rout each compartment to a final depth of $3/8$".

ROUND CORNERS. To create the rounded corners at the bottom of each compartment, switch to a $1/2$" core box bit combined with a $1/2$"-dia. pin *(Fig. 8)*. Set the depth of cut so the bit is well shy of the bottom and make a pass around the perimeter of each compartment.

Then increase the depth of cut a little at a time (sneaking up on the final depth) until the round corner profile meets the flat bottom of the compartments.

Note: Although the corners of each compartment in the *template* are "square" (where the divider walls meet the circles), the routed pattern on the *tray* will have rounded corners because the bits are round. This is the pattern I wanted.

CUT OUT TRAY. When all the compartments are routed, remove the blank from the holding box, and trim the tray to its final circular shape.

To do this, tack the blank (face down) to a piece of scrap plywood, nailing

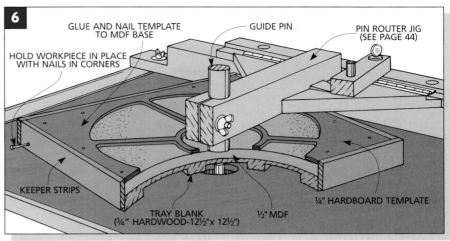

6   GLUE AND NAIL TEMPLATE TO MDF BASE   GUIDE PIN   PIN ROUTER JIG (SEE PAGE 44)

HOLD WORKPIECE IN PLACE WITH NAILS IN CORNERS

KEEPER STRIPS

TRAY BLANK ($3/4$" HARDWOOD-$12^1/2$" x $12^1/2$") $1/2$" MDF $1/4$" HARDBOARD TEMPLATE

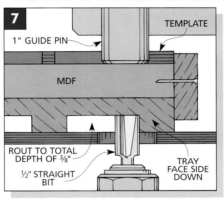

7   1" GUIDE PIN   TEMPLATE

MDF

ROUT TO TOTAL DEPTH OF $3/8$" $1/2$" STRAIGHT BIT   TRAY FACE SIDE DOWN

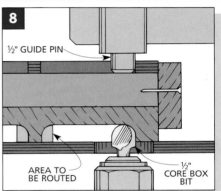

8   $1/2$" GUIDE PIN

AREA TO BE ROUTED $1/2$" CORE BOX BIT

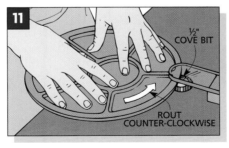

9   $1/4$" STARTER HOLE   LOCATE CENTER WITH DIAGONAL LINES

$6^3/8$

NAIL ONLY IN CORNERS

ATTACH ROUTED TRAY FACE DOWN TO SCRAP PLYWOOD

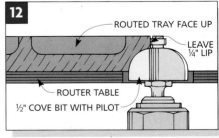

10   ROUT CIRCUMFERENCE WITH $1/4$" STRAIGHT BIT

FINISH DIAMETER $12^1/2$"   TACK FOUR CORNERS

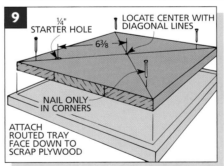

11   $1/2$" COVE BIT

ROUT COUNTER-CLOCKWISE

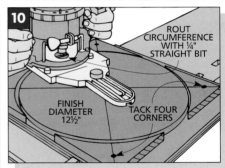

12   ROUTED TRAY FACE UP

LEAVE $1/4$" LIP

ROUTER TABLE $1/2$" COVE BIT WITH PILOT

through the corner waste areas *(Fig. 9)*. Draw diagonal lines from corner to corner to locate the center of the blank.

Now set the trammel attachment on the router to cut a $6^1/4$" radius. Then, using a $1/4$" straight bit, make several successively deeper passes with the router to free the tray from the blank *(Fig. 10)*.

COVE MOLDING. With the snack tray cut out, rout a cove for a finger hold on the outside edge using a $1/2$" cove bit on the router table *(Figs. 11 and 12)*.

FINISHING. Finally, sand each of the compartments to remove any marks left by the router bits. Then I finished the snack tray with a salad bowl finish. ∎

Pin routing is a technique used to make identical copies of a specific pattern. For the pin router to work, a pin is centered directly over the router bit. The pin traces a cutout in a template, while the router bit cuts the same design in a workpiece fastened to the template.

PIN ROUTERS. In most pin router setups, the router is mounted on an overhead arm that can be moved up and down to engage and disengage the workpiece.

Then to rout a pattern, a template is attached to the bottom of the workpiece, which is placed over a stationary pin mounted to the table of the pin router. The pin serves as a guide for the template.

ANOTHER VERSION. My version of a pin router is flipped upside down so it could be used on my router table. Since the router is already mounted (upside down) on the router table, it's necessary to have the pin on top.

Besides being inexpensive, this setup is a little easier to work with than the normal pin routing setup. The router remains stationary and out of the way so there's little chance of bumping it out of position while routing. Instead, the pin is conveniently moved out of the way when the workpiece has to be repositioned.

MOVABLE ARM

The key to this router table pin routing system is mounting the guide pin to an arm that can be easily moved out of the way for access. However, the guide pin (and the arm that holds it) must be held very stable during the routing operation.

If either the pin or the pin's support arm moves during the routing operation, there will be a "bump" in the routed piece.

To eliminate any movement, the guide pin is clamped in a thick support arm *(Fig. 1)*. Then the support arm is mounted to a triangular support piece that holds it steady. And finally the triangular support piece is hinged on a fixed plate so it can be flipped up out of the way.

CONSTRUCTION. There are three main parts for this set-up: a fixed plate (A), the triangular support (B), and the pin support arm (C). To start, cut the fixed plate (A) from a piece of $^3/_4$" plywood *(Fig. 1a)*.

FIXED PLATE. The fixed plate is sized to fit on the top of the router table's fence — 16" long and equal to the width of the fence ($2^1/_4$" on my router table).

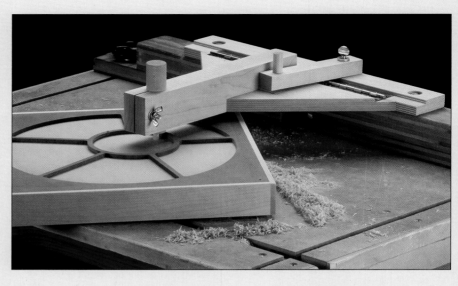

Then this plate is bolted to the fence with hex-head bolts screwed into threaded inserts so it's replaceable *(Fig 2)*.

To mount the plate to the fence, drill $^3/_4$" counterbored holes deep enough to accept the head of the bolt and a washer, and follow with $^1/_4$" holes for the bolts.

Then mark the position of these two holes on the top of the fence, and drill $^3/_8$" holes in the fence for the inserts.

TRIANGULAR SUPPORT. Before attaching the fixed plate to the fence, go ahead and make the triangular support (B). To make this support, first cut a piece of $^3/_4$" plywood to a length of $13^1/_2$" and a width of 6", and miter both ends at 45° *(Fig. 1a)*. When these miters are cut, they won't meet at the center — there will be a $1^1/_2$" "stub point" where the pin support arm will be attached *(Fig. 1)*.

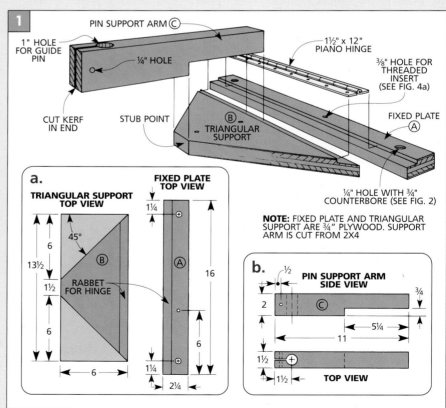

1

PIN SUPPORT ARM (C)

1" HOLE FOR GUIDE PIN

$^1/_4$" HOLE

$1^1/_2$" x 12" PIANO HINGE

$^3/_8$" HOLE FOR THREADED INSERT (SEE FIG. 4a)

CUT KERF IN END

STUB POINT

(B) TRIANGULAR SUPPORT

FIXED PLATE (A)

$^1/_4$" HOLE WITH $^3/_4$" COUNTERBORE (SEE FIG. 2)

NOTE: FIXED PLATE AND TRIANGULAR SUPPORT ARE $^3/_4$" PLYWOOD. SUPPORT ARM IS CUT FROM 2X4

a.

TRIANGULAR SUPPORT TOP VIEW

6 — 45°

$13^1/_2$

$1^1/_2$

6

(B) RABBET FOR HINGE

6

FIXED PLATE TOP VIEW

$1^1/_4$

(A)

16

6

$1^1/_4$

$2^1/_4$

b.

$^1/_2$

PIN SUPPORT ARM SIDE VIEW

$^3/_4$

2 (C)

$5^1/_4$

11

$1^1/_2$

$1^1/_2$

TOP VIEW

RABBET FOR HINGE. Later, the triangular support will be joined to the fixed plate with a piano hinge *(Fig. 2)*. To keep this hinge out of the way of the holddown lever (that's attached later), rout a shallow rabbet in both the plate and triangular support. (The rabbet is cut to match the size of the hinge you use.)

PIN SUPPORT ARM

Next, the pin support arm is cut to size and attached to the triangular support.

Note: The distance between the guide pin (at the end of the pin arm) and the router table fence determines the size of workpiece that can be built with this jig. So the longer the pin arm, the better.

To find the maximum length for the pin arm, move the fence back as far as it will go on the router table. Then measure the distance from the fence to the router bit, and add ¼". This is the length of the pin support arm (C) (11" in my case). This length also allows an extra ½" for adjusting the jig over the bit.

Make the pin arm from scrap 2x4, ripped 2" wide. Then cut a notch at one end to fit over the triangular support *(Fig. 1b)*.

HOLE FOR GUIDE PIN. Now, drill a hole for the guide pin through the 2" thickness of the arm to give the pin as much support as possible *(Fig. 3)*. It's very important that the hole is exactly perpendicular to the router table.

CLAMPING BOLT. To hold the guide pin tightly in this hole, I added a clamping bolt at the end of the pin arm.

First, drill a horizontal hole through the pin arm, centering it ½" from the front end of the arm. Then cut a kerf from the end of the pin arm into the 1"-dia. hole (the one for the guide pin) *(Fig. 3)*. To clamp the pin in place, use a carriage bolt, washer, and wing nut to pinch the two sides of the arm around the guide pin.

ASSEMBLY. Finally, glue and screw the pin arm to the triangular support, making sure to countersink the screws through the bottom of the support. Then install the piano hinge in the rabbets to join the triangular support to the fixed plate.

HOLDDOWN & GUIDE PINS

A holddown helps to keep the pin arm from lifting up and out of the template.

HOLDDOWN. To hold the pin arm in position while routing I added a small hold-down lever (D) with a ½" dowel at one end to use as a handle (E) for moving the lever back and forth *(Fig. 4)*.

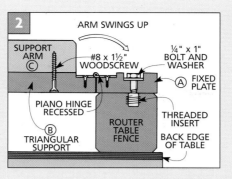

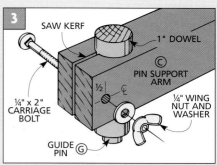

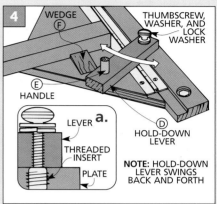

To attach this lever to the fixed plate, drill a ⅜" hole in the plate (A) for a threaded insert. Then use a thumbscrew, washer, and lock washer to hold the lever in place. Also, to compensate for any "play" in the hinge and to keep the pin arm firmly on the template, glue a wedge (F) to the top of the triangular support.

ATTACHING THE JIG. This completes the movable pin arm attachment. It can be mounted to the fence of the router table with two ¼" hex-head bolts and washers.

The only thing left to make is the guide pin — the key to the whole technique.

WOODEN PINS. To make the guide pins (G), I started with a 1" dowel and cut the end down to the diameter I wanted for each pin. This sounds difficult, but it's really just a matter of cutting a round tenon on the end of the dowel.

CUTTING JIG. To do this, you need a holding jig for the dowel *(Fig. 5)*. The jig is just a stop tacked to a plywood base so the stop is perpendicular to the saw blade.

To make the pin, hold the dowel against the stop. Then turn on the saw and gradually raise the rip blade until it cuts into the dowel the desired depth. Slowly rotate the dowel to "turn" the diameter of the dowel to the size you need.

As the dowel is being rotated, push it back and forth so the pin is cut to a length of about ⅜". (This length will keep the shoulder of the dowel above the surface of the ¼"-thick template.) You can make several sizes of pins this way, and each one will be exactly centered on the 1" dowel, making them interchangeable.

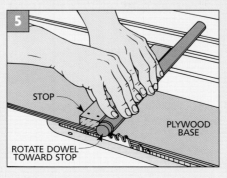

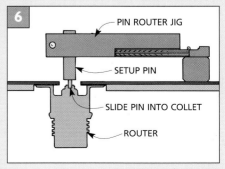

SET UP THE PIN ROUTER

To center the pin on the router bit, I use a ¼"-dia. "set-up" pin. Insert this pin in the pin arm and adjust the fence so the pin fits into the collet of the router *(Fig. 6)*.

The trick is to make sure the support arm is exactly parallel to the surface of the router table. (Measure the height of the support arm at the fence and out at the end of the arm. These two measurements should be equal.) When the set-up pin is centered on the collet, clamp the fence tightly on the router table.

Then replace the set-up pin with the pin that will be used to rout the workpiece. And place the template box (with the workpiece) under the pin. Once again, make sure the support arm is parallel to the router table by adjusting the height of the pin as it rests on the template. Then set the height (depth of cut) of the router bit, and you're ready to rout.

TV Trays and Stand

These trays are great for when you're entertaining guests or even when you're eating a snack in front of the television set. You can build a set of four and the stand for an attractive addition to your home.

The other day I was at a local discount store and saw a set of "solid wood" TV trays. They looked like what you'd expect from a discount store, but I wanted to see if they were sturdy. They weren't. When I touched the one on display, it wiggled like a duck at dinner time. Then I began to really wiggle when I saw the price tag for this wood set of four TV trays and a stand. That's when I decided to go ahead and come up with plans of my own for a set of trays.

ROTO-HINGE. At one point in the design process, I thought I'd use an arrangement of dowels and wooden nuts as a "pivot" so the legs could scissor open.

Then I learned about a hinge that I thought would be an ideal solution for my TV trays. It's called a Roto-Hinge. The Roto-Hinge is actually a very simple device that works great. It's just two wooden drums held together with a rivet. To learn more about them and where to buy them, see the Hardware box on page 49 and Sources on page 126.

LAMINATE TOP. Once I'd solved the wobbling problem, I turned my attention to the tray top. It's just a plywood panel that I sandwiched between two pieces of laminate. Then I wrapped the laminated top with solid wood rails and stiles using tongue and groove joinery.

T-MOLDING. There's also an option described in the Designer's Notebook on page 51 for a more economical tray top. As an alternative to a laminated top you could simply use a piece of oak plywood for the top. But instead of covering the edges with hardwood, use some plastic T-molding. This special molding hides the exposed edges of the plywood and it's really easy to install.

STORAGE STAND. Finally, I thought it would be nice to have some kind of storage for the TV trays, so I designed a stand that holds all four trays. It has a set of four swivel casters so you can roll it around for easy storage.

EXPLODED VIEW

OVERALL DIMENSIONS:
23³⁄₄W x 16D x 26H (OPEN TRAY)
21¹⁄₄W x 17¹⁄₈D x 37⁵⁄₈H (STAND)

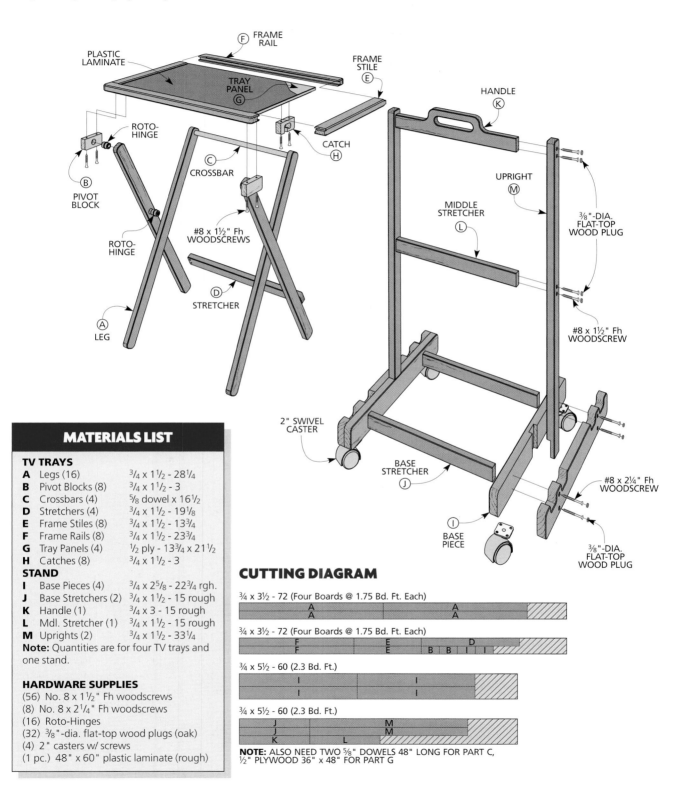

MATERIALS LIST

TV TRAYS

A	Legs (16)	³⁄₄ x 1¹⁄₂ - 28¹⁄₄
B	Pivot Blocks (8)	³⁄₄ x 1¹⁄₂ - 3
C	Crossbars (4)	⁵⁄₈ dowel x 16¹⁄₂
D	Stretchers (4)	³⁄₄ x 1¹⁄₂ - 19¹⁄₈
E	Frame Stiles (8)	³⁄₄ x 1¹⁄₂ - 13³⁄₄
F	Frame Rails (8)	³⁄₄ x 1¹⁄₂ - 23³⁄₄
G	Tray Panels (4)	¹⁄₂ ply - 13³⁄₄ x 21¹⁄₂
H	Catches (8)	³⁄₄ x 1¹⁄₂ - 3

STAND

I	Base Pieces (4)	³⁄₄ x 2⁵⁄₈ - 22³⁄₄ rgh.
J	Base Stretchers (2)	³⁄₄ x 1¹⁄₂ - 15 rough
K	Handle (1)	³⁄₄ x 3 - 15 rough
L	Mdl. Stretcher (1)	³⁄₄ x 1¹⁄₂ - 15 rough
M	Uprights (2)	³⁄₄ x 1¹⁄₂ - 33¹⁄₄

Note: Quantities are for four TV trays and one stand.

HARDWARE SUPPLIES

(56) No. 8 x 1¹⁄₂" Fh woodscrews
(8) No. 8 x 2¹⁄₄" Fh woodscrews
(16) Roto-Hinges
(32) ³⁄₈"-dia. flat-top wood plugs (oak)
(4) 2" casters w/ screws
(1 pc.) 48" x 60" plastic laminate (rough)

CUTTING DIAGRAM

³⁄₄ x 3¹⁄₂ - 72 (Four Boards @ 1.75 Bd. Ft. Each)

A		A
A		A

³⁄₄ x 3¹⁄₂ - 72 (Four Boards @ 1.75 Bd. Ft. Each)

F	E	D
F	E	B B I I

³⁄₄ x 5¹⁄₂ - 60 (2.3 Bd. Ft.)

I	I
I	I

³⁄₄ x 5¹⁄₂ - 60 (2.3 Bd. Ft.)

J	M
	M
K	L

NOTE: ALSO NEED TWO ⁵⁄₈" DOWELS 48" LONG FOR PART C, ¹⁄₂" PLYWOOD 36" x 48" FOR PART G

Begin constructing the trays by getting started on the legs. First, rip the four legs (A) for each tray to size (refer to *Fig. 2*). By the way, I went ahead and ordered the Roto-Hinges now to make sure I would have them on hand before starting this project. (For Sources, see page 126.)

The length for the legs will make the tray about 26" off the floor, which is an "in between" height. It's actually a little low if the tray is used when sitting in a chair, and it's a little high for use when sitting on a couch. But all in all, it's a good compromise for most uses.

ROUND ENDS. After the legs are cut to length, the four corners of each leg are rounded to a radius of $1/2$" (*Fig. 2a*). To do this, I used a quarter to draw the radius. Then I sanded the corners to shape on a disc sander.

Next, all the edges on both sides of the legs are chamfered. The easiest way to do this is on a router table using a chamfering bit with a pilot bearing.

MATCH UP LEGS. Before going any further, I found it's best to pair up the legs now to determine how they fit together best. If the legs are warped, they should be matched so the warp doesn't interfere with the folding action of the trays (*Fig. 1*). Test each pair and mark the sides that will face each other.

DRILL HOLES. Now, four sets of holes need to be drilled in the legs. Two sets of holes are for mounting the Roto-Hinges at the pivot point of the legs. Another set of holes is for a Roto-Hinge that connects the top of the leg to a pivot block and the fourth set is for a crossbar that is added later. (To learn more about how Roto-Hinges work, see the Hardware article on the next page.)

First, I drilled the holes on the marked sides of the legs to hold the Roto-Hinges (*Fig. 3*). These holes are located 12" down from the top of each leg (*Fig. 2b*).

Note: The holes aren't centered on the length of the legs. This gives it a wider stance at the bottom, so the hinge (pivot point) is shifted up a little.

HOLES AT TOP OF LEGS. Next, I drilled the holes at the top of each leg. On the outside legs, I drilled a $3/4$" hole for another Roto-Hinge that's used to join the outside leg to a pivot block (*Fig. 4*). Finally, at the top of the inside legs, a $5/8$" hole is drilled for the crossbar (*Fig. 2b*).

PIVOT BLOCK. Now pivot blocks (B) are needed to join the legs to the tray. To

make these blocks, first cut two pieces $1^1/2$" wide by 3" long (*Step 1 in Fig. 5*). Then drill another $3/4$"-dia. hole for the Roto-Hinge, this one centered on the length and width of the block.

Next, to mount the blocks to the tray bottom, counterbore $3/8$"-dia. holes in the pivot blocks (*Step 2 in Fig. 5*), and follow with $3/16$"-dia. shank holes (*Fig. 5a*).

Note: It's important to check the depth of the counterbore so $1^1/2$"-long screws extend only $3/8$" into the $1/2$" laminated plywood tray top.

Then after the holes have been drilled, you can round over the corners to a $1/4$" radius (*Step 3 in Fig. 5*).

MOUNT ROTO-HINGES. Before you mount the Roto-Hinges, finish sand the legs (especially the inside faces where it will be difficult to get to after the legs are joined). Then glue Roto-Hinges into the holes to join the two legs. Also, glue Roto-

Hinges in place to join the pivot blocks to the outside legs.

MOUNT CROSSBAR. Now the crossbar (C) can be mounted. To do this, I cut a $5/8$"-dia. dowel to fit in the holes in the

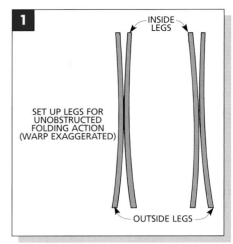

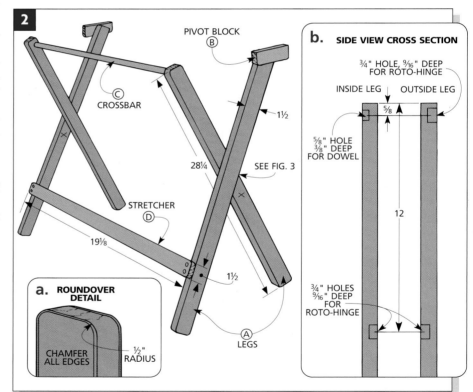

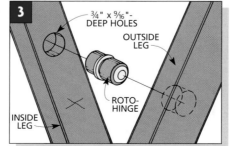

inside legs. This dowel should be cut to length so when it's in place, the inside legs are 15¾" apart *(Fig. 6)*. (This means, if the holes are ⅜" deep, then the dowel should be 16½" long.)

STRETCHER. The last step on the leg assembly is to add a single stretcher (D) *(Fig. 6)*. (The stretcher is what keeps the TV trays from racking.) Rip the stretcher 1½" wide and to rough length (about 20" long).

Then, to determine the final length of the stretcher, lay the leg assembly down onto a flat surface like a workbench *(Fig. 6)*. Then just measure the distance between the two *outside* edges of the outside tray legs.

Note: Take this measurement at the top of the leg assembly (where the dowel is). Then cut the stretcher to length so it equals this measurement.

To complete the stretcher, round all four of the corners to a ¼" radius and chamfer (or round over) the edges on both sides *(Fig. 7a)*. Then to mount the stretcher to the legs, counterbore the holes at the ends of the stretcher for No. 8 x 1½" woodscrews *(Fig. 7)*.

ADD WOOD PLUGS. After the stretcher is glued and screwed to the outside legs, fill the counterbores with wood plugs. Once the glue has set up, sand the plugs smooth with the surface of the stretcher.

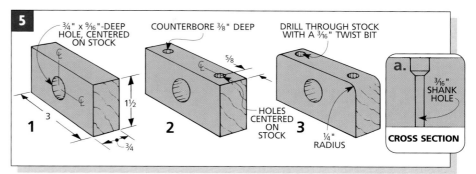

5

1 ¾" x 9/16"-DEEP HOLE, CENTERED ON STOCK 3 ¾" 1½"

2 COUNTERBORE ⅜" DEEP 5/8 HOLES CENTERED ON STOCK

3 DRILL THROUGH STOCK WITH A 3/16" TWIST BIT ¼" RADIUS

a. 3/16" SHANK HOLE **CROSS SECTION**

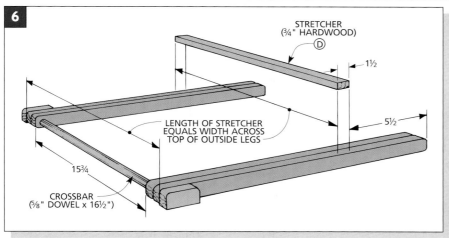

6

STRETCHER (¾" HARDWOOD) Ⓓ 1½

LENGTH OF STRETCHER EQUALS WIDTH ACROSS TOP OF OUTSIDE LEGS 5½

15¾

CROSSBAR (5/8" DOWEL x 16½")

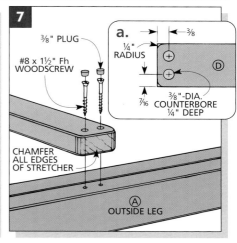

7

⅜" PLUG

#8 x 1½" Fh WOODSCREW

CHAMFER ALL EDGES OF STRETCHER

Ⓐ OUTSIDE LEG

a. 3/8 ¼" RADIUS Ⓓ ⅜"-DIA. COUNTERBORE ¼" DEEP 7/16

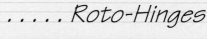

HARDWARE . . . . *Roto-Hinges*

The woodworking world is chock full of specialized hardware. While most hardware is developed for a single purpose, few are as simple to use (or work as well) as the Roto-Hinge.

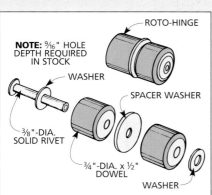

NOTE: 9/16" HOLE DEPTH REQUIRED IN STOCK
ROTO-HINGE
WASHER
SPACER WASHER
⅜"-DIA. SOLID RIVET
¾"-DIA. x ½" DOWEL
WASHER

The Roto-Hinge is perfect for folding chairs and cabinet doors. I used it on the TV trays because it gave me a sturdy, hidden pivot for the tray legs.

There's nothing really complicated about the hinges. They're just two wooden drums (or dowels) held together with a rivet. A spacer washer that's placed in between the two drums provides just the right amount of spacing to keep the legs from rubbing together.

Note: Some of the hinges may be a little loose. I wanted my tray legs to pivot smoothly, but to have a little friction so that they wouldn't swing open freely. So I gave each hinge a few healthy taps on the rivet with a small hammer to tighten it up.

The hinges are easy to install. All you need to do is drill a ¾"-wide hole, 9/16"

deep on the inside edge of the four legs where they pivot and another hole at the top of each leg where it joins with the pivot block. (The pivot block is needed to join the legs to the tray.)

After the legs are built, all that's needed is a tray top. The one shown in the photo on page 46 is an oak frame with a laminated panel. To make the tray, I started with the panel. (Or you could build the alternative tray top described in the Designer's Notebook on the next page.)

The panel is a piece of 1/2" plywood with plastic laminate on both sides. Cut the plywood tray panel (G) and the plastic laminate oversize (at least 1/2" in both directions) to allow for trimming.

PLASTIC LAMINATE. Then mount the laminate to the plywood by spreading contact cement on both surfaces. When the cement is dry to the touch, align the laminate at one end, placing dowels along the plywood *(Fig. 9)*. Then remove one dowel at a time, while pressing the laminate down as you go.

Note: The bottom of the plywood must also be covered with plastic laminate. If only one side is covered with laminate, moisture from the air can still penetrate the exposed plywood side, and the panel will warp.

CUT FRAME PIECES. Now the frame pieces can be cut to rough size. Rip the frame stiles (E) and frame rails (F) to a width of 1 1/2", and cut them about 1/2" longer than final length *(Fig. 8)*.

CUT GROOVES. Next, grooves are cut on the edges of the frame pieces to accept the rabbeted tray panel *(Fig. 10)*. To set up this cut on a table saw, use the laminate-covered panel to adjust the distance between the fence and the outside edge of the blade *(Step 1 in Fig. 11)*.

Set the depth of cut to 3/8" and make a pass on each frame piece *(Step 2)*. Then flip the piece around so the other face is against the fence, and make another pass on all pieces *(Step 3)*. Finally, adjust the fence to clean out the waste.

RABBET PANEL. After the grooves are cut, go back to working on the panel. First, trim the panel to final size *(Fig. 8)*. Then add the rabbet to the back (bottom) side *(Fig. 12)*. Sneak up on the depth of cut so the remaining tongue fits snugly in the grooves in the frame.

CUT TO LENGTH. Now the frame pieces can be cut to final length. The stiles (E) are cut to length to match the width of the panel (13 3/4"). The rails (F) are cut to length to match the distance between the shoulders of the rabbets on the panel (20 3/4") plus the width of the two stiles (1 1/2" each), for a total of 23 3/4" *(Fig. 8)*.

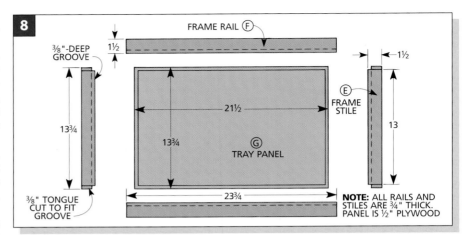

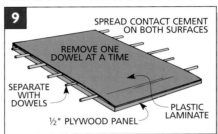

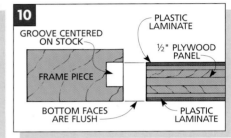

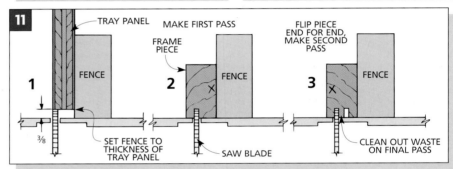

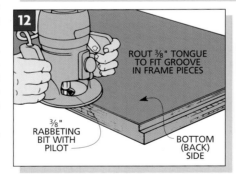

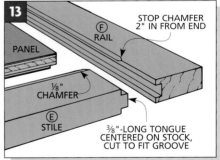

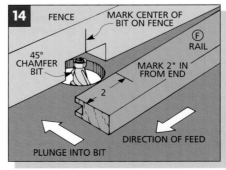

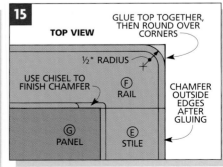

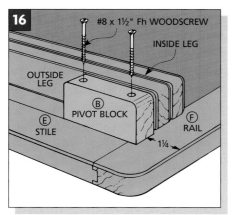

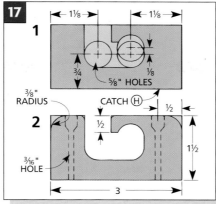

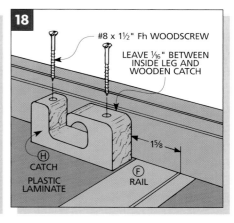

CUT TONGUES. To join the tray frame members, cut rabbets at the ends of the stiles to produce tongues to fit the grooves cut earlier *(Fig. 13)*.

CHAMFER EDGES. Next, chamfer the inside edges of the frame. This chamfer is routed along the entire length of the stiles, but the chamfer must be stopped on the rails *(Figs. 13 and 14)*.

Mark a stopping point on the rail and cut the chamfer so the cuts start and stop on these marks *(Fig. 14)*.

ASSEMBLE FRAME. Now, glue and clamp the frame pieces to the panel. Complete the chamfer on the inside edge of the frame with a sharp chisel *(Fig. 15)*. Then round the outside corners and chamfer the outsides of the frame.

ATTACH TRAY TOP

At last, the tray top can be attached to the legs. First, set the leg assembly on the tray and position the pivot blocks *(Fig. 16)*.

Then drill pilot holes and screw the pivot blocks in place.

WOODEN CATCH. To hook the crossbar in place, I made two wooden catches (H) *(Fig. 17)*. Drill three holes in each block, and cut out the shape of the catch.

Mount the catches with screws about $^1/_{16}$" from the inside legs and $1^5/_8$" from the back edge of the tray frame *(Fig. 18)*.

FINISHING. To finish the trays, I applied two coats of medium walnut oil to both stain and seal the wooden parts.

DESIGNER'S NOTEBOOK

Top your TV Trays with a plywood panel then add a hard finish and T-molding to complete the look.

CONSTRUCTION NOTES:

■ Start by cutting the plywood panel to size and rounding the corners *(Fig. 1)*.
■ Now use a slot-cutting bit to add a groove, centered on the stock all the way around the top *(Fig. 2)*.
■ A series of notches are cut in the T-molding to make it easier to wrap it around the corner of the plywood top *(Fig. 3)*.
■ Finally, use an adhesive to install the T-molding, cutting it to fit *(Figs. 4, 5, and 6)*.

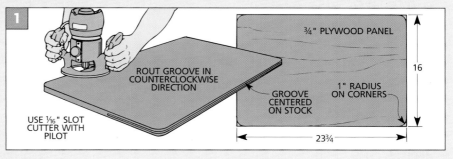

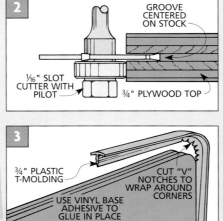

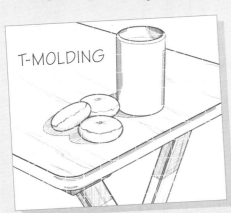

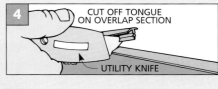

19

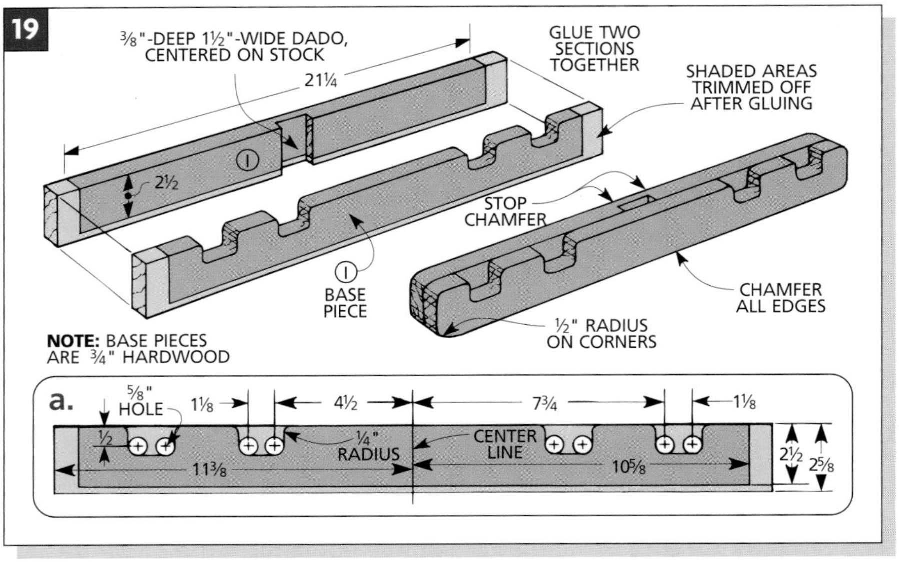
3/8"-DEEP 1½"-WIDE DADO, CENTERED ON STOCK
21¼
GLUE TWO SECTIONS TOGETHER
SHADED AREAS TRIMMED OFF AFTER GLUING
2½
I
STOP CHAMFER
I
BASE PIECE
CHAMFER ALL EDGES
½" RADIUS ON CORNERS
NOTE: BASE PIECES ARE ¾" HARDWOOD
a.
5/8" HOLE
1⅛
4½
7¾
1⅛
½
¼" RADIUS
CENTER LINE
11⅜
10⅝
2½
2⅝

STORAGE STAND

I thought it would be nice to have a stand to hold the set of four TV trays, so I designed a storage stand with casters.

This stand holds the trays "lean-to" fashion thanks to a series of notches cut into a couple of base pieces.

To keep the trays from tipping over, there's a center assembly that doubles as a handle. The handle allows you to easily move the stand around on the casters. Then a stretcher is added to strengthen the center assembly. To build the storage stand, start with the bases.

BASES. Each base consists of two base pieces (I) laminated together *(Fig. 19)*. First cut four pieces of stock to rough size. (This provides some room for trimming after they're laminated.)

NOTCHES. Now lay out the position of the notches that hold the ends of the tray legs. First mark a line centered on the length of two of the boards *(Fig. 19)*. Then mark the location of four pairs of $5/8$" holes to form the corners of the notches.

20

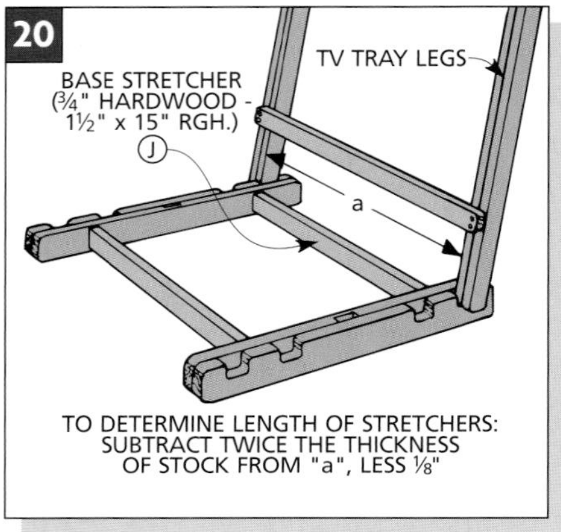
BASE STRETCHER (¾" HARDWOOD - 1½" x 15" RGH.)
J
TV TRAY LEGS
a
TO DETERMINE LENGTH OF STRETCHERS: SUBTRACT TWICE THE THICKNESS OF STOCK FROM "a", LESS ⅛"

Work from the centerline out, marking the center points of each hole *(Fig. 19a)*.

CUT OUT NOTCH. After the positions of the holes are marked on both boards, drill the holes. Then use a jig saw or band saw to cut all the notches to shape. Finally, sand or file the edges of the notches smooth, and round over the top corners.

SECOND BOARD. These notched boards are each laminated to a second board that has a large dado centered on its length.

When the two boards are laminated together, this dado actually creates a mortise for the stand upright *(Fig. 19)*.

Mark the position of this $1\frac{1}{2}$"-wide dado so it's centered on the length of the board. Then cut it by making multiple passes over the saw blade.

LAMINATE THE BASE. Now the boards can be glued and clamped together to form the bases, making sure to keep the top edges and the ends aligned.

Once the glue has set up overnight, cut the laminated pair to final size by trimming off the bottom edge and both ends. Then to complete the bases, round the corners to a $1/2$" radius, and chamfer all edges on a router table *(Fig. 19)*.

BASE STRETCHERS. The base pieces are joined to two base stretchers (J). Cut these stretchers $1\frac{1}{2}$" wide and to rough length (15"). Determine the final length by placing one of the tray leg assemblies in a notch on the bases *(Fig. 20)*. Measure the distance between the inside faces of the bases, subtract $1/8$" for clearance, and cut the stretchers to length.

HANDLE AND STRETCHER. Next, to join the uprights, the handle (K) and middle stretcher (L) are cut to width, and both pieces are cut to the same length as the base stretchers *(Fig. 21)*.

ACCESSORIES .... Portalign

For drilling holes that are perpendicular to a workpiece, my first choice is usually the drill press. But some pieces (like the stretchers of the tray stand and the side rails of the Magazine Rack on page 59) are too long to fit on a drill press without a special jig. That's where a Portalign attachment for your hand drill really shines (see photo).

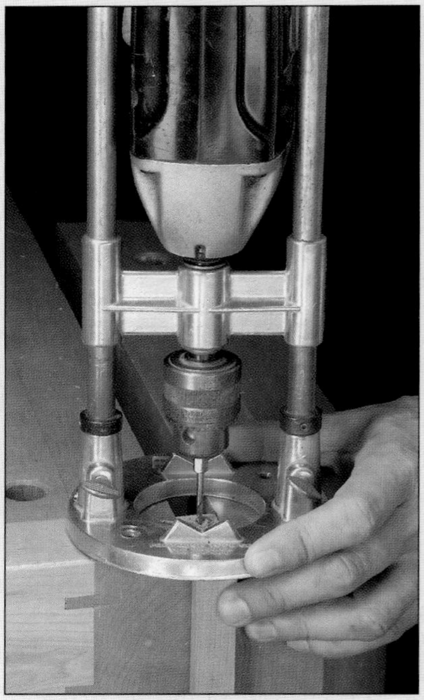

The Portalign operates much like a plunge router. It's mounted by tightening a collar on the guide to the drill itself. The collar and the drill slide up and down on two rods that are attached to the base of the guide.

Another real advantage when using a Portalign attachment becomes obvious when you need to drill a straight hole in the center of a large panel. It's then that the absence of a column for the drill stand makes this portability a real bonus.

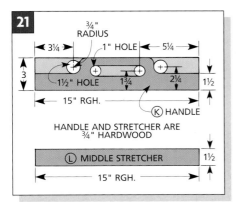

21

¾" RADIUS
3¼   1" HOLE   5¼
3
1½" HOLE   1¾   2¼   1½
15" RGH.
(K) HANDLE
HANDLE AND STRETCHER ARE ¾" HARDWOOD

(L) MIDDLE STRETCHER   1½
15" RGH.

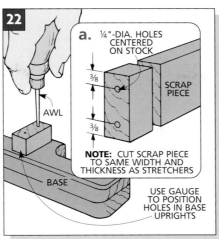

22

AWL

a. ¼"-DIA. HOLES CENTERED ON STOCK
⅜
⅜
SCRAP PIECE

NOTE: CUT SCRAP PIECE TO SAME WIDTH AND THICKNESS AS STRETCHERS

BASE

USE GAUGE TO POSITION HOLES IN BASE UPRIGHTS

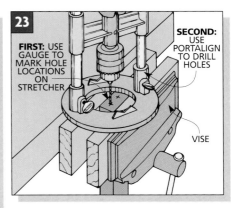

23

FIRST: USE GAUGE TO MARK HOLE LOCATIONS ON STRETCHER

SECOND: USE PORTALIGN TO DRILL HOLES

VISE

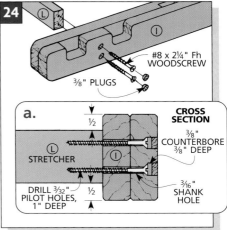

24

(L)
#8 x 2¼" Fh WOODSCREW
⅜" PLUGS
(I)

a.   ½
CROSS SECTION
(L) STRETCHER   (I)
⅜" COUNTERBORE ⅜" DEEP
DRILL 3/32" PILOT HOLES, 1" DEEP   ½
3/16" SHANK HOLE

HANDLE. After the handle blank is cut to size, drill holes to mark the shape of the hand-hold (*Fig. 21*). Then cut it out with a jig saw and sand the edges smooth. Finally, chamfer the top and bottom of the handle and the hand-hold.

UPRIGHTS. The last pieces to cut for the stand are the uprights (M). They're sized to match the width of the mortise (1½"), added in the base (refer to *Fig. 25b*).

First, cut them to a length of 33¼", and then cut half lap tenons on the bottom ends to fit the mortises. To complete the uprights, round each top corner to a ½" radius and chamfer the edges, stopping at the shoulder of the half lap on the bottom end (*Fig. 25*).

ASSEMBLY

Now that all the pieces are cut to final size, assemble them with glue and screws.

The only problem here is drilling the pilot holes for the screws exactly where you want them. Since there's no easy way to clamp the pieces together to drill the pilot holes, I made a drilling gauge to mark the position of the holes.

GAUGE. To make the gauge, cut a piece of ¾"-thick scrap to the same width as the handle and stretchers (1½") (*Fig. 22a*). Then mark two holes centered ⅜" from the edges of the stock. Drill ¼" holes at these points. Now cut off the end of the scrap to create the gauge.

MARK PILOT HOLES. To mark the position of the pilot holes on the base, center the block between the two notches, and equal distance (½") from the top and bottom edges (*Fig. 22*). Then use an awl to mark two points for the pilot holes. Use the same guide on the upright to mark the position of the pilot holes for the handle and the stretcher (*Fig. 25a*).

Now, drill pilot holes in the base and uprights, counterboring ⅜" deep for a wood plug (*Fig. 24*). The same gauge can

be used to mark the positions of the pilot holes in the ends of the stretchers and the handle (*Fig. 23*). (Use a Portalign to drill the pilot holes in the ends of these pieces.)

ASSEMBLY. To assemble the stand, glue and screw the stretchers between the bases. Then before mounting the uprights, I mounted the casters to the base (*Fig. 25c*). (It's a lot easier to do it before the uprights are in the way.) Finally, glue and screw the stretcher and handle between the uprights, and then glue the uprights in the mortises. ∎

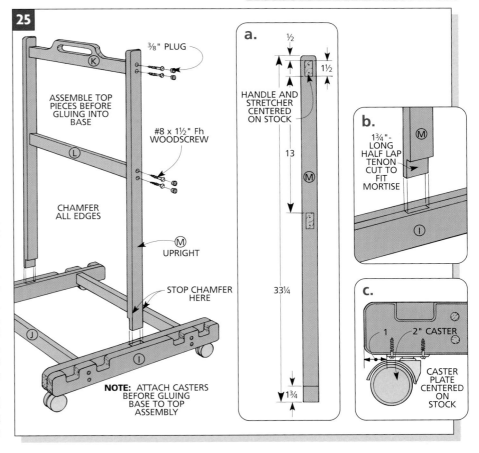

25

(K)
⅜" PLUG
ASSEMBLE TOP PIECES BEFORE GLUING INTO BASE
(L)
#8 x 1½" Fh WOODSCREW
CHAMFER ALL EDGES
(M) UPRIGHT
(J)
STOP CHAMFER HERE
(I)

NOTE: ATTACH CASTERS BEFORE GLUING BASE TO TOP ASSEMBLY

a.   ½   1½
HANDLE AND STRETCHER CENTERED ON STOCK
13
(M)
33¼
1¾

b.
1¾"-LONG HALF LAP TENON CUT TO FIT MORTISE
(M)
(I)

c.
1   2" CASTER
CASTER PLATE CENTERED ON STOCK

Magazine Rack

This piece is a perfect complement to your home's den or family room. Building the arched-top raised panels provides several interesting challenges, but you could use a solid wood panel instead.

Arched-top raised panels are often used to dress up cupboard doors. I've always wanted to try my hand at this technique and the Magazine Rack gave me the chance to make just two frames with arched-top raised panels instead of a whole kitchen full of them. That was *one* of the main reasons I wanted to build this project.

Another reason was the chance to use angled stub tenon and groove joinery to build the frames for the ends of the Magazine Rack. But this is not a true angled joint because, although the rails and stiles meet at an angle, the tenons fit into the mortises at 90°. Basically, it's just

a normal stub tenon and groove joint except the shoulders of the tenon are cut at an angle. To learn more about how I did this, see the Joinery article on page 61.

ARCHED-TOP RAISED PANEL. You'll find a complete description of how I cut arched-top raised panels in the Technique article on page 62. All it takes is a shop-built auxiliary fence that cradles the panel and allows you to swing it past the table saw blade in an arc.

STORE-BOUGHT SPINDLES. If you don't have a lathe to turn spindles, no problem. I bought the spindles that I used in this Magazine Rack from a woodworking supply store (see Sources, page 126).

DESIGN OPTIONS. If you don't want to use frame and panel construction for the rack, there is an easier way. You could make the end panels by gluing up solid stock. In fact, I've offered two variations of the rack with solid wood panels.

The first option is just to build the rack with solid panels on the ends. The second option is a more contemporary look. Instead of turned spindles, I used dowels and a wider (taller) bottom rail in the side. This gives the rack a sleek look that makes it the perfect place to store all your magazines and newspapers. Turn to the Designer's Notebooks on pages 56 and 58 for more on both these options.

EXPLODED VIEW

OVERALL DIMENSIONS:
12W x 13⅝D x 18⅜H

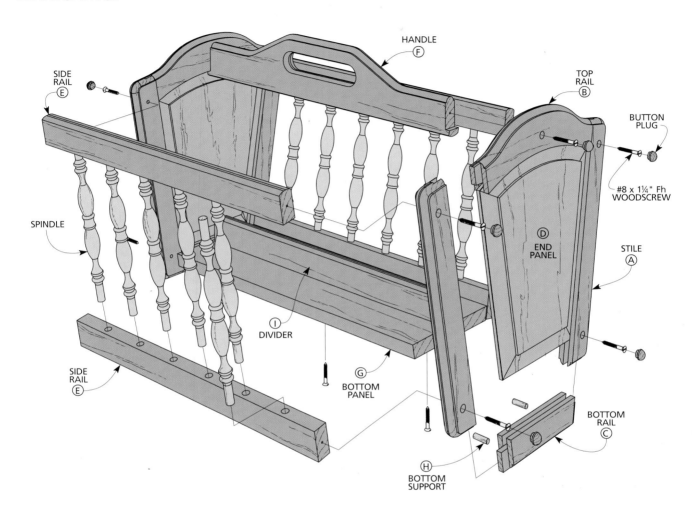

SIDE RAIL (E)

SPINDLE

SIDE RAIL (E)

HANDLE (F)

DIVIDER

BOTTOM PANEL

TOP RAIL (B)

BUTTON PLUG

#8 x 1¼" Fh WOODSCREW

END PANEL (D)

STILE (A)

BOTTOM RAIL (C)

BOTTOM SUPPORT (H)

MATERIALS LIST

WOOD

A	Stiles (4)	¾ x 1½ - 12¼
B	Top Rails (2)	¾ x 3¼ - 11 rough
C	Bottom Rails (2)	¾ x 1½ - 6¾ rgh.
D	End Panels (2)	¾ x 9½ - 11 rough
E	Side Rails (4)	¾ x 1½ - 16¾
F	Handle (1)	¾ x 3½ - 17¼ rgh.
G	Bottom Panel (1)	¾ x 7 - 16¾
H	Bottom Supports (4)	¼ dowel x ¾
I	Divider (1)	¾ x 1½ - 16¼

HARDWARE SUPPLIES

(13) No. 8 x 1¼" Fh woodscrews
(10) Button plugs
(12) ⅞"-dia. spindles (9" long)

CUTTING DIAGRAM

¾ x 3½ - 36 (Two Boards @ .9 Bd. Ft. Each)

¾ x 3½ - 36 (.9 Bd. Ft.)

¾ x 5½ - 48 (Two Boards @ 1.8 Bd. Ft. Each)

ALSO NEED: ¼"-DIA. DOWEL, ABOUT 4" LONG FOR BOTTOM SUPPORTS

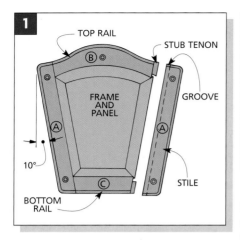

1

TOP RAIL

B

STUB TENON

FRAME AND PANEL

GROOVE

A

A

STILE

10°

BOTTOM RAIL

C

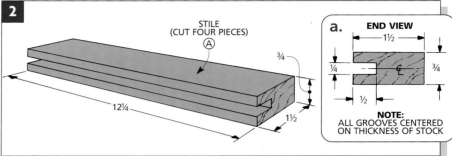

2

STILE (CUT FOUR PIECES)
A

3/4

12¼

1½

a. END VIEW

1½

¼

3/4

C

½

NOTE: ALL GROOVES CENTERED ON THICKNESS OF STOCK

END FRAMES

I've always wanted to try my hand at making arched-top raised panel doors, so I made the ends of my rack with frame and panel construction *(Fig. 1)*. But if you'd rather build solid-wood end panels, see the Designer's Notebook below for more details on how to do this.

STILES. Begin work on the frame by cutting the stiles (A) to size *(Fig. 2)*.

CUT GROOVES. After the stiles are cut to size, rout a $\frac{1}{4}$"-wide groove centered on the inside edge of the stiles. Because a groove needs to be cut in the arched top rail later, I used a $\frac{1}{4}$" slot cutter on the router table to do this.

Note: Leave the router table set up so identical grooves can be cut in the top and bottom rails later.

LAYOUT TOOLS. Before going to work on the top rail though, I made two layout tools: the first is a block with a 10° angle cut on one end for setting up the miter gauge; the second is a cardboard template with a 10"-radius arc cut out. The arc

sets the radius of the bottom edge of the rail. (There are more details about this in the Joinery article on page 61.)

LAY OUT TOP RAIL. Now the top rail (B) can be laid out. To establish the overall length of the rail, begin by drawing a centerline on the workpiece and then mark a shoulder-to-shoulder distance of $8\frac{5}{8}$" ($4\frac{5}{16}$" from the centerline on each side) on the bottom edge of the workpiece *(Fig. 3)*.

Then use the angled block layout tool to extend a line at 10° from these marks across the face of the top rail. (These marks are the shoulder lines of the

DESIGNER'S NOTEBOOK

Frame and panels can be a challenge, even when they're not arched. So a solid panel is a good alternative.

CONSTRUCTION NOTES:

■ Start by gluing up stock to form the blanks for the end panels (see drawing). Trim the ends square and mark a centerline on the bottom edge of the blank.

■ Then mark a point 4" to each side of the centerline, and trim the sides off at 10° at these marks (see drawing).

■ Now use the template to lay out the top (refer to *Fig. 3*), then cut it to shape. Next rout a profile on all of the edges (refer to *Fig. 9a*) and drill holes for attaching the side rails (refer to *Fig. 14* on page 60).

■ To keep the handle from pivoting, cut it to length (mine's $16\frac{3}{4}$" without shoulders; refer to *Fig. 17*). Then use brads to toe-nail the handle to the end panels.

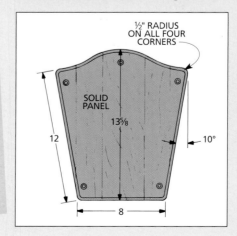

SOLID PANELS

½" RADIUS ON ALL FOUR CORNERS

SOLID PANEL

$13\frac{5}{8}$

12

10°

8

angled tenons.) To establish the length of the tenon, draw a second set of parallel lines 1/2" from the shoulder lines.

DRAW PROFILE. Now the curved profiles can be drawn on the top and bottom edges of the rail. I used the arch template described in the Joinery article on page 61 to draw the curve on the bottom edge of the rail. Then make another template (shown in the 1/2" grid in *Fig. 3*) to draw the shape on the top edge.

Although the profiles are laid out, they won't be cut until later. That's because you'll need straight edges to steady the rail against the miter gauge when the tenons are cut to length.

CUT RAILS TO LENGTH. To do this, set the miter gauge to 10° (using the angle block) and cut off both ends at the outside (tenon) lines *(Fig. 4)*.

BOTTOM RAIL. Next, I made the bottom rail (C). This rail is 1 1/2" wide by about 7" long with one end trimmed off at 10° *(Fig. 4)*. (It's cut to final length later to fit between the stiles.)

JOINING THE FRAME

Once the top and bottom rails are cut to length, stub tenons are cut on the ends. These tenons fit the grooves on the inside edge of the frame *(Fig. 5)*, rather than fitting in a full mortise. (This process is described in more detail in the Joinery article on page 61.)

When cutting the stub tenons, I cut both ends of the top rail but only one end of the bottom rail. To cut the tenon on the other end of the bottom rail, clamp the rest of the frame together *(Fig. 6)*.

Then lay the bottom rail in place, mark where it meets the opposite stile, and cut the tenon on this end of the rail.

CUT TO SHAPE. After the tenons are cut, the top rail can be cut on the band saw and sanded to shape. Then rout the 1/4"-wide groove for the panel on the inside edges of the top and bottom rails *(Fig. 7)*.

END PANELS

At this point, the frame is complete, so you can move on to constructing the end panels (D). First, glue up enough stock for two panels *(Figs. 8 and 8a)*. When the glue is set up, cut each panel to fit inside the angled frame.

After that, the edges are chamfered to raise a field on each face of the panel. (The Technique article on page 62 walks you through this procedure.)

ASSEMBLE FRAME. Now each frame can be assembled with a panel inside. (Refer to the Shop Tip on page 59.)

Note: Don't glue the panels into the grooves; they should be able to expand and contract with changes in humidity.

When the glue is set up, trim the bottom ends of the stiles flush with the bottom rail *(Fig. 9)*. Then round the corners *(Fig. 9)* and rout a roundover with a shoulder on the outside edges *(Fig. 9a)*.

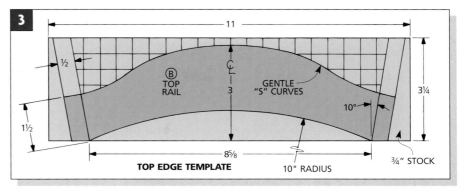

3 — 11 — 1/2 — ⓑ TOP RAIL — GENTLE "S" CURVES — 3 — 3 1/4 — 1 1/2 — 8 5/8 — 10° — **TOP EDGE TEMPLATE** — 10" RADIUS — 3/4" STOCK

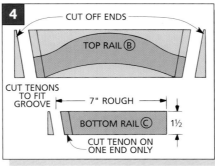

4 CUT OFF ENDS — TOP RAIL ⓑ — CUT TENONS TO FIT GROOVE — 7" ROUGH — BOTTOM RAIL ⓒ — 1 1/2 — CUT TENON ON ONE END ONLY

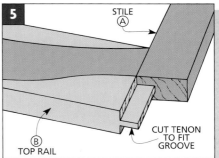

5 STILE ⓐ — CUT TENON TO FIT GROOVE — ⓑ TOP RAIL

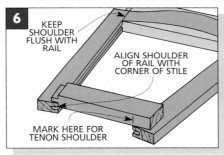

6 KEEP SHOULDER FLUSH WITH RAIL — ALIGN SHOULDER OF RAIL WITH CORNER OF STILE — MARK HERE FOR TENON SHOULDER

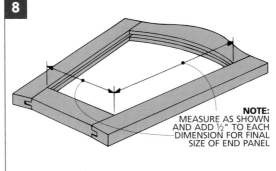

7 BOTTOM RAIL — TOP RAIL — CUT GROOVE SAME AS ON STILES (SEE FIG. 2a)

8 — **NOTE:** MEASURE AS SHOWN AND ADD 1/2" TO EACH DIMENSION FOR FINAL SIZE OF END PANEL

a. — 9 1/2 — GLUE UP 3/4" STOCK FOR END PANELS — ⓓ END PANEL — LENGTH + 1/2" — 11 — 10° — WIDTH + 1/2"

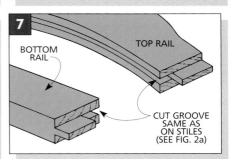

9 1/2" R. ALL FOUR CORNERS — STILE — BOTTOM RAIL — TRIM OFF EARS FLUSH WITH BOTTOM RAIL — **a.** OUTER EDGE PROFILE — 3/32 — 1/4" ROUND-OVER BIT

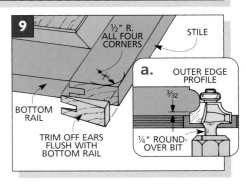

DESIGNER'S NOTEBOOK

Here's a magazine rack that fits well in any home. Instead of frame and panel sides, it's made with solid wood end panels. And the spindles in the side panels have been replaced with wood dowels.

CONSTRUCTION NOTES:

■ Building this Contemporary Rack is really simple — that's because I used solid wood end panels for a cleaner look. And instead of adding a separate wood handle, I decided to place cutouts in the ends to make construction even easier.

■ Start construction by gluing up the two ³⁄₄"-thick blanks for the end (J) panels.

Then once the glue has completely set up, go ahead and lay out the end panels with the same 10° tapers as before, but with a slightly different profile on the top edge. I used an 11" radius for the top edge of the Contemporary Rack (*Fig. 1*).

■ Next, lay out the location of the handles and the ⁵⁄₁₆"-dia. shank holes for the screws used to attach the sides (*Fig. 1*).

■ Go ahead and cut the panels to size and soften each corner of the end panels by adding a ¹⁄₂" radius (*Fig. 1*). Then drill pilot holes and use a jig saw to cut the holes for the handles.

■ Finally, drill the holes on the inside edges of the sides for the bottom supports (added later) (*Fig. 1*).

■ After the end panels are complete, the sides of the rack can be made. Each side consists of six dowels mounted between a top side rail (K) and bottom side rail (L). Begin by ripping all the rails to size and cutting each of them to length (*Fig. 2*).

■ Now drill ¹⁄₂"-dia. holes for the dowel spindles (M) on one edge of each top and bottom side rail (*Fig. 2*).

■ Next, drill ⁷⁄₃₂" pilot holes for the screws used to fasten the side frames to the end panels (*Fig. 2a*). Mark the centerpoint with an awl first, then use the drill press (or a Portalign attachment on a hand drill) to drill them perpendicular to the rails.

■ The last step is to rout the bullnose profile on the upper edge of the top rail (and on all four edges of the end panels). Use a ¹⁄₂" roundover bit, and raise it ⁵⁄₁₆" high in the router table (refer to *Fig. 12* on page 59).

■ Glue the dowel spindles into the rails when assembling the sides. This strengthens the assembly and you won't need to add any glue to the end grain of the bottom rail where it joins the sides. Then screw them to the end panels with 2"-long Confirmat screws (*Fig. 2a*).

■ Next, install the four bottom support (H) dowels for the bottom panel (G) to rest on. I sized the bottom to fit down between the end panels and loosely between the bottom rails.

■ Finally, I added the divider (I) to the top side of the bottom panel. Rip it to size, add the bullnose detail and screw it in place.

MATERIALS LIST

NEW PARTS

J	Ends (2)	³⁄₄ x 13 - 14 rgh.
K	Top Side Rail (2)	³⁄₄ x 1¹⁄₂ - 16³⁄₄
L	Bottom Side Rail (2)	³⁄₄ x 6 - 16³⁄₄
M	Dowel Spindles (12)	¹⁄₂ dowel x 4¹⁄₂

Note: Do not need parts A, B, C, D, E, and F.

HARDWARE SUPPLIES

(3) No. 8 x 1¹⁄₄" Fh woodscrews
(8) 2" Confirmat screws

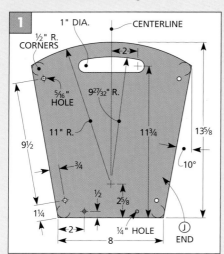

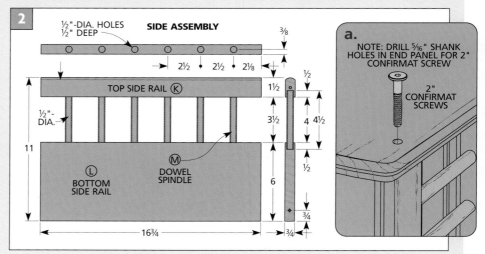

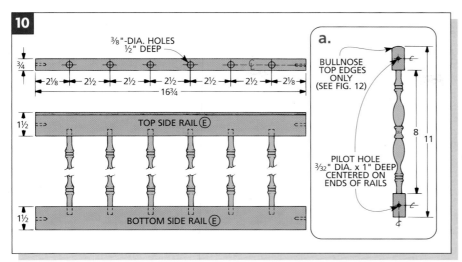

SIDES

After the ends are assembled, the sides of the rack can be made. Each side consists of a top and bottom rail with six spindles mounted between them. Begin by ripping the side rails (E) to size *(Fig. 10)*.

SPINDLE HOLES. After the rails are cut to size, 3/8" holes for the spindles are drilled 1/2" deep on the inside edges of the rails. To position the spindles, begin by drilling a hole 2 1/8" from each end. Then drill the remaining holes 2 1/2" apart *(Fig. 10)*.

RAIL MOUNTING HOLES. The next step is drilling pilot holes for the screws that fasten the side rails to the end frames. Begin by marking the centerpoint on the ends of each rail *(Fig. 11)*. Then drill a 3/32" pilot hole 1" deep.

Note: To make sure the rail ends are drawn tight to the end frames, these pilot holes have to be absolutely perpendicular. I secured the rail in a bench vise and used a Portalign to drill the holes *(Fig. 11)*. (Refer to the Accessories box on page 52.)

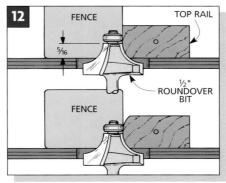

TOP RAIL PROFILE. The last step on the side rails is forming a bullnose profile on the upper edge of the top rails. I did this by using a 1/2" roundover bit set only 5/16" high in the router table *(Fig. 12)*.

DRILL MOUNTING HOLES. With the rails completed, drill five counterbored holes on the end frames. Four of them are for the screws that secure the end frames to the side rails and one is for the handle.

Bore these holes in two stages. Begin by drilling 3/8"-deep counterbores with a

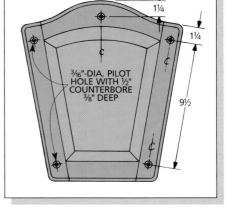

1/2" brad point bit. Then drill a 3/16" pilot hole the rest of the way *(Fig. 13)*.

ASSEMBLE SIDES. Next, assemble the rails and spindles to form the sides. Since the spindles aren't glued into the holes, I strapped each side assembly together with rubber bands so I could attach them to the end frames easily.

Now the rails can be screwed to the end frames. Begin by attaching the top rails. Then align the bottom holes with the bottom rail and screw the parts together.

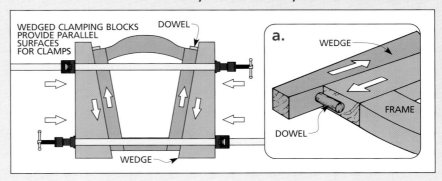

SHOP TIP . . . . *Clamping a Tapered Frame*

A pair of wedged clamping blocks provides parallel surfaces for clamping and applies even pressure across a tapered panel during glue-up (see drawing).

To concentrate clamping pressure inward, I used two 10° wedges (see drawing). Then to keep the wedges from slipping when the clamps are tightened, I inserted a dowel at the top end of each one (detail 'a').

HANDLE

After assembling the pieces to form the rack, I made a carrying handle with an elongated hole for a handhold.

CUT TO SIZE. Begin by cutting the handle blank (F) $3^1/_2$" wide and about 1" longer than the inside dimension of the assembled rack *(Fig. 14)*.

HANDLE ENDS. To make sure the handle doesn't pivot, I cut shoulders on its ends. They fit under the top rail of the end frame, and are flush against the chamfered border of the panel *(Fig. 17a)*.

Begin by marking on the workpiece the inside dimension between the top rails of the assembled rack. Then to make sure the shoulders fit tight against the panels, add $^1/_2$" and cut the handle to its final length *(Fig. 14)*.

Now, measure down to mark the top edge of the support shoulder. Then stand the workpiece on edge and cut a $^1/_4$"-wide notch to the marked line *(Fig. 15)*.

CUT SHOULDER ANGLE. Next, I trimmed the end of the shoulders off to match the chamfer on the panel *(Fig. 16)*. To do this, set the miter gauge at 10° and trim off the end so the distance to the long point of the shoulder equals the distance from the face of the rail to the face of the chamfered panel *(Fig. 17a)*.

HANDHOLD. Now a handhold can be added. Begin by marking a centerline on the workpiece. Then drill two centered holes and cut out the waste between them *(Fig. 14)*. Then contour the inside edges with a $^1/_2$" roundover bit.

Finally, cut the curved profile on the top edge of the handle to shape *(Fig. 14)*.

BOTTOM

The bottom panel (G) rests on two pairs of bottom supports (H) glued into holes in the end frame bottom rails *(Fig. 18)*.

CUT PANEL. The bottom panel is sized so it's slightly less than the length of the side rails, and so it fits loosely between the bottom rails (to allow for expansion).

But measuring the width is difficult because the side rails are at a 10° angle. So to cut it, begin by setting the saw blade to 10°. Then trim the edges and test fit the panel until it rests on the dowels with about a $^1/_{32}$" space on either side *(Fig. 19)*.

DIVIDER. Finally, I added a divider (I). To make the divider, first cut the stock to size. Then bullnose the top and the ends and fasten it with screws through the bottom panel *(Fig. 20)*. ■

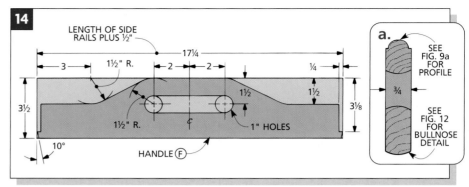

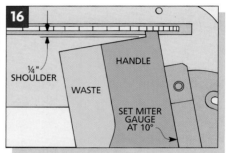

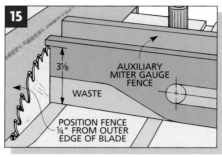

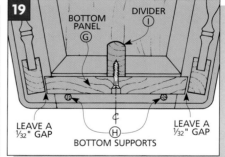

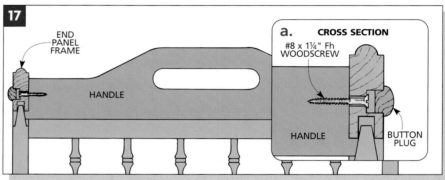

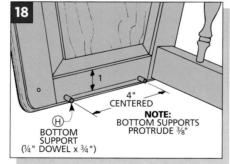

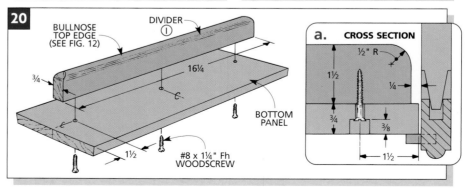

The frames for the ends of the Magazine Rack call for an angled stub tenon on each rail to fit a groove in the stiles (see photo). This angled cut is easier than it looks because it's really not cut at an angle at all.

Although the rails and stiles meet at an angle, the stub tenons fit into the grooves at 90°. This means it's just a normal tenon and groove joint except the shoulders of the stub tenon are cut at an angle.

ANGLE-SETTING BLOCK. Cutting angled shoulders on a tenon means getting the shoulders on both sides to turn out even and parallel. The trick is in setting and resetting the miter gauge to keep it consistent. To accomplish this, I made an angle-setting block. (This block also helps when laying out the tenons on the rails.)

To make this block, cut one end off a piece of plywood at the angle you want for the shoulders (10°). I cut my block out of a 6" x 8" piece of plywood *(Fig. 1)*.

SETTING MITER GAUGE. To set up for the cut, first I added an auxiliary fence to the miter gauge to support the workpiece all the way to the blade *(Fig. 1)*.

Then to set the angle of the miter gauge, simply slide the rip fence over next to the miter gauge and press the angle-setting block tight against it (with the angle facing it) and adjust the miter gauge to the correct angle *(Fig. 1)*.

To cut the opposite side, just flip the angle-setting block over and reset the miter gauge *(Fig. 2)*. Then the angle will

be exactly the same for this second setting as it was on the first.

ARCH TEMPLATE. Before actually cutting the stub tenons, I made a large arch template out of a piece of cardboard. I used the template to trace the arches on the top rails and on the tops of the panels *(Fig. 3)*. For the Magazine Rack, I drew an arc with a radius of 10".

Note: This template will also be used later for making the jig to cut the arched tops on the panels. See the Technique article starting on page 62.

CUT THE TENONS

Before you can cut the tenons, you need to set up the saw. The tenons are cut to length and thickness by making multiple passes over a dado blade.

SET UP SAW. There are two steps to setting up the saw. First, position the rip

fence so the distance between it and the *outside* (left) edge of the dado blade is equal to the length of the tenon *(Fig. 4)*. (The fence acts as a stop to cut all tenons to the same length.)

The second step is raising the dado blade so it cuts the tenon the right thickness. Set the blade a little low so the tenon is a hair thick. It will be fine-tuned later.

FIRST PASS. When the saw is set up, cut the face of the stub tenon by making multiple passes over the dado blade *(Fig. 5)*. Then flip the rail over and repeat on the *opposite end (Fig. 5a)*.

SECOND PASS. After one face has been cut on each end, the opposite face is cut to bring the tenon to thickness *(Fig. 5b)*. To do this, again use the angle-setting block to reset the miter gauge to the *opposite angle (Fig. 5)*. Then make passes on the other side. Test the fit. If necessary, raise the blade and shave off just enough until the tenon fits the groove.

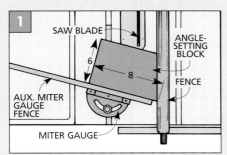

4 SET FENCE FROM OUTSIDE EDGE OF DADO BLADE TO EQUAL TENON LENGTH

FENCE

SNEAK UP ON FINAL HEIGHT OF DADO BLADE

DADO BLADE

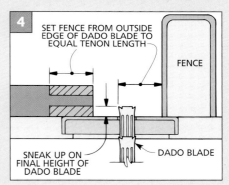

1 SAW BLADE

ANGLE-SETTING BLOCK

FENCE

AUX. MITER GAUGE FENCE

MITER GAUGE

2 AUX. MITER GAUGE FENCE

ANGLE-SETTING BLOCK

MITER GAUGE

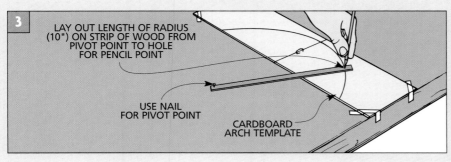

3 LAY OUT LENGTH OF RADIUS (10") ON STRIP OF WOOD FROM PIVOT POINT TO HOLE FOR PENCIL POINT

USE NAIL FOR PIVOT POINT

CARDBOARD ARCH TEMPLATE

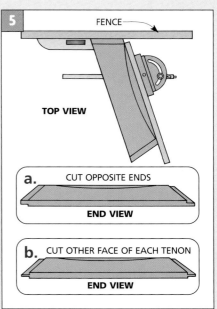

5 FENCE

TOP VIEW

a. CUT OPPOSITE ENDS

END VIEW

b. CUT OTHER FACE OF EACH TENON

END VIEW

Making raised panels on a table saw isn't difficult. It's just a matter of standing the panel on edge and running it through a tilted blade on the table saw.

However, the frames for the Magazine Rack have arched-top panels, which means they have to have an arched border to match. Although this can be done on a router table, it would require a very expensive bit, so I decided to try it on the table saw instead.

The idea is to make a jig to swing the panel in an arc (as though on a pendulum) as the blade trims the edge. But first, I cut the workpiece for the panel.

CUT PANEL TO SIZE

Start by cutting the panel to size, using the same angle block and template from the Joinery article on page 61 to help lay it out and set the miter gauge. First, glue up the stock for the panel to get an oversized workpiece (about 9½" wide by 11" long). When the glue has finished set-

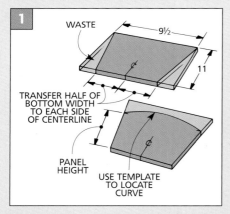

1
WASTE
9½
11
TRANSFER HALF OF BOTTOM WIDTH TO EACH SIDE OF CENTERLINE
PANEL HEIGHT
USE TEMPLATE TO LOCATE CURVE

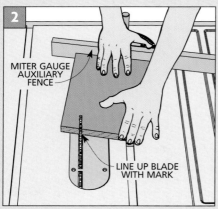

2
MITER GAUGE AUXILIARY FENCE
LINE UP BLADE WITH MARK

ting up, square up the panel and mark a centerline on a wide edge (*Fig. 1*).

Then cut the angled sides on the panels. To do this, work from dimensions that you've transferred to the panel directly from the inside of the frame.

BOTTOM WIDTH. The first dimension is the bottom width of the panel. To get this dimension, measure between the stiles along the inside edge of the bottom rail and add ½" (refer to *Fig. 8* on page 57 and *Fig. 1* at left).

Now to lay out the cuts on the panel, divide this measurement in half and mark it on each side of the centerline on the bottom edge of the panel workpiece.

SET UP MITER GAUGE. In order to cut the angled sides, use the angle-setting block to set the miter gauge at the same angle as the tenon shoulders. Next, cut one side of the panel, aligning the blade with one of the marks on the bottom edge of the panel (*Figs. 1 and 2*). Then flip the panel over and cut off the other edge.

TOP ARCH. The next step is establishing the height of the panel. Again,

take the measurement from the frame. Measure the distance between the inside edges of the top and bottom rails (refer to *Fig. 8* on page 57). Add ½" to this measurement and mark this distance up from the bottom on both edges of the panel workpiece (*Fig. 1*). Then position the arch template so it touches both marks, trace the top curve, and cut away the waste.

MAKE CURVED CHAMFERING JIG

After the panels are cut to shape, the edges are ready for chamfering. To do this, I made a jig with a high auxiliary fence and a curved "runner" that guides the arched top in a curved path through the blade (see photo).

FENCE. The auxiliary fence is a piece of ¾" plywood about 8" wide and as long as the rip fence (*Fig 3*). Draw a vertical centerline on it to help align the runner (made next).

MAKE RUNNER. After cutting the fence to size, I laid out the runner on another piece of ¾" plywood. First, lay the arch template on the plywood so the low point of the arch is about 1½" from the bottom edge of the plywood (*Fig. 3a*). Then align the two centerlines, trace the curve, and cut away the waste.

The next step is to position this curved runner on the plywood auxiliary fence so the bottom of the curve just touches the bottom of the fence (*Fig. 3*). When they're aligned, screw the pieces together. Then trim the bottom of the runner so the curve is flush with the bottom edge of the vertical fence (*Fig. 4*).

REFERENCE MARKS. Before attaching the jig to the saw's rip fence I made a reference mark on the saw table to indi-

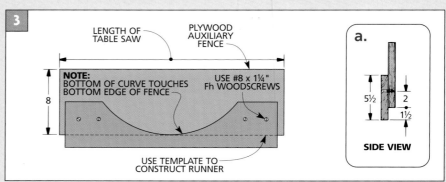

3
LENGTH OF TABLE SAW
PLYWOOD AUXILIARY FENCE
NOTE: BOTTOM OF CURVE TOUCHES BOTTOM EDGE OF FENCE
USE #8 x 1¼" Fh WOODSCREWS
8
USE TEMPLATE TO CONSTRUCT RUNNER

a.
5½
2
1½
SIDE VIEW

cate the very front of the saw blade (where the leading saw tooth is level with the table) *(Fig. 6)*.

To locate this mark, first tilt the blade to 10°, and raise the blade to the height of the chamfer shoulder (the angled border around the panel).

Note: The height of the blade is not the same as the width of the chamfer because of the way the jig and saw blade are aligned *(Fig. 5)*. (The blade has to be raised to 1⅝" for the 1"-wide border.)

BLADE CLEARANCE. Now cut a chamfer off the bottom of the back part of the runner to allow blade clearance. Stop cutting as the blade comes to the centerline on the fence, and make multiple passes until the width of the runner is about ⅜" at the bottom *(Fig. 6a)*.

ATTACH JIG. After the back half of the runner is chamfered, line up the centerline on the jig with the reference mark on the table saw *(Fig. 6)*. Then screw the jig to the rip fence.

CHAMFER THE EDGES

Cutting the chamfers on the panels will take a lot less time to cut than it did to make the jig. But getting a feel for using the jig takes practice. I warmed up on a few plywood test panels.

SETTING UP. To set up the jig to cut the arched chamfer, slide the fence over so the top of the blade is outside the face of the panel *(Fig. 7)*.

CUT THE CURVE. Making the arched cut requires a light touch. Begin by letting the panel rest in the curve of the runner *(Fig. 10)*. Then press the panel against the fence just hard enough to keep it upright and slide it along the runner.

When doing this, I think of the vertical fence as the table. That is, concentrate on pressing the panel against the face of the fence — not down on the saw.

Note: Use a zero-clearance insert here so the workpiece won't catch.

After cutting the first chamfer, repeat the process on the opposite side of the panel. Next, to get the edge to fit the groove, adjust the fence and jig toward the blade *(Fig. 8)*. Then keep making passes on both sides until the edge of the panel fits about halfway to the bottom of the groove *(Fig. 9)*.

CUT STRAIGHT CHAMFERS. To chamfer the straight sides, unscrew the curved runners and lower the blade. Then cut a

test piece to make sure that the width of the chamfers on the straight edges is the same as on the arched part *(Fig. 11)*.

CLEAN UP SHOULDER. There's one last step before the panel is ready to be mounted in the frame. Lightly sand the shoulder so it's perpendicular to the panel face. I used a sanding block cut at the same angle as the chamfer *(Fig. 12)*. It straightens the shoulder and smooths the chamfer at the same time.

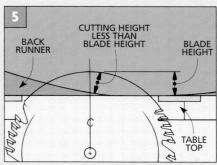

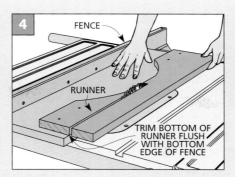

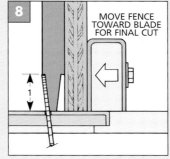
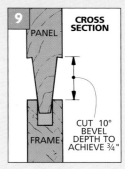

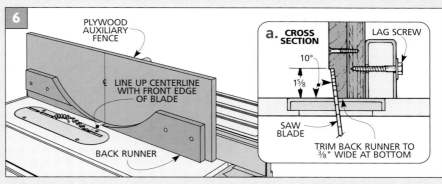

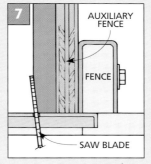

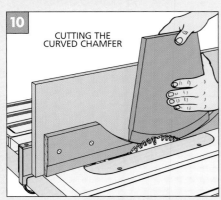

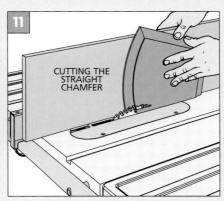

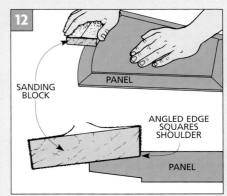

Folding Table

The Folding Table features simple construction techniques like splined miters, tapered legs, and a unique spring and wedge assembly made from hardwood that helps make the table both sturdy and "storable."

Y ou could say that the first designs for this Folding Table were a bit slow to "unfold." Not because it's all that complicated. But because I wanted the legs of the table to fold up for storage, yet still provide sturdy support when they're fully extended.

As it turned out, that's easier said than done. I tried several types of hardware that are specially designed for folding legs. But none of them kept the legs from wobbling. So I experimented with different ways to *lock* the legs in place.

SPRING. And, as is often the case, the solution was as close as the scrap bin — a thin, wood strip that works like a spring

to apply pressure against each leg (see photos on the opposite page). The spring holds the leg securely in place in both the extended and folded position. But don't worry, it's not that difficult to make the leg fold up or down — just press down on the spring and swing the leg past.

KEEP IT SQUARE. The table top and the rails below it feature attractive mitered corners. I used splined miters for the rail corners. The secret to keeping the four mitered corners of the rails square is to glue them up one at a time. And to make it easy to do this, I made another trip to the scrap bin. There I found a block of wood that I could make into a squaring

block. For more on how I did this, see the Technique article on page 67.

BUFFET TABLE. Finally, learn about how to build a longer, narrower version of the Folding Table — a Buffet Table — in the Designer's Notebook on page 69.

EXPLODED VIEW

OVERALL DIMENSIONS:
38¼W x 38¼D x 29¼H

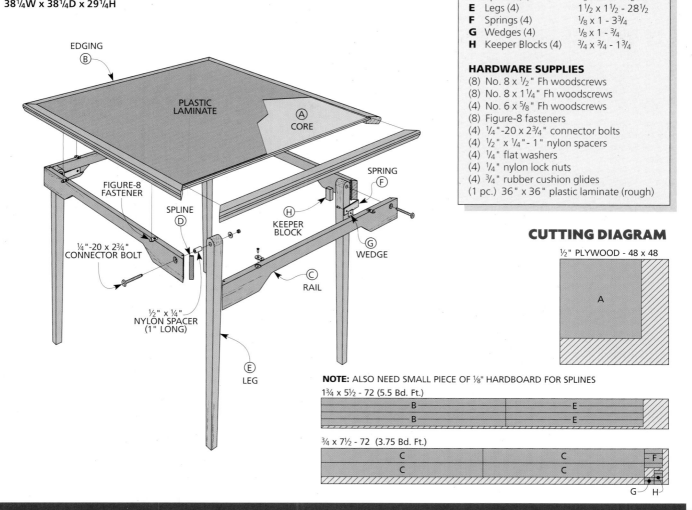

EDGING ⓑ

PLASTIC LAMINATE

ⓐ CORE

FIGURE-8 FASTENER

SPLINE ⓓ

SPRING ⓕ

KEEPER BLOCK ⓗ

WEDGE ⓖ

¼"-20 x 2¾" CONNECTOR BOLT

½" x ¼" NYLON SPACER (1" LONG)

RAIL ⓒ

LEG ⓔ

CUTTING DIAGRAM

½" PLYWOOD - 48 x 48

A

NOTE: ALSO NEED SMALL PIECE OF ⅛" HARDBOARD FOR SPLINES

1¾ x 5½ - 72 (5.5 Bd. Ft.)

B	E
B	E

¾ x 7½ - 72 (3.75 Bd. Ft.)

C	C	F
C	C	

G H

FOLDING LEGS

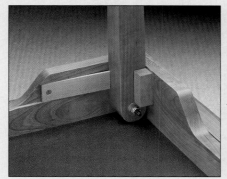

Leg Extended. *When each leg is extended, a thin wood "spring" holds it in place. And a small block helps add rigidity.*

Folding the Leg. *To fold up the legs when it's time to store the table away, press the spring down and swing the leg past.*

Locking Spring. *Once you fold the leg all the way down, the spring pops back out to wedge the leg securely in place.*

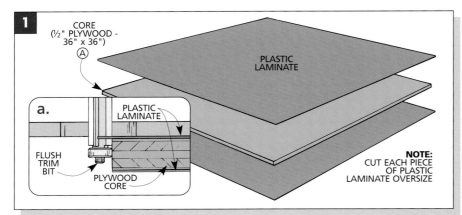

1
CORE
(½" PLYWOOD -
36" x 36")
Ⓐ

PLASTIC
LAMINATE

a.
PLASTIC
LAMINATE

FLUSH
TRIM
BIT

PLYWOOD
CORE

NOTE:
CUT EACH PIECE
OF PLASTIC
LAMINATE OVERSIZE

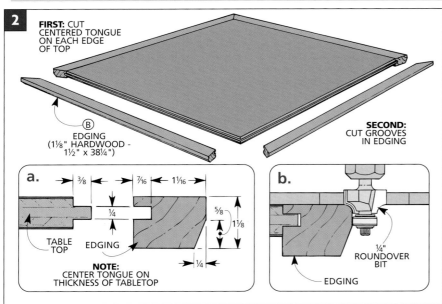

2
FIRST: CUT
CENTERED TONGUE
ON EACH EDGE
OF TOP

Ⓑ
EDGING
(1⅛" HARDWOOD -
1½" x 38¼")

SECOND:
CUT GROOVES
IN EDGING

a.
⅜   ⁷⁄₁₆   1¹⁄₁₆
¼
TABLE
TOP   EDGING
¼
5/8   1⅛

NOTE:
CENTER TONGUE ON
THICKNESS OF TABLETOP

b.
¼"
ROUNDOVER
BIT

EDGING

TABLE TOP

I began work by building the top of the table. Basically, it's a plywood core that's covered with plastic laminate and then wrapped with hardwood edging.

CORE. To reduce the weight of the top, I cut a core (A) piece from ½" plywood (*Fig. 1*). Then to ensure that the top stays flat, oversize pieces of plastic laminate are glued to both sides of the core. I like to use contact cement which creates a strong, instant bond as soon as the two surfaces touch. So I've found it's best to get the workpieces aligned *before* you stick them together.

To do this, apply the plastic laminate to one side at a time. And use wood strips to raise the laminate above the core. This way it's easy to position the laminate so it overhangs the core piece on all sides.

Once the laminate is in place, I used a flush trim bit and a hand-held router to trim the plastic laminate flush (*Fig. 1a*).

TONGUE. The next step is to form a tongue on all four edges of the top that will help align the edging (*Fig. 2a*). Rabbeting both sides of the top all the way around makes quick work of this.

EDGING. All that's left to complete the top is to add the hardwood edging (B) (*Fig. 2*). To make the top appear thicker than it is, the edging is made from 1⅛"-thick stock (I used cherry) (*Fig. 2a*).

GROOVES. After cutting four extra-long pieces of edging, you'll need to cut a

TECHNIQUE . . . . *Gluing Mitered Corners*

Gluing up a mitered picture frame can be tricky. Of course, there are special clamps that make this process a lot simpler. Unfortunately, gluing up a mitered frame the size of the Folding Table top presented another challenge.

DRY-CLAMP. For example, I wanted to make sure all the mitered corners for the top fit nice and tight. So to do this, I first dry-clamped the four hardwood edging pieces to the table top after mitering them to final length (*Fig. 1*).

GLUE-UP. Then I removed two of the clamps and glued the two opposite pieces of edging to the table at a time (*Fig. 2*). These pieces then help to position the remaining pieces, ensuring that the miters stay tight all the way around the top.

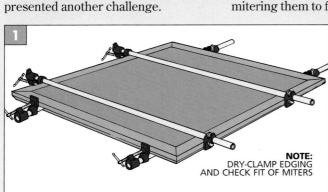

1
NOTE:
DRY-CLAMP EDGING
AND CHECK FIT OF MITERS

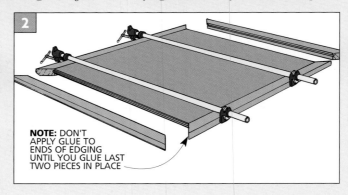

2
NOTE: DON'T
APPLY GLUE TO
ENDS OF EDGING
UNTIL YOU GLUE LAST
TWO PIECES IN PLACE

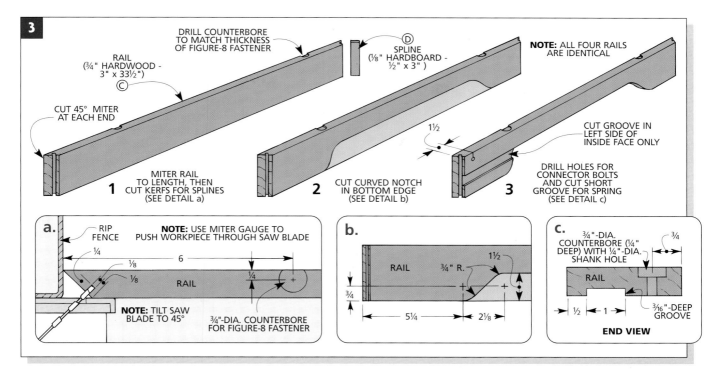

3

DRILL COUNTERBORE TO MATCH THICKNESS OF FIGURE-8 FASTENER

RAIL (¾" HARDWOOD - 3" x 33½")
Ⓒ

CUT 45° MITER AT EACH END

MITER RAIL TO LENGTH, THEN CUT KERFS FOR SPLINES (SEE DETAIL a)

1

SPLINE (⅛" HARDBOARD - ½" x 3")
Ⓓ

CUT CURVED NOTCH IN BOTTOM EDGE (SEE DETAIL b)

1½

2

NOTE: ALL FOUR RAILS ARE IDENTICAL

CUT GROOVE IN LEFT SIDE OF INSIDE FACE ONLY

DRILL HOLES FOR CONNECTOR BOLTS AND CUT SHORT GROOVE FOR SPRING (SEE DETAIL c)

3

a.
RIP FENCE
NOTE: USE MITER GAUGE TO PUSH WORKPIECE THROUGH SAW BLADE
¼
⅛
⅛
6
¼
RAIL
NOTE: TILT SAW BLADE TO 45°
¾"-DIA. COUNTERBORE FOR FIGURE-8 FASTENER

b.
RAIL   ¾" R.   1½
¾
5¼   2⅛

c.
¾"-DIA. COUNTERBORE (¼" DEEP) WITH ¼"-DIA. SHANK HOLE
¾
RAIL
½   1
³⁄₁₆"-DEEP GROOVE
END VIEW

groove in each one to fit the tongue on the top *(Fig. 2a)*. The important thing here is to locate this groove so the top of the edging is flush with the plastic laminate.

Next, to create an angled profile, I ripped a bevel on the bottom outside edge of each piece *(Fig. 2a)*. Then the pieces are simply mitered to length.

Note: To get the miters to fit tight, it's best to sneak up on the final length.

Once the miters fit tight, the trick is to get them to stay that way as you glue on the edging. To do this, I used a simple assembly sequence, shown in the Technique article on the previous page.

Then I eased the tops by routing a ¼" roundover all the way around *(Fig. 2b)*.

APRON

The top of the table is supported by an apron with a tapered leg in each corner.

SPLINED MITERS. The apron consists of four identical rails (C) that are held together with splined miter joints. (I used cherry for the rails.)

After mitering the rails to finished length, cut a kerf in the end of each piece for a spline that will help strengthen the corners of the apron *(Step 1 in Fig. 3)*.

Before gluing the rails together, a few more things need attention. To create a recess for a figure-8 fastener that will be used to attach the top, two shallow counterbores are drilled along the top outside

edge *(Fig. 3a)*. And there's a curved notch in the bottom edge to provide leg clearance *(Step 2)*. (See the Shop Tip on page 97 for details on how to rout a clean straight edge after you've cut the notch.)

Also, drill a single counterbored shank hole at this time for a fastener that will be used to attach the legs later *(Step 3)*. Finally, to create a recess for the spring, cut a short groove in each rail.

ASSEMBLY. Now you're ready to glue up the apron. To do this, you'll need to cut four hardboard splines (D) that fit the kerfs in the mitered ends *(Fig. 3)*.

Note: To ensure that the corners of the apron are square, refer to the Technique box below.

TECHNIQUE . . . . *Squaring Mitered Corners*

When you're gluing up all four corners of the mitered rails for this project (or for any mitered frame, for that matter), the slightest amount of extra pressure from one of the clamps can cause the frame to rack — which can create gaps in the corners.

So when gluing up the rails for the Folding Table, I decided it was best to work on *one* mitered corner at a time.

SQUARE CORNERS. In this case, what I used to keep each corner square is a simple block of wood (see photo at right).

I found my block of wood in the scrap bin. And since I needed a block for all four corners, I went ahead and picked out a long piece of scrap. Then I made sure to square up the scrap piece before cutting the four blocks to length.

Now after you've added glue to the ends of the mitered rails and inserted a spline, the block is clamped to the inside of the corner (see photo).

Note: I also thought it was a good idea to chamfer the corner of the block to provide a relief area for glue squeeze-out.

4

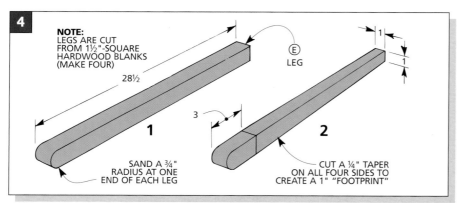

NOTE: LEGS ARE CUT FROM 1½"-SQUARE HARDWOOD BLANKS (MAKE FOUR)

28½

E
LEG

1

3

2

1
1

SAND A ¾" RADIUS AT ONE END OF EACH LEG

CUT A ¼" TAPER ON ALL FOUR SIDES TO CREATE A 1" "FOOTPRINT"

5

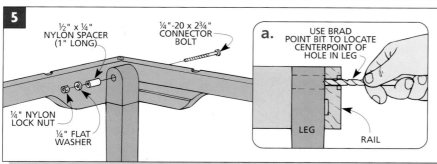

½" x ¼" NYLON SPACER (1" LONG)

¼"-20 x 2¾" CONNECTOR BOLT

¼" NYLON LOCK NUT

¼" FLAT WASHER

a.

USE BRAD POINT BIT TO LOCATE CENTERPOINT OF HOLE IN LEG

LEG

RAIL

6

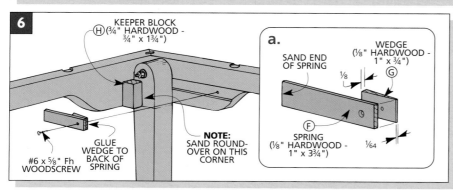

KEEPER BLOCK (H) (¾" HARDWOOD - ¾" x 1¾")

a.

SAND END OF SPRING

WEDGE (⅛" HARDWOOD - 1" x ¾")

⅛

G

⅛

F

SPRING (⅛" HARDWOOD - 1" x 3¾")

1/64

GLUE WEDGE TO BACK OF SPRING

NOTE: SAND ROUND-OVER ON THIS CORNER

#6 x ⅝" Fh WOODSCREW

TECHNIQUE ...... Cutting Wedges

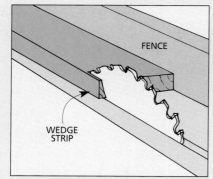

FENCE

WEDGE STRIP

1 To make the wedges, first tilt the table saw blade to the desired angle and rip a thin strip on a long workpiece. (Note direction of grain.)

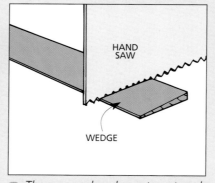

HAND SAW

WEDGE

2 Then, use a hand saw to cut each wedge to the desired width from the long strip. Go ahead and cut all four wedges from the strip.

LEGS

Now, you can turn your attention to building and installing the tapered legs.

Each leg (E) starts out as a 1½"-square blank *(Fig. 4)*. (I used cherry.) To provide clearance for the the leg when it folds, sand a ¾"-radius roundover on the top end of each blank *(Step 1 in Fig. 4)*.

TAPER LEGS. Then all four sides of the blank are tapered. This gives the legs a lightweight look and feel, without taking away from their sturdiness.

There are two things to keep in mind here. First, the taper begins 3" down from the top of the leg. And second, you want to end up with a 1"-square footprint at the bottom *(Step 2 in Fig. 4)*.

Note: I used a manufactured adjustable tapering jig on the table saw to taper the legs. (See Sources on page 126.)

ATTACH LEGS. Now you're ready to attach the legs to the apron frame. But rather than just screw the leg to the apron, I came up with a way for the legs to pivot easily up and down: each one pivots on a nylon spacer that keeps the threads on a bolt from digging into the leg *(Fig. 5)*.

An easy way to locate the hole for the spacer is to clamp each leg in place and use a brad point bit to mark the center-point *(Fig. 5a)*. Now drill the hole and slip in the spacer, then install the connector bolt and secure it with a lock nut.

SPRING. Now it's easy to fold up the leg — in fact it's too easy. So to lock the legs in place (in the extended or the folded position), I added a thin wood "spring."

Each spring (F) is just a ⅛"-thick strip of hardwood that fits in the groove on the inside of the apron *(Fig. 6)*. With the leg fully extended (or folded) the spring sticks out from the apron and holds it in place *(Fig. 7a)*. Pressing the spring into the groove lets you swing the leg up or down.

What makes this work is a small wood wedge (G) that's glued to one end of the spring *(Fig. 6a)*. The wedge pushes the opposite end of the spring away from the apron until you're ready to fold the leg.

To locate the spring, fit it tight against the leg when the leg is fully extended. After screwing the spring in place, glue a keeper block (H) to the apron to fit tight against the adjacent side *(Figs. 6 and 7a)*. This provides firm support on both sides of the leg to keep it from wobbling.

ATTACH TOP. All that's left to complete the table is to attach the top. It's held in place by screwing the figure-8 fasteners to the apron and the top *(Fig. 7b)*. ∎

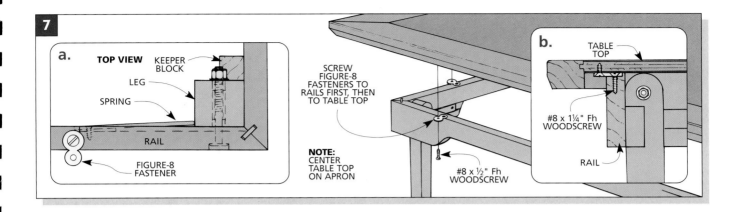

7

a. TOP VIEW

KEEPER BLOCK

LEG

SPRING

RAIL

FIGURE-8 FASTENER

SCREW FIGURE-8 FASTENERS TO RAILS FIRST, THEN TO TABLE TOP

NOTE: CENTER TABLE TOP ON APRON

#8 x ½" Fh WOODSCREW

b. TABLE TOP

#8 x 1¼" Fh WOODSCREW

RAIL

DESIGNER'S NOTEBOOK

Here's a perfect solution for those times when you need a little more space when dining or entertaining.

CONSTRUCTION NOTES:

■ This table is narrower and longer than the Folding Table. It's just the right size for serving dishes when space is limited.

■ Begin by building the table top. I started by cutting the core (A) to size and covering it with laminate (see drawing).

■ Next, rout the tongue around the core (refer to *Fig. 2a* on page 66). Then make the new side (I) and end (J) edging. Rout and cut the details as before (refer to *Figs. 2a and 2b* on page 66), and glue them to the core (see drawing below).

■ The side rails (K) are longer, while the end rails (L) are shorter. Miter them to length now. Instead of cutting a curved notch in all four rails, only the side rails (K) get notches (see drawing).

■ Finally, drill the holes for the connector bolts at each end of the side rails and cut the short groove for the spring at *both* ends on the inside edge of each side rail. (The legs fold up pointing toward each other, instead of in a domino fashion.)

Plus, drill the recesses for the figure-8 fasteners, but this time do it on the inside edge of the apron (see drawing). Complete the table by adding the legs, springs, wedges, and the spacer blocks.

BUFFET TABLE

MATERIALS LIST

CHANGED PART

A	Core (1)	½ ply - 18 x 61¼

NEW PARTS

I	Side Edging (2)	1⅛ x 1½ - 63½
J	End Edging (2)	1⅛ x 1½ - 20¼
K	Side Rails (2)	¾ x 3 - 58¾
L	End Rails (2)	¾ x 3 - 17

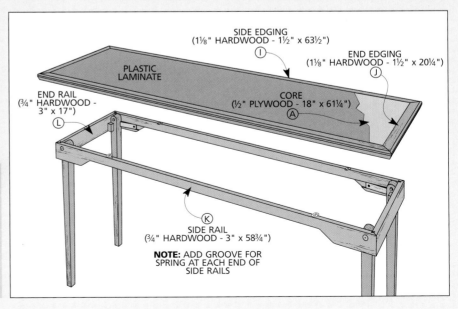

SIDE EDGING (1⅛" HARDWOOD - 1½" x 63½")
Ⓘ

END EDGING (1⅛" HARDWOOD - 1½" x 20¼")
Ⓙ

PLASTIC LAMINATE

END RAIL (¾" HARDWOOD - 3" x 17")
Ⓛ

CORE (½" PLYWOOD - 18" x 61¼")
Ⓐ

SIDE RAIL (¾" HARDWOOD - 3" x 58¾")
Ⓚ

NOTE: ADD GROOVE FOR SPRING AT EACH END OF SIDE RAILS

Plant Stand

This project offers a woodworker two distinct challenges. The first is bending the legs to shape and the second is cutting perfectly round shelves. Fortunately, a couple of simple jigs make each job easy.

Y ou might think that making bent legs — especially legs with a bend on each end — would require a complicated jig, hours of set up, and maybe a special technique that involves steaming the wood.

Actually, the bent legs on this Plant Stand are bent laminations. That means each leg is made of six thin strips of oak with two strips of walnut in the center for accent. Then these strips are laminated (glued) together and shaped on a special bending jig. (For more on bent laminations in general, see the Technique article on page 77.)

BENDING JIG. To bend the curves on both ends of the legs, all you need are ten clamps that open to at least 4", and a simple bending jig that's made out of plywood. Since this project isn't too large, you can get by with inexpensive C-clamps while you're learning the ropes.

And best of all, the jig is designed with gentle curves so the strips of wood can be bent to shape without steaming, soaking, or any special preparation. To learn more about it, see the Shop Jig box on page 76.

SHELVES. Once you've mastered bending the legs, they get attached to three round shelves with glue and woodscrews. (I added decorative wood plugs to hide the screws.) And I sized the shelves to hold a medium sized (6"-dia.) flower pot, but the shelf diameter can be varied to almost any size.

Cutting the shelves into perfect circles is the second challenge on this project. But again, it's easier than it might seem, thanks to a special router jig. All I used is a router fitted with a shop-made base plate that has a pivot hole drilled in it. When the hole is set over a pivot pin in the workpiece, the router swings around it to cut perfect circles.

FINISH. As for the finish, since this stand is designed to be a place to show off your plants, the primary requirement is that it resist moisture. So I applied two coats of satin polyurethane.

EXPLODED VIEW

OVERALL DIMENSIONS:
15½W x 15½D x 37½H

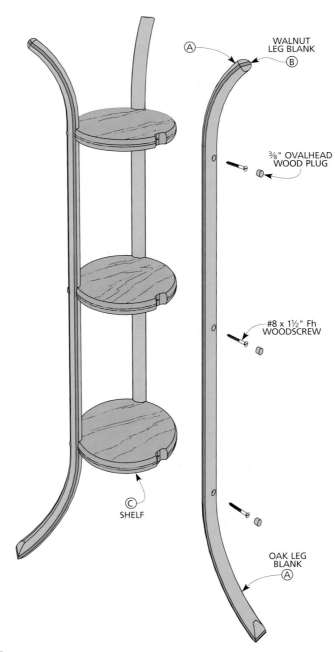

WALNUT
LEG BLANK

Ⓐ Ⓑ

⅜" OVALHEAD
WOOD PLUG

#8 x 1½" Fh
WOODSCREW

Ⓒ
SHELF

OAK LEG
BLANK
Ⓐ

MATERIALS LIST

WOOD
A Oak Leg Blanks (7) ¾ x 1¹/₁₆ - 44
B Walnut Leg Blanks (3) ¾ x 1¹/₁₆ - 44
C Shelves (3) ¾ x 8 - 8
Note: Each oak and walnut blank yields three strips. Minimum of 18 oak strips and 6 walnut strips needed for three legs.

HARDWARE SUPPLIES
(9) No. 8 x 1½" Fh woodscrews
(9) ⅜" ovalhead wood plugs

CUTTING DIAGRAM

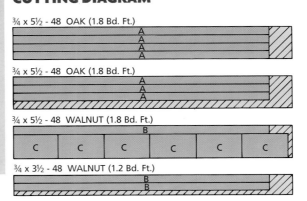

¾ x 5½ - 48 OAK (1.8 Bd. Ft.)

¾ x 5½ - 48 OAK (1.8 Bd. Ft.)

¾ x 5½ - 48 WALNUT (1.8 Bd. Ft.)

¾ x 3½ - 48 WALNUT (1.2 Bd. Ft.)

CUTTING THE STRIPS

The first step in building the stand is to make the bending jig described in the Shop Jig box on page 76.

Once it was built, I cut seven blanks (A) of ³/₄"-thick oak and three blanks (B) of ³/₄"-thick walnut 1¹/₆" wide. Then I set up the table saw to resaw the blanks into ³/₃₂"-thick strips *(Fig. 1)*. (See the Technique article at the bottom of this page for more on ripping thin strips.)

Note: Before cutting any oak or walnut, be sure your table saw is set up correctly by test cutting eight strips of scrap stock. Then stack the strips and measure the combined thickness *(Fig. 2)*.

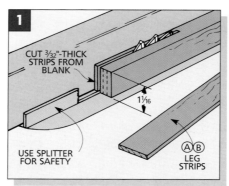

CUT ³/₃₂"-THICK STRIPS FROM BLANK

USE SPLITTER FOR SAFETY

1¹/₆

(A)(B) LEG STRIPS

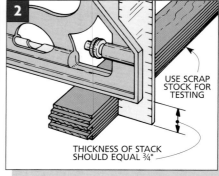

USE SCRAP STOCK FOR TESTING

THICKNESS OF STACK SHOULD EQUAL ³/₄"

If the setting is correct, the stack you've cut will be exactly ³/₄" thick.

Now, when you're sure the setting for the table saw is correct, go ahead and resaw a total of twenty oak strips and eight walnut strips.

Note: I cut two extra strips of each in case some of the strips break.

TECHNIQUE .... *Ripping Thin Strips*

One key to a successful bent lamination project is using wood strips that have square edges and are uniform in thickness. The easiest and safest way I've found to cut them is on a table saw with a zero-clearance insert with a splitter, and a simple push block.

INSERT. The zero-clearance insert has so little clearance on each side of the blade that the thin strips can't fall down into the slot. Plus, the splitter keeps the kerf open the same width as the blade, so it reduces kickback and binding on the back edge of the blade.

SHAPING THE BLANK. To make a zero-clearance insert, first resaw or plane a hardwood blank to the thickness of the insert opening in the saw table so the new insert will lie flush.

Now remove the original insert from your saw and trace the outline of the insert onto the blank. Then rough cut to within ¹/₁₆" of the outline *(Fig. 1)*.

To trim the new insert to the exact shape of the original, I use the original as a template. Start by taping the original

insert to the new blank with double-sided carpet tape. Then mount a flush trim bit in the router table and, with the bearing riding on the original insert, trim the new one to shape *(Fig. 1a)*.

Note: If you don't have a flush trim bit, you can sand or file the insert until it fits snugly in the opening.

The next step is to cut the blade slot. To do this, replace the original insert in the saw table and carefully align the fence with the edge of the insert *(Fig. 2)*. Then rip the slot, stopping and turning off the saw 3" from the end of the new insert.

THE SPLITTER. To make the splitter, rip a piece of stock to the exact thickness of the saw blade kerf. Then cut it 1" high (wide) and 3" long. Sand the end that will be closest to the blade to a point, and then glue the splitter into the slot *(Fig. 3)*.

Finally, bore a 1"-dia. hole in the insert to make it easier to lift it out of the table.

PUSH BLOCK. Of all the push blocks I've used in the past, the one that works the best for me is extremely simple. I like to use a wide push block when rip-

ping thin stock. The reason I like a wide push block is because of safety. It straddles the blade so the heel on the bottom edge of the block pushes *both* the workpiece and the waste past the blade, eliminating any chance of kickback. For more on how to make a wide push block, see the Shop Tip box on page 108.

NO SANDING. Once you've finished ripping the strips needed for the Plant Stand, it may be tempting to sand them before you glue them up — but don't. The table saw will cut the strips so the edges are square and the thickness is uniform. Plus, sanding the edges may round them over or even create depressions in the thickness of the strips.

So instead of sanding, I use a sharp combination blade in my saw to eliminate many of the marks before they occur. But even then, you may still have some blade marks on the faces of the strips. You can plane these pieces by hand. Or if you have a thickness planer that will plane thin stock, rip the strips slightly thicker and then run them through the planer.

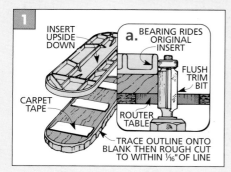

INSERT UPSIDE DOWN

a. BEARING RIDES ORIGINAL INSERT

FLUSH TRIM BIT

CARPET TAPE

ROUTER TABLE

TRACE OUTLINE ONTO BLANK THEN ROUGH CUT TO WITHIN ¹/₁₆" OF LINE

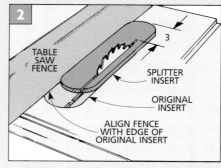

TABLE SAW FENCE

3

SPLITTER INSERT

ORIGINAL INSERT

ALIGN FENCE WITH EDGE OF ORIGINAL INSERT

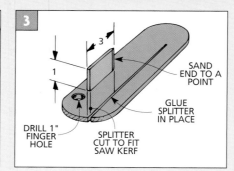

3

1

SAND END TO A POINT

GLUE SPLITTER IN PLACE

DRILL 1" FINGER HOLE

SPLITTER CUT TO FIT SAW KERF

LEGS

After ripping all the oak and walnut strips, the next step is to glue up the legs.

GLUING THE STRIPS. Start by spreading the glue on one side of each strip. Then, stack the strips like a sandwich: three oak, two walnut, and three oak *(Fig. 3a)*. Now lay the stack on its side against the straight form on the bending jig.

CLAMPING. Now, add the other straight form and clamp everything together, starting in the center and working toward the ends *(Fig. 3)*. Be sure to align the top edges flush.

BENDING THE STRIPS. Next, bend the strips around the fixed curved pieces, using the loose curved piece to press the strips against the curved forms. Now place a clamp, centered on the curved section, and tighten it down *(Fig. 3)*.

Add the remaining clamps to the curved sections, tightening them so the pressure is even along the entire leg. (For more tips on how to use the bending jig, see the article on page 77.)

CLEAN-UP. Once the glue has set up, remove the leg from the jig and scrape off the dried glue with a paint scraper.

Now the legs can be planed to their final width of 1". To avoid tearout, I used a low angle block plane.

CUT TO LENGTH. To finish the leg it must be cut to length. You'll need to mark the top and the bottom ends of each leg, and then cut off the excess.

To keep all three legs uniform, mark the cut-off locations on the jig, marking the location of the top of the leg from one end of the fixed curved form *(Fig. 4)*. Then mark the location of the leg bottom from the end of the other form *(Fig. 5)*.

Now, replace the leg and transfer the cut-off locations from the jig to the leg. Then saw off the extra stock.

SHAPING THE ENDS. Now, round over the top end of the leg *(Fig. 4a)*. The bottom end needs a second cut for a flat foot. To do this, draw a line on the bottom of the leg, centered on the squared end *(Fig. 5a)*. Cut off the excess and then shape the tip with a file.

SHAPING THE SIDES. Now, before drilling the screw holes, I used a ³⁄₈" roundover bit mounted in the router table and took a series of light passes on the legs to soften the corners *(Figs. 6 and 6a)*.

SCREW HOLES. Finally, mark the locations for the screws that attach the legs to the shelves. Here again I used the jig to lay out the screw hole locations *(Fig. 7)*. Then drill a counterbored shank hole *(Fig. 8a)*.

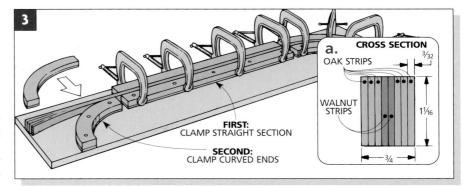

3

FIRST: CLAMP STRAIGHT SECTION
SECOND: CLAMP CURVED ENDS

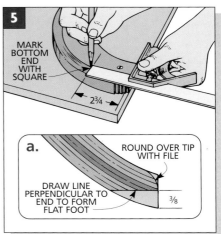

a. CROSS SECTION
OAK STRIPS
³⁄₃₂
WALNUT STRIPS
1¹⁄₁₆
³⁄₄

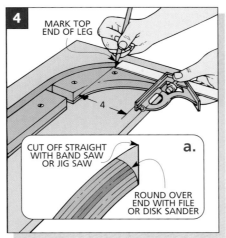

4 MARK TOP END OF LEG
4
a. CUT OFF STRAIGHT WITH BAND SAW OR JIG SAW
ROUND OVER END WITH FILE OR DISK SANDER

5 MARK BOTTOM END WITH SQUARE
2³⁄₄
a. ROUND OVER TIP WITH FILE
DRAW LINE PERPENDICULAR TO END TO FORM FLAT FOOT
³⁄₈

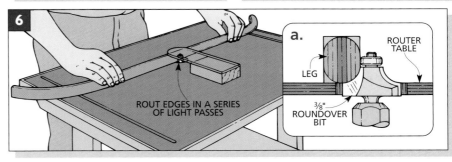

6 ROUT EDGES IN A SERIES OF LIGHT PASSES
a. ROUTER TABLE
LEG
³⁄₈" ROUNDOVER BIT

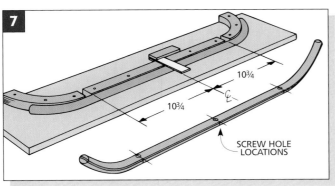

7
10³⁄₄
10³⁄₄
SCREW HOLE LOCATIONS

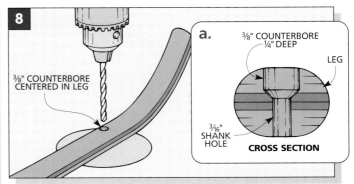

8 ³⁄₈" COUNTERBORE CENTERED IN LEG
a. ³⁄₈" COUNTERBORE ¹⁄₄" DEEP
LEG
³⁄₁₆" SHANK HOLE
CROSS SECTION

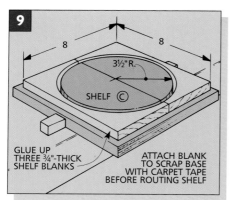

9

8   8

3½" R.

SHELF Ⓒ

GLUE UP THREE ¾"-THICK SHELF BLANKS

ATTACH BLANK TO SCRAP BASE WITH CARPET TAPE BEFORE ROUTING SHELF

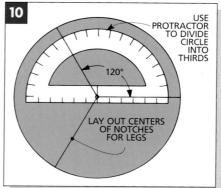

10

USE PROTRACTOR TO DIVIDE CIRCLE INTO THIRDS

120°

LAY OUT CENTERS OF NOTCHES FOR LEGS

SHELVES

When all three legs are complete, begin working on the shelves. The circular shelves (C) are cut from ¾"-thick walnut blanks. To make them, start by gluing up three squares *(Fig. 9)*.

ROUT CIRCLES. To cut the blanks into perfect 7"-dia. circles, I used my router fitted with a special base plate. This base is slightly larger than the original base to accommodate a pivot hole 3½" from the router bit (see Shop Jig box below).

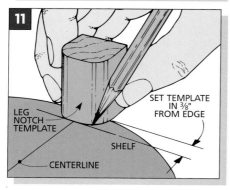

11

SET TEMPLATE IN ⅜" FROM EDGE

LEG NOTCH TEMPLATE

SHELF

CENTERLINE

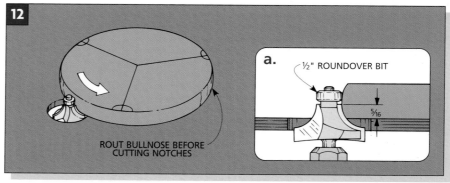

12

ROUT BULLNOSE BEFORE CUTTING NOTCHES

a.

½" ROUNDOVER BIT

⁵⁄₁₆

SHOP JIG .... *Router Trammel*

Replacing the base plate on your router with a larger shop-made base makes cutting the three round shelves for the Plant Stand a lot easier. The new base plate acts as a trammel attachment for cutting and routing circles.

BASE PLATE. While ¼"-thick hardboard will work for the base plate, I used a piece of ¼" acrylic plastic so I could easily see what I was routing. To cut circles, the new base needs to be extra long. (See page 126 for sources of acrylic plastic.)

To attach this piece of acrylic to your router, position your router's original base plate over the new plate and use it as a template to locate the holes for the

mounting screws and also the large center opening for the bit.

PIVOT HOLE. The next step is to drill a ¹⁄₁₆"-dia. hole in the new base plate to fit over a pivot pin *(Fig. 2)*.

To locate the pivot pin for the Plant Stand shelf, first mount a ¼" straight bit in the router. Then measure from the cutting edge of the bit to the hole. This distance is equal to the radius of the circle you want to cut. For the pivot pin, use a brad and drive it into the workpiece, snipping it off ¼" above the surface.

ROUTING CIRCLES. Once the pin is in place, you can start routing. To keep the bit from cutting into the bench when

routing through the blank, I screwed through the waste section in each corner into a piece of plywood. Then I clamped the plywood to my bench *(Fig. 3)*.

To rout a circle, set the bit ¼" deep and place the base plate over the pivot pin. Then, tip the router so the bit is above the workpiece and turn on the router *(Fig. 2)*.

Note: If you're using a plunge router, you won't have to tip it.

Now, slowly plunge the bit into the blank. Then move the router clockwise until you reach the starting point. Keep repeating this process, lowering the bit ¼" (or less) between passes until the bit cuts through the blank *(Fig. 3)*.

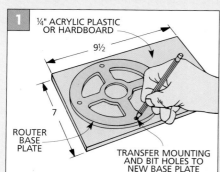

1

¼" ACRYLIC PLASTIC OR HARDBOARD

9½

7

ROUTER BASE PLATE

TRANSFER MOUNTING AND BIT HOLES TO NEW BASE PLATE

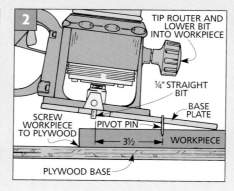

2

TIP ROUTER AND LOWER BIT INTO WORKPIECE

¼" STRAIGHT BIT

BASE PLATE

SCREW WORKPIECE TO PLYWOOD

PIVOT PIN

3½

WORKPIECE

PLYWOOD BASE

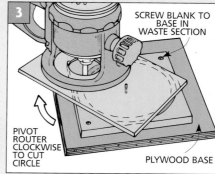

3

SCREW BLANK TO BASE IN WASTE SECTION

PIVOT ROUTER CLOCKWISE TO CUT CIRCLE

PLYWOOD BASE

LEG NOTCHES. The legs are screwed into notches cut into the edges of the shelves. To mark the centers of these notches, mark every 120° *(Fig. 10)*.

NOTCH TEMPLATE. Each notch is cut to fit the side of a leg. It's easiest to lay them out by first making a template that's the same shape as the legs *(Fig. 11)*. To do this, round over the edges of a long scrap piece, using a $\frac{3}{8}$" roundover bit.

Now, to mark the notches on the shelves, center the leg template over the 120° marks on a shelf. Set it $\frac{3}{8}$" in from the edge, and draw a line around the template onto the shelf *(Fig. 11)*.

BULLNOSE EDGES. Before cutting the notches, I routed a bullnose edge on each shelf *(Fig. 12)*. To do this, mount a $\frac{1}{2}$" roundover bit in the router table, adjust it so it's $\frac{5}{16}$" above the table, and rout both the top and bottom edges *(Fig. 12a)*.

CUT OUT NOTCHES. Now the notches for the legs can be cut out of the shelves

(Fig. 13). I used a band saw to remove the stock, but a jig saw or coping saw would also work for this small job.

Then, to smooth the inside surface of the notch, use a $\frac{3}{4}$"-diameter sanding drum on the drill press *(Fig. 14)*. Now, test the legs in the notches to be sure they fit.

ASSEMBLY. Now it's time to put everything together. Start by drilling a pilot hole centered in each notch. To do this, clamp the shelf into a large hand screw or between two pieces of scrap stock so the shelf is held securely at 90° to the drill press table *(Fig. 15)*.

SCREW LEGS TO SHELVES. Next, screw the legs into the shelf notches *(Fig. 16)*. Then, check to see that the shelves are perpendicular to the legs. If the stand isn't, loosen the screws, adjust the stand and re-tighten the screws.

PLUG HOLES. Fill the screw holes with ovalhead walnut wood plugs *(Fig. 16a)* (see the Technique article below). ■

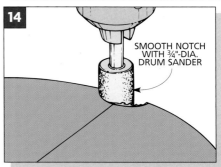

CUT OUT LEG NOTCH ON BAND SAW

SHELF

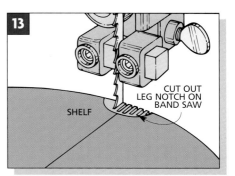

SMOOTH NOTCH WITH ¾"-DIA. DRUM SANDER

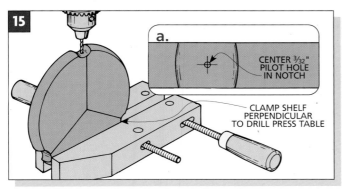

a. CENTER 3/32" PILOT HOLE IN NOTCH

CLAMP SHELF PERPENDICULAR TO DRILL PRESS TABLE

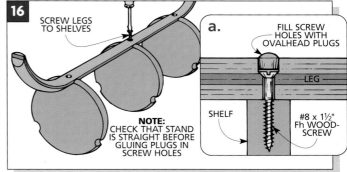

SCREW LEGS TO SHELVES

NOTE: CHECK THAT STAND IS STRAIGHT BEFORE GLUING PLUGS IN SCREW HOLES

a. FILL SCREW HOLES WITH OVALHEAD PLUGS

LEG

SHELF

#8 x 1½" Fh WOOD-SCREW

TECHNIQUE .... *Installing Wood Plugs*

Wood plugs are commonly available in three styles *(Fig. 1)*. And they're readily available in $\frac{1}{4}$", $\frac{3}{8}$", and $\frac{1}{2}$" diameters.

INSTALLING PLUGS. Each type of plug is unique in the way it's installed.

Flathead and button plugs are simple to install. Ovalhead plugs, however, can be driven in too far, flattening the top.

Since I used $\frac{3}{8}$" ovalhead plugs for the Plant Stand, I needed a simple way to install the plugs without flattening the tops. So I made a plug setter that matched the plug's rounded top *(Fig. 2)*.

CONSTRUCTION. To make the plug setter, I first cut a $\frac{3}{4}$" dowel, $1\frac{1}{2}$" long. Then I drilled a shallow hole in one end of the dowel with a $\frac{7}{16}$" twist drill bit *(Fig. 2)*.

SET THE PLUGS. Once you've completed the plug setter, it's easy to use. First, position an ovalhead plug in a hole and place the setter over the plug. Then, tap the setter just until it bottoms out on the workpiece *(Fig. 3a)*.

Note: Don't continue tapping the setter after it bottoms out or you could leave a doughnut-shaped dent in the work surface.

WOOD PLUGS

FLATHEAD

OVALHEAD

BUTTON

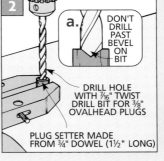

a. DON'T DRILL PAST BEVEL ON BIT

DRILL HOLE WITH 7/16" TWIST DRILL BIT FOR 3/8" OVALHEAD PLUGS

PLUG SETTER MADE FROM ¾" DOWEL (1½" LONG)

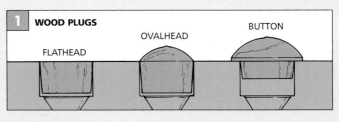

PLACE SETTER ON PLUG AND TAP

a. OVAL-HEAD PLUG

PLUG SETTER

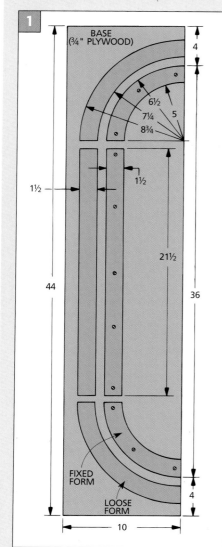

1

BASE
(3/4" PLYWOOD)

6½
7¼   5
8¾

1½

1½

1½

21½

44

36

FIXED
FORM

LOOSE
FORM

10

4

4

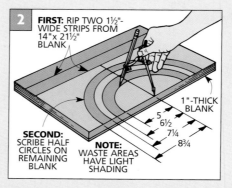

2

FIRST: RIP TWO 1½"-
WIDE STRIPS FROM
14"x 21½"
BLANK

1"-THICK
BLANK

5
6½
7¼
8¾

SECOND:
SCRIBE HALF
CIRCLES ON
REMAINING
BLANK

NOTE:
WASTE AREAS
HAVE LIGHT
SHADING

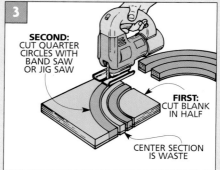

3

SECOND:
CUT QUARTER
CIRCLES WITH
BAND SAW
OR JIG SAW

FIRST:
CUT BLANK
IN HALF

CENTER SECTION
IS WASTE

4

STRAIGHT FORM

CURVED FORM

6½

18

18

¾" PLYWOOD BASE

a.   1½

FORM

1

FORM

BASE

B efore you can start building the legs, you have to make a bending jig. To do this, begin by cutting a base for the jig from ³/₄" plywood *(Fig. 1)*.

BLANK FOR FORMS. The next step in building the jig is to add sections of straight and curved forms to bend the thin strips to shape. Since the strips are 1¹/₁₆" wide, these forms should be at least 1" thick. I made the forms by gluing a piece of ¹/₄" plywood to a piece of ³/₄" plywood to produce a 1"-thick blank *(Fig. 2)*.

STRAIGHT FORMS. Six pieces are cut out of the blank to make the bending form: four curved pieces and two straight pieces *(Fig. 2)*. I cut the straight pieces from the blank first.

CURVED FORMS. To make the curved sections, scribe four half-circles on the

remaining part of the blank *(Fig. 2)*. After you've completed drawing the half-circles, cut the blank in half *(Fig. 3)*. Then cut out the quarter-circle forms with a band saw or a jig saw.

MOUNTING THE FORMS. After all the form pieces have been cut, the bending jig is ready to be assembled. Start by screwing the inside (smaller) curved pieces to the base.

To align the ends of the two curved pieces, draw a line down the length of the base, 6½" from one edge *(Fig. 4)*. Then mark reference lines 18" to each side of the centerline *(Fig. 4)*. Now screw down the curved pieces so the outside of the curve touches the 18" reference marks at the ends and the line down the length of the jig.

Next, screw one of the straight pieces on the line so it's aligned with the ends of the curved pieces *(Fig. 4)*.

Note: The other straight piece and curved pieces are not screwed to the base. They're used to clamp the strips to the fixed forms.

Finally, to prevent the strips from sticking to the base and bending forms, rub paraffin (or paste wax) on the surfaces that will come in contact with the strips during gluing.

Bending Jig. *You don't need a lot of fancy tools to bend thin strips of wood. Once the jig is made, all that's needed are clamps, glue, and some patience.*

TECHNIQUE .... *Bent Lamination*

Bent lamination is a process of bending several thin strips of wood together — using lots of glue and lots of clamps. It's messy, but rewarding to see a gracefully bent piece of wood emerge from a glue-encrusted form.

The process starts with ripping some thin strips of wood and applying glue to each strip. Then it's a matter of stacking all the strips together like a sandwich and laying the sandwich on its side in a bending jig. Then the strips are pushed around the curves on the jig, and clamped every few inches.

STRENGTH. Although bent laminations can provide an attractive piece of wood, there are more reasons to use it than just appearance. It's also strong. While it would be much easier to make a curved piece by simply cutting it out of solid stock, it's not always a good idea. This creates a lot of waste. And there will be a weak spot where the grain runs across the narrow face (from edge to edge) *(Fig. 1)*.

STRAIGHT GRAIN. Any wood will bend if it's cut thin enough. And hardwoods will bend better than softwoods. But, whatever kind of wood you use, remember that wood with grain that runs in a fairly straight line is best for bending around tight curves. Highly figured woods can break before they bend and more often than not, splitting can occur *(Fig. 2)*.

RIPPING. To cut strips to a consistent thickness, and do it safely, I cut them on the table saw using a special shop-made zero-clearance insert with a splitter. (For more on this special insert, see the Technique article on page 72.)

Note: If the straight grain is on the edge of a board, cutting it is a two-step process. First, rip a piece to the *width* of the finished strips (plus a little for clean up). Then turn that piece on its edge and resaw the strips with the straight grain up *(Fig. 3)*. This way the straightest grain will appear on the edge of the workpiece.

KEEP IN ORDER. To minimize color variation in the laminated pieces, arrange the strips in the order they're cut off the board. This way you won't see joint lines.

GLUE UP. Bent lamination uses lots of glue. It's hard to predict just how much you'll need, but it is usually more than you expect.

Note: To keep the glue from sticking to the jig, rub on a heavy coat of paraffin wax before starting.

Apply the glue in thin layers to one side of the workpiece only, stacking them as you go *(Fig. 4)*. Then pick up the stack and lay it on its side in the form.

Start by clamping in the middle and moving out toward each end, wrapping the strips around the curves. Use a wood block to keep the strips flush as you tighten down the clamps *(Fig. 5)*. Once the glue has had time to completely dry (I leave the clamps on overnight), remove the clamps and use a paint scraper to remove most of the squeeze-out. Finish up with a block plane or drum sander to remove the remaining glue *(Fig. 6)*.

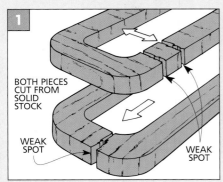
1
BOTH PIECES CUT FROM SOLID STOCK
WEAK SPOT
WEAK SPOT

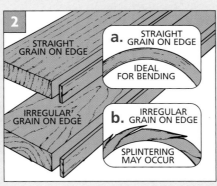
2
STRAIGHT GRAIN ON EDGE
a. STRAIGHT GRAIN ON EDGE
IDEAL FOR BENDING
IRREGULAR GRAIN ON EDGE
b. IRREGULAR GRAIN ON EDGE
SPLINTERING MAY OCCUR

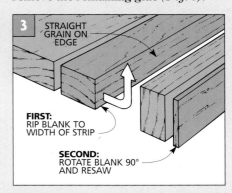
3
STRAIGHT GRAIN ON EDGE
FIRST: RIP BLANK TO WIDTH OF STRIP
SECOND: ROTATE BLANK 90° AND RESAW

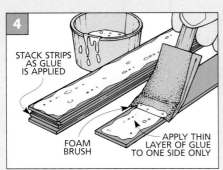
4
STACK STRIPS AS GLUE IS APPLIED
FOAM BRUSH
APPLY THIN LAYER OF GLUE TO ONE SIDE ONLY

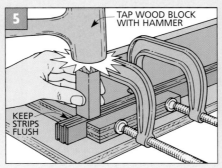
5
TAP WOOD BLOCK WITH HAMMER
KEEP STRIPS FLUSH

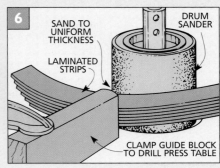
6
SAND TO UNIFORM THICKNESS
DRUM SANDER
LAMINATED STRIPS
CLAMP GUIDE BLOCK TO DRILL PRESS TABLE

TV & CD CABINETS

Have you ever entertained the thought of a custom-built cabinet to hold your media components? Make it a reality with the projects in this section.

Tabletop TV Stand

Easy enough to build in a weekend, this swivel-top TV stand looks good from any angle. And it's perfectly sized to hold a computer monitor. Add a drawer below for even more convenience.

When I was growing up, we had one television set. It was a big floor model that sat against the wall in the living room and everyone in the house watched the same show.

Today of course, it's common to have additional television sets in a den, a bedroom, a kitchen, or even the workshop.

But unlike a TV in the living room, television sets in other rooms of the house don't usually occupy a central spot in the room. They often wind up sitting on top of a table, a dresser, or maybe a night stand. And they get moved around a lot in an effort to find the best viewing angle.

That's why I came up with this TV stand. It's designed to hold a small to medium-size television (13" to 19" screen). And it has an open compartment below that's just the right size to hold a VCR or DVD player.

LAZY SUSAN. But the neatest thing (I think) about this stand is the fact that the top is mounted on a lazy Susan turntable. This allows you to swivel the TV easily so it can be seen from just about any spot in the room.

COMPUTERS. This project isn't just for TVs, however. When set on a desk, it makes a great place for a computer monitor (see the photo on the facing page). And the compartment beneath the top can be used for storing computer disks, CDs, or other accessories.

CONSTRUCTION. If you look at the Exploded View on the next page, you'll see that there's not much to this project. Just five pieces. So you can probably com-

plete it in a few evenings. (Even if you're building several stands.)

The joinery is as simple as the rest of the project. Long mortises and tenons join the top and bottom of the base to the sides. The mortises are cut on the router table so you don't have to spend a lot of time drilling or chiseling. And the tenons are created with just a couple of passes over the table saw blade.

DRAWER OPTION. To give you even more storage, you might want to consider adding a drawer below the compartment. It's a convenient place to store tapes, DVDs, or the remote control. You can add the drawer and still have the project completed in about a weekend. Details about this option are in the Designer's Notebook on page 85.

EXPLODED VIEW

OVERALL DIMENSIONS:
18W x 20D x 7⅜H

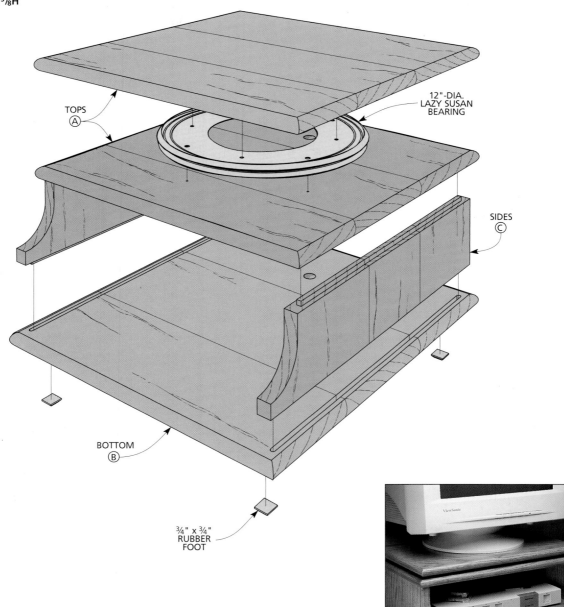

TOPS
Ⓐ

12"-DIA.
LAZY SUSAN
BEARING

SIDES
Ⓒ

BOTTOM
Ⓑ

¾" x ¾"
RUBBER
FOOT

Use the stand to raise a computer monitor to a comfortable viewing height. The swivel top makes it easy to turn the monitor so others can see it, and peripherals can be stored in the compartment.

MATERIALS LIST

WOOD

A	Tops (2)	¾ x 18 - 18
B	Bottom (1)	¾ x 20 - 18
C	Sides (2)	¾ x 19¼ - 4½

HARDWARE SUPPLIES

(1) 12"-dia. lazy Susan w/ screws
(4) ¾" x ¾" rubber feet

CUTTING DIAGRAM

¾ x 7¼ - 72 (3 Boards @ 3.6 Bd. Ft. Each)

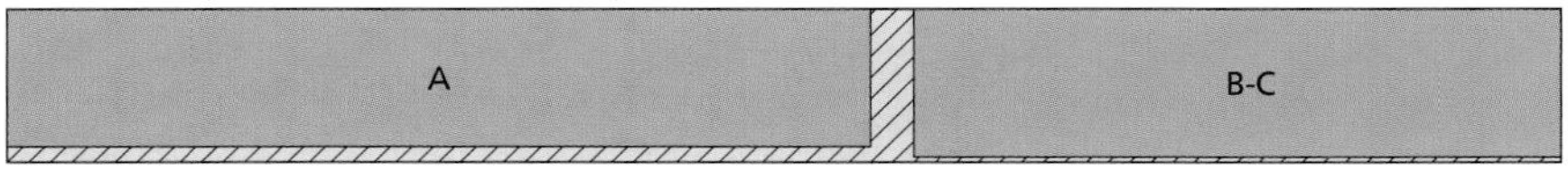

A		B-C

NOTE: PARTS B AND C ARE CUT FROM THE SAME GLUED-UP BLANK.
REFER TO FIG.1A ON PAGE 82

1

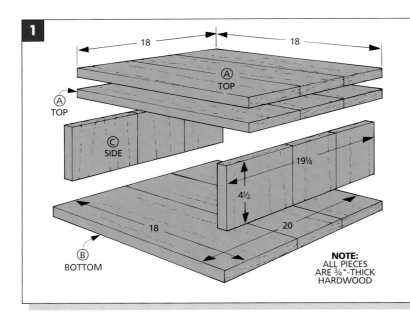

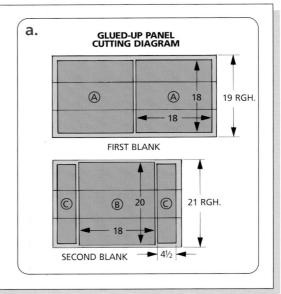

a.

GLUED-UP PANEL CUTTING DIAGRAM

FIRST BLANK

19 RGH.

18

18

SECOND BLANK

21 RGH.

20

18

4½

18 · TOP

18

TOP · A

A · TOP

C · SIDE

19¼

4½

18 · BOTTOM

20

B

NOTE:
ALL PIECES
ARE ¾"-THICK
HARDWOOD

PANEL BLANKS

This stand is made out of solid, ¾"-thick stock, so it's strong enough to support quite a bit of weight. And I used a heavy-duty lazy Susan turntable so that even with the weight of a television it will still swivel smoothly and with very little effort. At the same time, I managed to keep the construction straightforward.

FIVE EASY PIECES. This entire project consists of just five parts *(Fig. 1)*. Two sides are sandwiched between a top panel and a bottom panel. Then a second top panel is added on top of a lazy Susan to allow the TV to be turned.

Some TV sets have a wider base than others. Therefore, it's best to check the actual dimensions of your television before you begin building, then alter the measurements of the stand if necessary.

TECHNIQUE .... *Gluing Up Panels*

Gluing up a bunch of narrow boards to make a wide panel of solid wood seems like such a simple thing. But there's a little more to it than first meets the eye.

The goal is to end up with a panel that looks like a single, wide piece of wood. But it also has to be perfectly flat (and stay that way). Reaching this goal is a two-step process — first, the boards are arranged to consider appearance and movement. Then the boards can be glued up.

ARRANGEMENT. The first step is to arrange your boards for uniformity. This means matching the color and grain pattern of adjacent boards (see photos below).

In addition to appearance, you'll also need to consider how the panel will move with changes in humidity. This depends on the growth rings on the end of each board. If you alternate the rings, each board moves in opposite directions. The end result is a panel that stays flat.

GLUE-UP. After you have the boards arranged, you still have to glue them up. Once you start, you need to work quickly to get the panel flat — and to keep it that way while the clamps are applied.

One trick that will save some assembly time is to apply glue to only one edge of each joint (detail 'a').

Then, to keep the panel from bowing as you tighten the clamps, alternate clamps above and below the panel every 6" (see drawing).

Finally, if the boards aren't exactly flush, whack them with a mallet and a block of wood (detail 'b').

Curved Grain. Arrange adjacent boards so curved grain patterns "merge."

Straight Grain. Side by side, straight-grained boards create an invisible joint.

a.

APPLY GLUE TO ONE EDGE ONLY

SPACE CLAMPS 6" APART

b.

SCRAP BLOCK

Because all of the pieces are fairly wide (at least 18"), they have to be glued up from narrower boards. (Refer to the Technique article on the opposite page for some tips on doing this.)

Rather than gluing up an individual panel for each piece, however, I decided to glue up two long panels and then cut the individual pieces to length *(Fig. 1a)*. This cut down on the amount of gluing and clamping I had to do. Plus it made it much easier to match the color and grain pattern between all of the pieces.

Two identical pieces for the tops (A) are cut from the first blank *(Fig. 1a)*. The bottom (B) and sides (C) are cut from the second blank.

There's just one thing to keep in mind while you're laying out the parts on your blanks. To allow all sides of the stand to expand and contract evenly, it's important to keep the grain orientation the same on all the pieces. This means that the bottom (B) and the sides (C) are actually going to be wider than they are long.

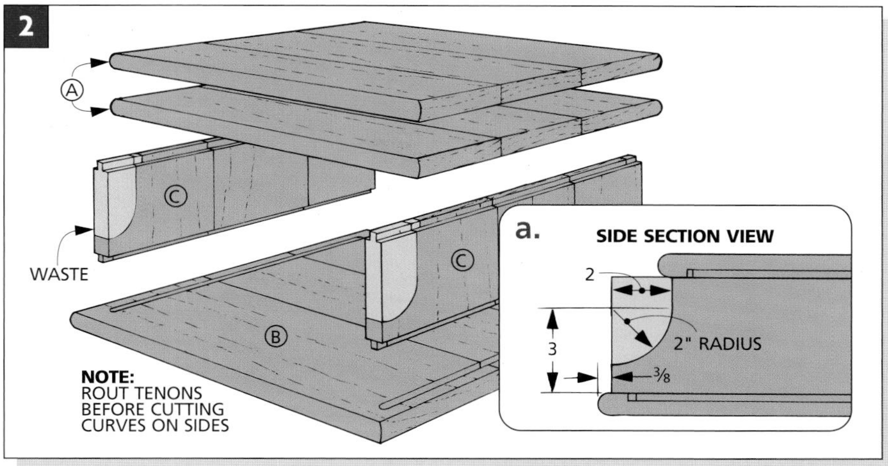
2
A
C
WASTE
C
B
NOTE:
ROUT TENONS
BEFORE CUTTING
CURVES ON SIDES
a.
SIDE SECTION VIEW
2
3
2" RADIUS
3/8

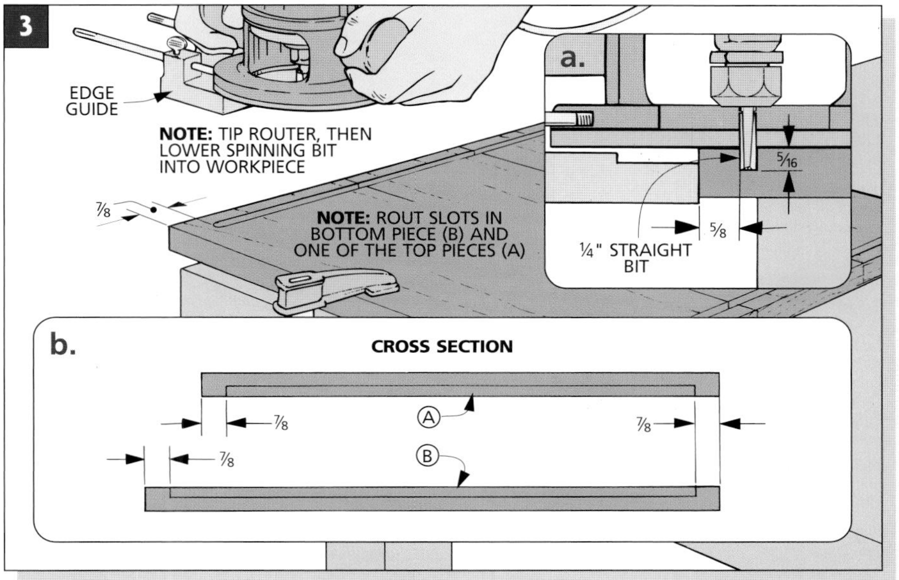
3
EDGE
GUIDE
NOTE: TIP ROUTER, THEN
LOWER SPINNING BIT
INTO WORKPIECE
7/8
NOTE: ROUT SLOTS IN
BOTTOM PIECE (B) AND
ONE OF THE TOP PIECES (A)
a.
5/16
5/8
1/4" STRAIGHT
BIT
b.
CROSS SECTION
7/8
A
7/8
7/8
B

ASSEMBLING THE BASE

Once all five pieces are cut to size, you can begin on the joinery. The sides are joined to the top and bottom with tenons. These tenons are cut on the ends of the sides to fit in shallow slots that are cut in the top and bottom *(Fig. 2)*.

I started by making the slots in the top and bottom panels. Note that only one of the tops receives these slots.

Since the slots are stopped, I couldn't use the table saw to make them. Instead, I routed the slots with a hand-held router equipped with a $\frac{1}{4}$" straight bit and an edge guide *(Figs. 3 and 3a)*.

If you have a plunge router, this is a good chance to use it. If not, you can still rout the slots with an ordinary router. You'll just have to tip the router and carefully lower the rotating bit into the wood, keeping the guide fence tight against the edge of the workpiece *(Fig. 3a)*.

ROUNDOVERS. Once the slots were cut, I created a round-nose profile on both top panels and the bottom panel *(Figs. 4 and 4a)*. You can do this by simply routing a $\frac{3}{8}$" roundover on both sides of the panels. Once you finish routing this profile, you can place the tops and bottom aside for the time being while you work on the sides.

TENONS. Both sides have tenons cut on the ends to fit in the slots in the top and bottom. To do this, I cut a rabbet on both sides of the workpiece, leaving a tenon centered on the edge *(Fig. 5)*.

CURVES. The front edge of each side piece is curved to provide a transition from the top to the large bottom panel *(Fig. 2a)*. After laying out these curves, I cut them on a band saw. (If you don't have a band saw, you could also use a jig saw or a coping saw.)

Regardless of the saw you use, the edges of the curves will likely be less than perfect. But a few minutes with a drum sander mounted in the drill press will take care of this.

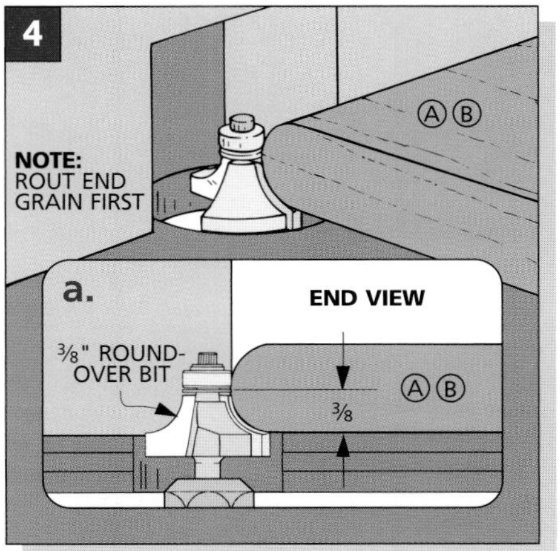
4
A B
NOTE:
ROUT END
GRAIN FIRST
a.
END VIEW
3/8" ROUND-
OVER BIT
A B
3/8

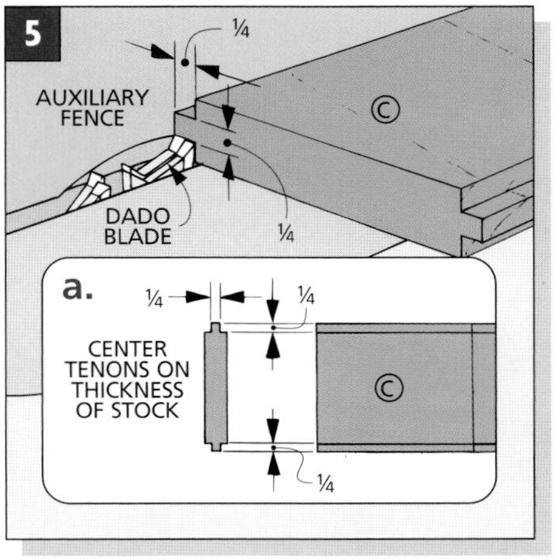
5
1/4
AUXILIARY
FENCE
C
DADO
BLADE
1/4
a.
1/4
1/4
CENTER
TENONS ON
THICKNESS
OF STOCK
C
1/4

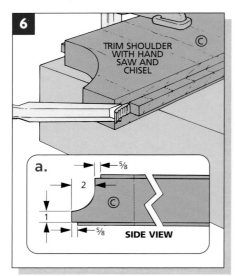

6 TRIM SHOULDER WITH HAND SAW AND CHISEL

a. SIDE VIEW

5/8 2 1 5/8

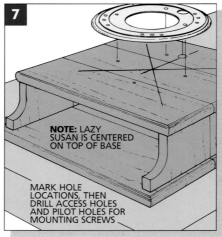

7 NOTE: LAZY SUSAN IS CENTERED ON TOP OF BASE

MARK HOLE LOCATIONS, THEN DRILL ACCESS HOLES AND PILOT HOLES FOR MOUNTING SCREWS

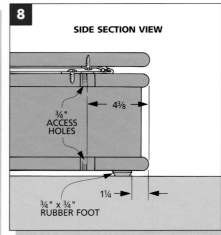

8 SIDE SECTION VIEW

3/4" ACCESS HOLES

4 3/8

3/4" x 3/4" RUBBER FOOT

1 1/4

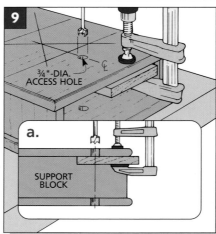

9 3/4"-DIA. ACCESS HOLE

a. SUPPORT BLOCK

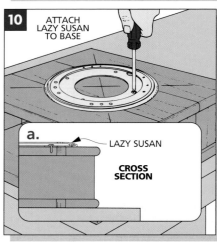

10 ATTACH LAZY SUSAN TO BASE

a. LAZY SUSAN

CROSS SECTION

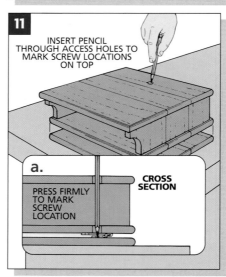

11 INSERT PENCIL THROUGH ACCESS HOLES TO MARK SCREW LOCATIONS ON TOP

a. PRESS FIRMLY TO MARK SCREW LOCATION

CROSS SECTION

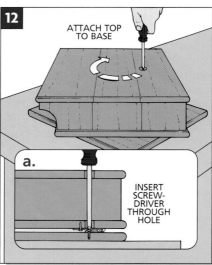

12 ATTACH TOP TO BASE

a. INSERT SCREW-DRIVER THROUGH HOLE

TRIM THE TENONS. There's one more step before the sides can be glued into the top and bottom. The tenons need to be trimmed back about 5/8" from each end *(Fig. 6a)*. This is just a matter of first removing most of the waste with a small hand saw. Then the rest of the waste can be pared back with a sharp chisel *(Fig. 6)*. When you're finished with this, you can glue up the sides, top, and bottom.

ADDING THE TOP

If you've never installed a lazy Susan before now, you might not have stopped to think about how one is fastened to a project. Once you screw the lazy Susan down to the base, how do you attach the top? The trick lies in drilling a small access hole through the base. This hole lines up with a similar hole in the mechanism that allows you to attach the upper top panel *(Figs. 7 and 8)*.

The first step is attaching the lazy Susan to the base. The turntable is centered on top of the base. A simple way to do this is to draw diagonal lines from corner to corner *(Fig. 7)*.

With the lazy Susan centered on the base, mark the location of the screw holes and the large access hole *(Fig. 7)*.

Note: I positioned the lazy Susan so the access hole was at the back.

When you've finished marking the holes, set the lazy Susan aside and drill a 3/4"-dia. access hole through the top of the base *(Fig. 9)*. To help prevent splintering when the bit exits the hole, I clamped a piece of scrap to the base before drilling the hole *(Fig. 9a)*. Then transfer the hole location and drill an identical hole in the bottom of the base.

After drilling pilot holes, the lazy Susan turntable can be screwed to the top of the base *(Figs. 10 and 10a)*.

ATTACHING THE TOP. There's not much to adding the top of the stand. You can start by setting the top face-down on your workbench. Then place the base (upside-down) on the top, making sure the edges

line up. Now slowly rotate the base while looking through the access holes. When you come to the first mounting hole, mark it with a pencil *(Fig. 11)*. Keep rotating the base until you've marked all the locations for the mounting screws.

Now just remove the base and drill pilot holes in the top for the mounting screws. Then reach through the access holes with a screwdriver to screw the lazy Susan to the top *(Fig. 12)*. At this point, the turntable is hard to reach, so see the Shop Tip at right for a way to get the screws into place easily.

FEET. Before finishing the stand, I added four rubber stick-on "feet" to the bottom of the base *(Fig. 8)*. These keep the base from turning along with the TV and will prevent the stand from scratching up the top of a dresser or table. ∎

DESIGNER'S NOTEBOOK

Add a drawer to the TV stand to help corral clutter.

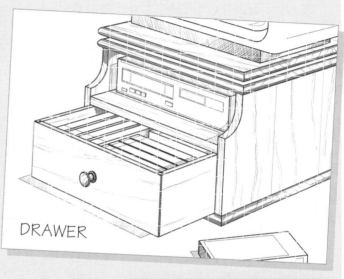

DRAWER

CONSTRUCTION NOTES:

∎ On this version of the TV stand, the case sides are taller (longer) *(Fig. 1a)*. The joinery is the same, but you'll also need to cut a stopped dado near the middle of each side *(Fig. 1)*. This dado accepts a divider that forms the top of the drawer compartment.

∎ The case divider (D) is a glued-up panel. Rabbets are cut on each face to leave a tongue on each end that fits the dadoes in the sides *(Fig. 1a)*.

∎ Once all the pieces and joinery are cut, the base can be glued together.

∎ The drawer fits below the divider with a $1/32$" gap on each side and a $1/16$" gap above. So the widths of the drawer sides (E), front (F), and back (F) are $1/16$" less than the height of the opening ($4^{15}/16$" for me) *(Fig. 2)*. The lengths of the front and back are $1/16$" less than the width of the opening ($15^{11}/16$").

∎ The lengths of the drawer sides are $1/2$" less than the length of the case sides ($18^3/4$" in my case). This allows for the joinery and for a drawer stop at the back of the case that keeps the front of the drawer flush with the sides of the base.

∎ Once the drawer pieces are cut to size, cut a groove $1/4$" from the bottom edge of each piece to accept the $1/4$" plywood drawer bottom *(Fig. 2)*.

∎ Next, cut the locking rabbet joint for the drawer pieces *(Fig. 2a)*.

∎ The last piece for the drawer is the $1/4$" plywood bottom (G) *(Fig. 2)*.

∎ Glue a drawer stop (H) to the case bottom across the back of the drawer opening.

MATERIALS LIST

CHANGED PART

C	Sides (2)	$3/4$ x $19^1/4$ - $10^5/16$

NEW PARTS

D	Case Divider (1)	$3/4$ x $19^1/4$ - $16^1/4$
E	Drawer Sides (2)	$1/2$ x $4^{15}/16$ - $18^3/4$
F	Drawer Ft./Bk. (2)	$1/2$ x $4^{15}/16$ - $15^{11}/16$
G	Drawer Bottom (1)	$1/4$ ply - $18^7/16$ x $15^1/8$
H	Drawer Stop (1)	$1/4$ x $1/4$ - 12

HARDWARE SUPPLIES

(1) 1"-dia. cherry knob w/ screw

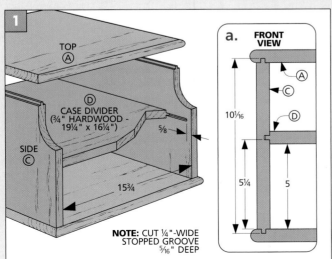

1

TOP Ⓐ

CASE DIVIDER ($3/4$" HARDWOOD - $19^1/4$" x $16^1/4$")

Ⓓ

SIDE Ⓒ

$5/8$

$15^3/4$

NOTE: CUT $1/4$"-WIDE STOPPED GROOVE $5/16$" DEEP

a. FRONT VIEW

Ⓐ

Ⓒ

Ⓓ

$10^1/16$

$5^1/4$

5

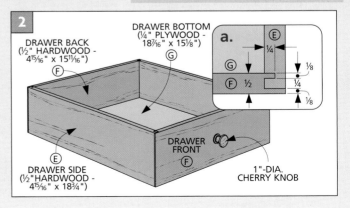

2

DRAWER BACK ($1/2$" HARDWOOD - $4^{15}/16$" x $15^{11}/16$")

Ⓕ

DRAWER BOTTOM ($1/4$" PLYWOOD - $18^7/16$" x $15^1/8$")

Ⓖ

DRAWER SIDE ($1/2$" HARDWOOD - $4^{15}/16$" x $18^3/4$")

Ⓔ

DRAWER FRONT Ⓕ

1"-DIA. CHERRY KNOB

a.

Ⓔ

$1/4$

Ⓖ

Ⓕ $1/2$

$1/8$

$1/4$

$1/8$

Barrister's CD Cases

The doors flip up and slide into the case — just like the doors of a full-size barrister's bookcase. But unlike a bookcase, this project can be built on a bench top and stacked on a table top.

Sometimes working on a smaller scale can be a real treat. While building these cases, I really liked the fact that I didn't have to find room all over the shop to store the workpieces. When I stopped for the day, all the parts fit right on my bench top.

Although these cases are scaled-down versions of a barrister's bookcase, there's more to it than just shrinking all the pieces. The smaller size meant using different joinery than might be used on its "big brother." In fact, all the joinery is cut on the router table with just a couple of straight bits.

FEATURES. But even though it's smaller and the joinery is a bit different, this CD case has all the features of a full-size bookcase. As you'd expect, the doors pivot up and slide into the case to allow access. And the cases can be stacked on top of each other. A raised field on the top of each case "locks" into a recess in the case above it (see inset photo).

BASE. As for the base of this project, there are a couple of options. The first is the pedestal base shown in the main photo. Since a stack of cases filled with CDs will be rather top-heavy (each case holds 32 discs), this base has a compartment that's filled with sand to help keep the stack stable.

The second option is a simple, low-profile base, shown in the photo on page 92. (An optional top is shown in the Designer's Notebook on page 93.)

EXPLODED VIEW

OVERALL DIMENSIONS:
16½"W x 7¼"D x 13¹/₁₆"H (Base & One Case)

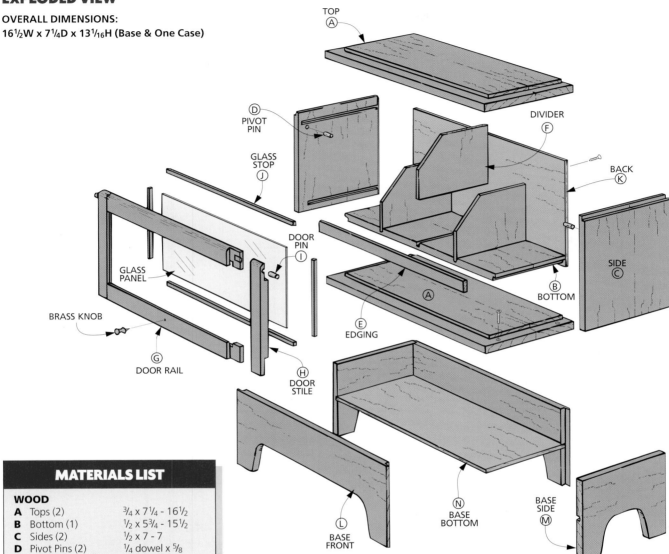

TOP
Ⓐ

DIVIDER
Ⓕ

Ⓓ
PIVOT
PIN

BACK
Ⓚ

GLASS
STOP
Ⓙ

DOOR
PIN
Ⓘ

SIDE
Ⓒ

GLASS
PANEL

Ⓑ
BOTTOM

BRASS KNOB

Ⓐ

Ⓔ
EDGING

Ⓖ

DOOR RAIL

Ⓗ
DOOR
STILE

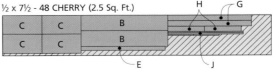

Ⓛ
BASE
FRONT

Ⓝ
BASE
BOTTOM

BASE
SIDE
Ⓜ

MATERIALS LIST

WOOD
A	Tops (2)	¾ x 7¼ - 16½
B	Bottom (1)	½ x 5¾ - 15½
C	Sides (2)	½ x 7 - 7
D	Pivot Pins (2)	¼ dowel x ⅝
E	Edging (1)	¼ x ¾ - 15
F	Dividers (3)	¼ x 5¾ - 4
G	Door Rails (2)	½ x 1 - 14¹⁵/₁₆
H	Door Stiles (2)	½ x 1 - 6⁹/₁₆
I	Door Pins (2)	¼ dowel x ⅝
J	Glass Stop (1)	¼ x ¼ - 42
K	Back (1)	¼ ply - 7 x 15½
L	Base Front/Back (2)	½ x 5 - 16
M	Base Sides (2)	½ x 5 - 6¾
N	Base Bottom (1)	¼ ply - 6½ x 15½

Note: Materials listed are for one case and
one base.

HARDWARE SUPPLIES
(4) No. 6 x 1" Fh woodscrews
(4) No. 4 x ¾" Fh woodscrews
(1) ½" x ½" brass knob w/ screw stud
(1) ⅛"-thick glass panel (4¹⁵/₁₆" x 13⁵/₁₆")
(10) ⅝" wire brads
(2) ¼" felt dots

CUTTING DIAGRAM

¾ x 7½ - 48 CHERRY (2.5 Bd. Ft.)

A	A
A	A

½ x 7½ - 48 CHERRY (2.5 Sq. Ft.)

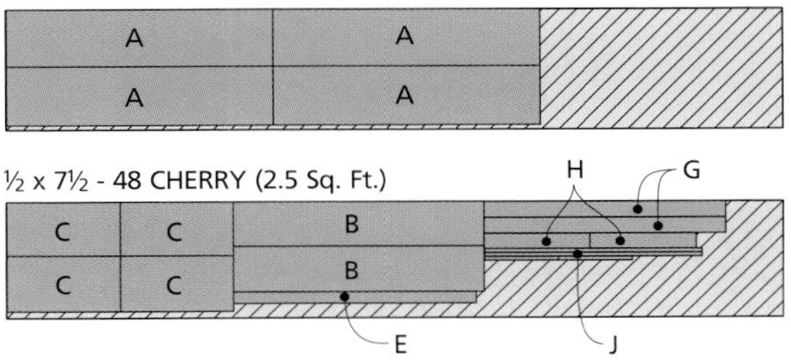

H   G

C	C	B
C	C	B

E   J

½ x 5½ - 24 CHERRY
(2 Bds. @ .9 Sq. Ft. Each)

L	M

¼ x 6 - 24 CHERRY (1 Sq. Ft.)

F	F	F	

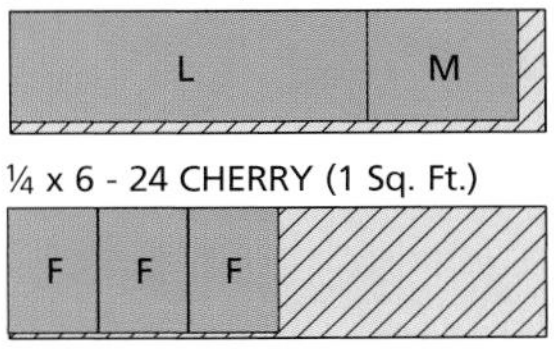

ALSO NEEDED: ONE 18" x 18"
PIECE OF ¼" PLYWOOD FOR PARTS
K AND N, AND 4" LENGTH OF ¼"
DOWEL FOR PARTS D AND I

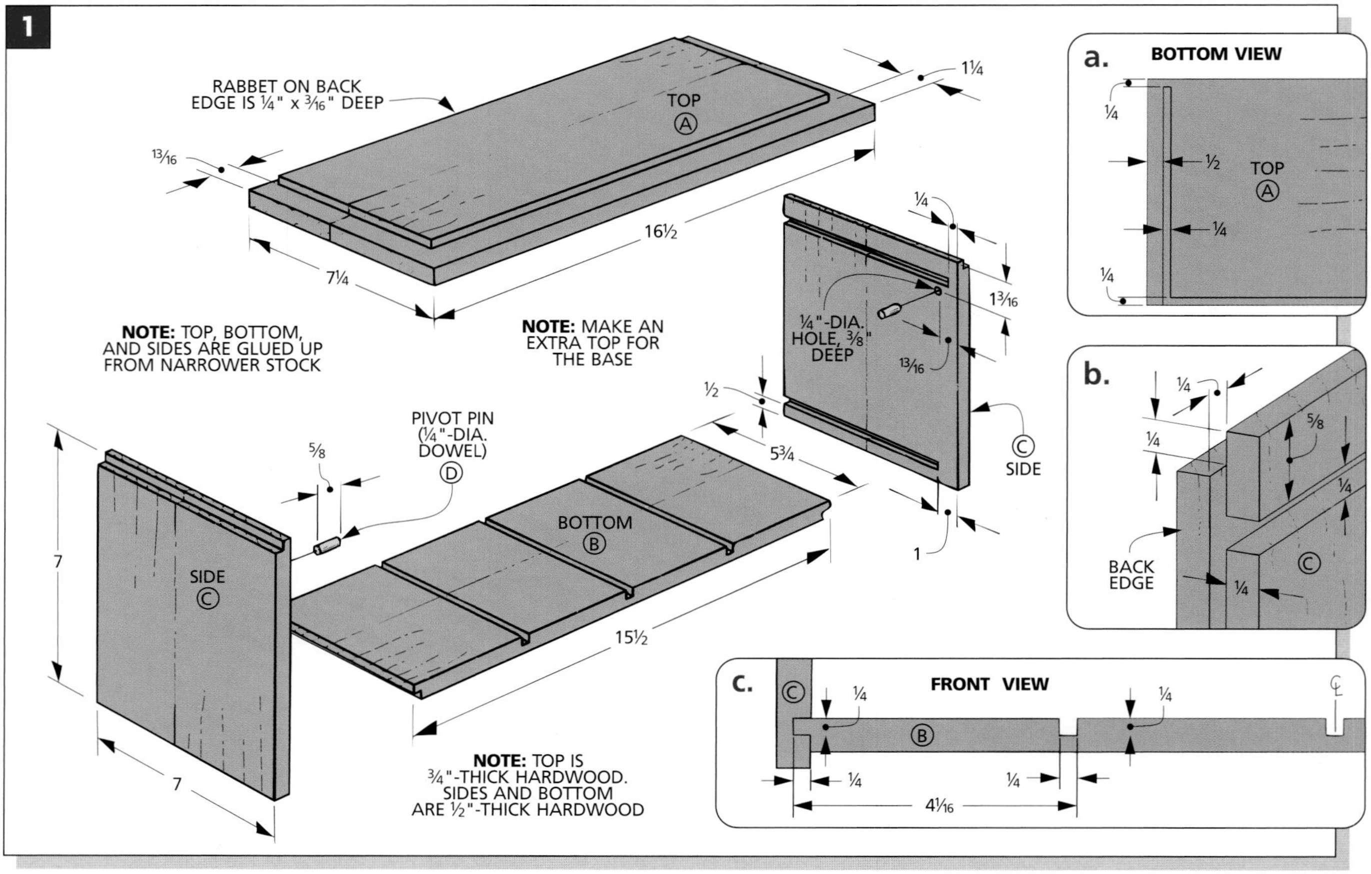
1
RABBET ON BACK EDGE IS 1/4" x 3/16" DEEP
TOP
A
13/16
1 1/4
16 1/2
7 1/4
NOTE: TOP, BOTTOM, AND SIDES ARE GLUED UP FROM NARROWER STOCK
NOTE: MAKE AN EXTRA TOP FOR THE BASE
1/4
1/4"-DIA. HOLE, 3/8" DEEP
1 3/16
13/16
1/2
5 3/4
C
SIDE
1
PIVOT PIN (1/4"-DIA. DOWEL)
D
5/8
BOTTOM
B
7
SIDE
C
15 1/2
7
NOTE: TOP IS 3/4"-THICK HARDWOOD. SIDES AND BOTTOM ARE 1/2"-THICK HARDWOOD
a.
BOTTOM VIEW
1/4
1/2
TOP
A
1/4
1/4
b.
1/4
5/8
1/4
1/4
BACK EDGE
1/4
C
c.
FRONT VIEW
C
1/4
1/4
B
1/4
1/4
4 1/16
℄

CASE

Just like full-sized barrister's bookcases, these CD cases are built in sections that stack up. A recessed bottom in each case fits over a raised field on the case below. (See the inset photo on page 86.)

TOP PANELS. Start by gluing up a panel for a top (A) for each case, plus one extra to be used later for the base.

TOP FACE. After cutting the top panels to size *(Fig. 1)*, the first thing I worked on was the raised field on the top face. I decided to make this with a straight bit on the router table. This means making a few more passes than with a dado blade, but you'll save a lot of sanding time.

Note: An optional treatment for the top can be found on page 93.

To start, I made a skim cut around each top panel to prevent chipout. Then I set the fence to cut the shoulder of the rabbets on the ends *(Fig. 2a)*. Then I removed the waste to the end of the panel.

Once the ends were done, I moved the fence to cut the rabbets on the front edge *(Fig. 2b)* and back edge *(Fig. 2c)*. (If some sanding is needed to clean up the rabbets, refer to the Shop Tip below.)

At this point, the extra top you made for the base is complete and can be set aside. The case top though, still needs some dadoes and a rabbet for joining with the other case pieces *(Fig. 1a)*. I started with the dadoes.

STOPPED DADOES. The dadoes stop short of the front edge, and are easy to cut on the router table.

Note: There are three pairs of stopped dadoes on this project. While their lengths and the distances from the edges are different, the procedure for cutting them is the same. For more details, refer to the Technique box on page 90.

Routing one dado of each pair involves pushing the piece into the bit and stopping before it cuts through the opposite edge *(Fig. 3)*. The matching dado is routed by plunging the workpiece onto the bit and pushing it through *(Fig. 4)*.

After the dadoes are cut, a rabbet is routed between them. You can use the same bit used to cut the dadoes. Just position the fence flush with the back edge of

SHOP TIP ..... *Sanding Rabbets*

When sanding a rabbet, it's easy to tip the sander slightly and round over the edge.

To prevent this, clamp the workpiece in a bench vise with a piece of scrap flush with the top of the rabbet. This supports the sander and keeps the edges square.

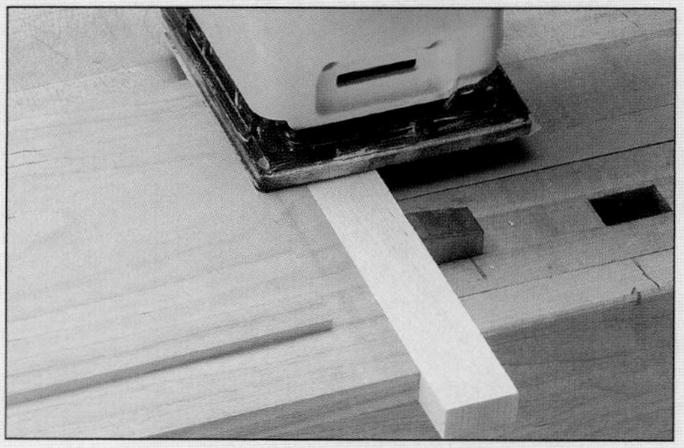

the bit *(Fig. 5)*. This time, instead of drawing start and stop lines on the fence, I marked the top of the workpiece to show the locations of the dadoes cut earlier. Then swing the workpiece into the spinning bit. and rout until you hear the bit reach the dado at the other end.

BOTTOMS. Next, a ½"-thick panel can be glued up for each bottom (B). The bottom is narrower than the sides and top *(Fig. 1)*. This leaves room for the door to hang in front of the bottom panel.

After cutting the bottom panel to size, a rabbet is routed on each end to leave a ¼"-thick tongue *(Fig. 1c)*.

Later, three dividers will be added to support the CDs. Each divider will rest in a dado routed all the way across the bottom *(Fig. 1c)*. (The front edge gets covered by a piece of edging later.)

SIDES. Now you can work on the sides (C). Like the other pieces, these are glued-up panels with stopped dadoes and rabbets. But the sides aren't identical — they're mirror images of each other.

RABBETS. I routed the rabbets on the top and back edges first *(Fig. 1b)*. A rabbet along the top creates a tongue that fits the dado in the top piece. And the rabbet along the back edge will accept the plywood back panel later.

DADOES. The next things to work on are the two stopped dadoes — one near the top for the door to slide in, and another to hold the bottom panel.

The technique for routing these dadoes is the same one used earlier (refer to page 90). Just remember to make new marks on the router fence each time. Note that the lower dadoes stop farther from the front edge than the upper ones *(Fig. 1)*. Also, the lower dadoes are positioned so the bottom panel sits above the bottom of the sides. This creates the recess that will fit over the raised field on the top panel below *(Fig. 1c)*.

PIVOT PIN. There's just one more thing to do before assembling the case. To support the door when it's slid into the case, a pivot pin (D) needs to be added to the inside of each side *(Fig. 1)*. Then the four case pieces can be glued together.

EDGING. To form the front edge of the recess under the case, edging (E) is cut to fit between the sides *(Fig. 6)*. The edging is then glued flush with the top edge of the bottom panel.

DIVIDERS. Lastly, I added three dividers (F). To make it easy to grab a CD, I cut away the front corner of each divider before gluing them in place *(Fig. 6)*.

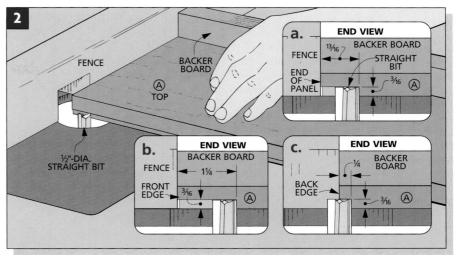

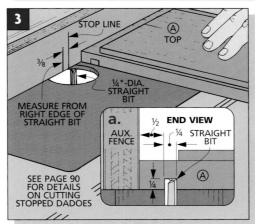

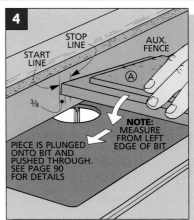

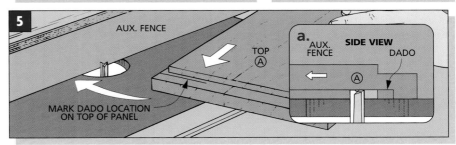

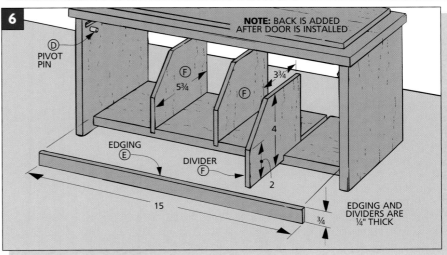

Each CD case has three pairs of stopped dadoes (two in the sides, the third in the top). The easiest way to cut these is with a $1/4$" straight bit on the router table.

Even though each pair of dadoes is a different length, the procedure for cutting them is the same. To cut one dado, you push the workpiece into the bit. To cut the second dado, the workpiece is plunged onto the spinning bit and pushed through.

STOP LINE. First, you'll need to position the fence and set the bit height. Then for the first cut, you'll need to know where to stop the workpiece before the bit cuts through the back edge.

So mark a stop line on the fence to the *right* side of the bit (*Fig. 1*). I allow some "fudge room." If the cut is supposed to stop $1/4$" from the end, I'll mark the line $3/8$" from the bit (refer to *Fig. 3* on page 89). Since the end of the dado needs to be squared up with a chisel anyway, it's easy enough to complete the length of the dado as you do that.

START LINE. For the matching dado in the pair, you'll need to make a start line on the *left* side of the bit (*Fig. 2*). (But don't move the fence.)

Note: On the side pieces, one dado of the pair is cut in each side piece. The matching dado is cut on the other side piece. On the top, both dadoes are on the same workpiece.

And since each pair of dadoes stops a different distance from the edge, each pair will need new start and stop lines.

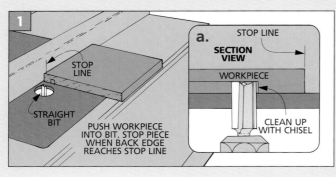

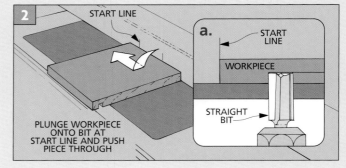

DOOR

Whenever I stand next to a barrister's bookcase, it's hard to resist opening and closing the doors at least once. The same holds true for this scaled-down version.

Although this door works the same way as the full-size one, it's built differently. Instead of mortises and tenons, the small doors can be joined with half laps. It's plenty strong — plus there's just one setup needed to cut the joint.

To start, the rails (G) can be cut to length so they're $1/16$" less than the opening at the front of the case (*Fig. 7*). The stiles (H) are cut to length to allow the back corner to clear the bottom panel when the door is opened (*Fig. 7b*).

HALF LAPS. Like the other joints on this project, I cut the half laps on the router table with a straight bit (*Fig. 8*). (Refer to the Technique box on the next page for more details about cutting half laps.) Once the joints are cut, you can glue up the door frame.

After the glue has dried, a roundover is routed along the top outside edge of the door (*Fig. 7a*). This allows the door to clear the top as the door is swung open.

DOOR PINS. The doors pivot and slide into the case with the help of a pair of door pins (I) that travel in the stopped dadoes in the side panels. The holes for the pins

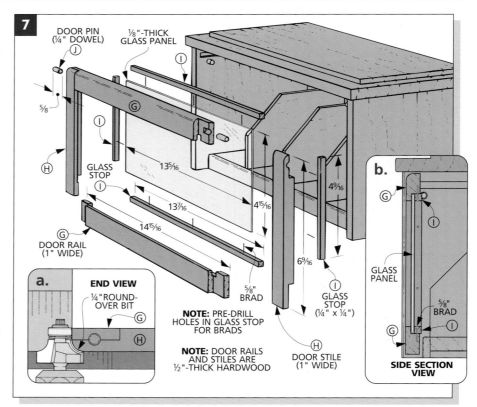

are centered on the thickness of the door (*Fig. 7a*). This puts the hole right in the joint line. So to prevent any splitting, I did a couple of things. First, I clamped the door to my bench (*Fig. 9*). Then I

clamped across each joint while I drilled the hole. And lastly, since my pin still fit a bit tight, I chucked it in my drill, turned the drill on, and sanded the dowel lightly to reduce its diameter.

ADD GLASS. The next thing to do is add the glass panel. First, you'll need to rout a rabbet around the inside face of the door to accept the glass. This is done on the router table with a rabbet bit *(Fig. 10)*. Then the corners of the rabbet can be squared up with a sharp chisel.

Next, I made some glass stop (J) to hold the glass in the rabbet. You can do this safely on the table saw by following the steps in the Shop Tip below right. Once you've ripped enough glass stop to size to fit around the door, it can be cut to finished length *(Fig. 7)*.

Although it's tempting to install the glass now, it's a good idea to apply a finish to the case, door, and glass stop first. I

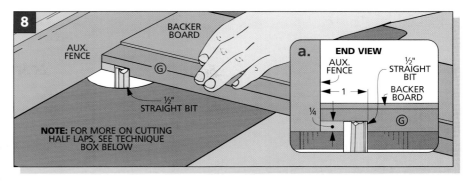

wiped on a couple of coats of a one-step oil and urethane top coat.

After the finish has dried on these pieces, the glass can be installed and the glass stop secured with brads *(Fig. 7b)*.

To prevent the glass stop from splitting, I pre-drilled the brad holes.

Note: Don't use glue, just brads. That way you can remove the glass stop to replace the glass should it break.

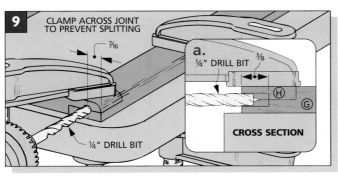

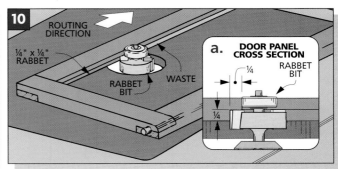

NOTE: FOR MORE ON CUTTING HALF LAPS, SEE TECHNIQUE BOX BELOW

TECHNIQUE .... *Cutting Half Laps*

When cutting half laps on small pieces, like the door of the CD case, I use a straight bit in the router table to get a smoother surface.

SETUP. I check my setup by cutting a test joint on some scrap the same thickness as the door pieces. Just raise the bit ¼" above the table. Then make a pass on one end of each scrap (see drawing). Check the setup by fitting the pieces together (detail 'a'). If the faces are perfectly flush, the bit is at the right height.

CUTTING JOINT. Using a ½" straight bit, I took three passes to cut the 1" width of each joint. The first pass defined the shoulder of the joint. The second pass is a light cut with the end of the workpiece pressed against the router table fence and a small part of the bit exposed (detail 'b'). This cut helps prevent chipout as you clean up the remaining waste on the third pass.

As you make each pass, press down firmly on the workpiece so the cuts are all the same depth.

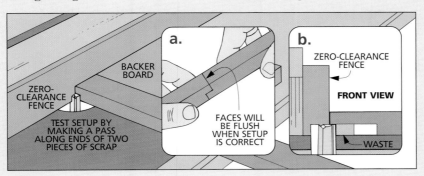

SHOP TIP
Glass Stop

The glass stop can be cut from a larger blank with two passes on the table saw *(Figs. 1 and 2)*. A zero-clearance insert around the blade will prevent the stop from falling into the saw.

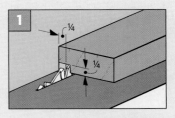

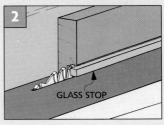

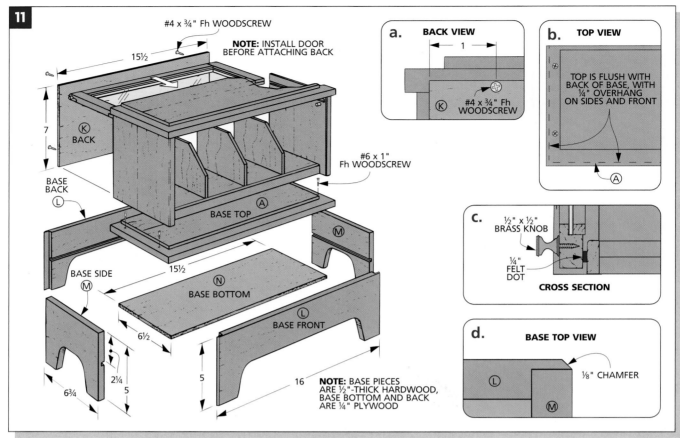

11

#4 x ¾" Fh WOODSCREW

15½

NOTE: INSTALL DOOR
BEFORE ATTACHING BACK

7

ⓚ
BACK

BASE
BACK
ⓛ

BASE TOP

ⓐ

#6 x 1"
Fh WOODSCREW

BASE SIDE
ⓜ

15½

ⓝ
BASE BOTTOM

ⓜ

6½

ⓛ
BASE FRONT

2¼

6¾

5

5

16

NOTE: BASE PIECES
ARE ½"-THICK HARDWOOD,
BASE BOTTOM AND BACK
ARE ¼" PLYWOOD

a. BACK VIEW

1

ⓚ

ⓐ

#4 x ¾" Fh
WOODSCREW

b. TOP VIEW

TOP IS FLUSH WITH
BACK OF BASE, WITH
¼" OVERHANG
ON SIDES AND FRONT

ⓐ

c.
½" x ½"
BRASS KNOB

¼"
FELT
DOT

CROSS SECTION

d. BASE TOP VIEW

ⓛ

⅛" CHAMFER

ⓜ

The last few items have to be added to the door after it's in place, so go ahead and slide the door into the case from the back *(Fig. 11)*. (If the door doesn't slide smoothly, wax the dadoes and the door pins *after* applying a finish.) Once the door was installed, I centered a screw-in brass knob on the bottom rail *(Fig. 11c)*. I also added two felt dots to the back face of the rail to keep the door from banging.

BACK. Now to complete the case, a ¼" plywood back (K) can be added. It's cut

For a case that sits on a desk top, just use the extra top as a base. It will lift the case enough to make it easy to grab the knob and open the door.

to fit the opening in the back and is held in place with small screws *(Fig. 11)*. Just like with the glass stop, you don't want to glue this piece in place. That way, you'll be able to remove the back if the door ever needs repair.

BASE

There are a couple of options for the base, depending on where you'll be setting the case. If you plan to stack several cases (especially on a carpeted floor), the weighted pedestal base is a good idea *(Fig. 11)*. For a single case sitting on a desk top, the extra top you made earlier will work just fine (see the photo at left).

PEDESTAL BASE. The pedestal base starts with four pieces of ½"-thick stock. The base front and back (L) and sides (M) can all be cut to size *(Fig. 11)*. As for the joinery, the side pieces fit into rabbets cut in the front and back, so I routed these next *(Fig. 13)*.

After that, a groove needs to be cut in each piece to accept the plywood bottom that's added later. I did this on the table saw with a regular blade *(Fig. 14)*. Just move the rip fence slightly between passes to widen the groove.

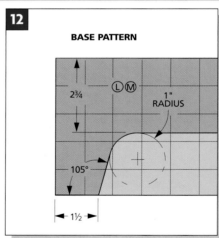

12

BASE PATTERN

2¾

ⓛⓜ

1"
RADIUS

105°

1½

CUTOUT. To lighten the look of the base, a cutout on each piece forms "legs" at the corners. To make the cutout the same at each corner, I made a pattern out of a scrap of hardboard *(Fig. 12)*. Then I used the pattern to lay out the shape on each workpiece. The shape can be roughed out on the band saw or with a jig saw. I then fastened the pieces together with carpet tape and sanded to the line with a drum sander.

BOTTOM. Now you can dry-assemble the base pieces and measure for the base

SHOP TIP .... *Weighted Base*

The Barrister's CD Cases are designed to allow several cases to be stacked on top of each other. But by the time you add CDs, a stack of cases will become top-heavy and could topple over easily.

To provide a solid foundation for several cases, I designed the base to have a hollow compartment (see drawing). Before screwing the top in place, I filled the compartment with sand. This lowers the center of gravity of a stack of cases, making them more stable.

If the cases will be stacked on a carpeted surface, it's best not to place more than two or three cases on top of each other.

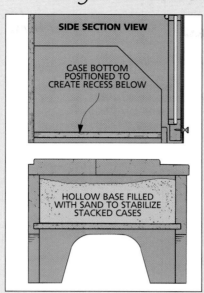

SIDE SECTION VIEW

CASE BOTTOM POSITIONED TO CREATE RECESS BELOW

HOLLOW BASE FILLED WITH SAND TO STABILIZE STACKED CASES

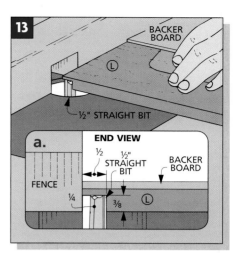

13

BACKER BOARD

½" STRAIGHT BIT

a. END VIEW

½ ½" STRAIGHT BIT

BACKER BOARD

FENCE

¼

⅜

L

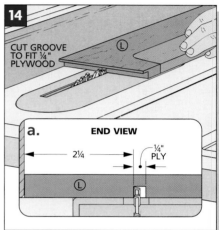

14

CUT GROOVE TO FIT ¼" PLYWOOD

a. END VIEW

2¼

¼" PLY

L

bottom (N). Once it's cut to size from ¼" plywood, the four base pieces can be glued together around the bottom.

Building the base with a rabbet joint makes assembly easier but leaves a small line of end grain exposed on the sides. There's a simple trick that will make this end grain virtually disappear. Just

chamfer the corners of the base so the chamfer ends at the joint line *(Fig. 11d)*.

Finally, before screwing on the extra top that was made earlier, I filled the base with sand (see the Shop Tip above). Then I softened all the exposed edges of the base with a light sanding and applied a couple of coats of a wipe-on finish. ∎

DESIGNER'S NOTEBOOK

This optional top takes only a little extra time to make and adds a "crowning" touch to your case.

CONSTRUCTION NOTES:

∎ This top is meant to go on the top case in a stack. Since it doesn't have a raised field, you won't be able to "lock" another case in place on top of it.

∎ The case top (A) is the same size, but is only ½" thick (see drawing). All the joinery is the same, but no rabbets are cut around the top face.

∎ After the case is completed, a molded top (O) is glued to the top. This is a glued-up panel with a ⅜" cove routed around three sides (see detail 'a').

∎ The molded top is glued to the top of the case with their back edges flush and an equal over-hang on the ends.

MATERIALS LIST	
CHANGED PART	
A Top (1)	½ x 7¼ - 16½
NEW PART	
O Molded Top (1)	½ x 7¾ - 17½

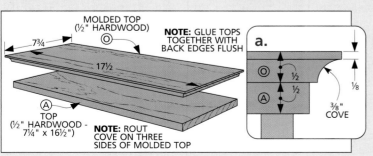

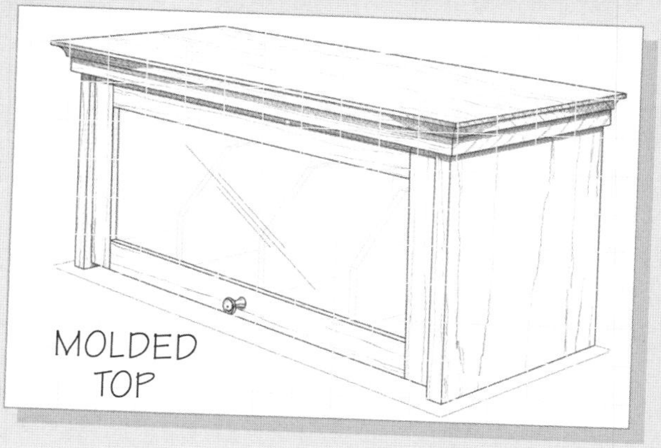

MOLDED TOP (½" HARDWOOD)

O

7¾

17½

A

TOP (½" HARDWOOD - 7¼" x 16½")

NOTE: ROUT COVE ON THREE SIDES OF MOLDED TOP

NOTE: GLUE TOPS TOGETHER WITH BACK EDGES FLUSH

a.

O

A

½

½

⅛

⅜" COVE

MOLDED TOP

Roll-Around TV Stand

Build this stand and your eyes will no longer be glued to the TV set. Instead, they'll be checking out the handsome cherry cabinet with black accents that it sits on. Plate joinery makes it quick to build.

This project gave me a chance to solve some frustrations I had with my old TV stand. First off, it was a "bear" to move — whether you were just turning the set so everyone could see or moving it to rearrange the room. But this stand "floats" on casters, so moving it is no trouble at all.

The casters also allow you to get at the back of the stand easily, which was another problem I had. Plus, the back panel is removable, so you can expose all the cords and cables when you need to get at them. And when you're done, there's no tangle of cords hanging out, either. The back covers all the "spaghetti."

So even if the stand sits away from a wall, you won't see all the unsightly cords.

Finally, the stand has four drawers that are sized just right for keeping all of my favorite videos, CDs, and DVDs well-organized. This eliminates "leaning towers" of videos stacked on top of the TV.

PLATE JOINERY. This is quite a few features to "pack into" a project. But that doesn't mean it has to be complicated. The stand is built in sections: a base, two drawer cases, and a top. And to keep it as simple to build as possible, I used plywood construction and plate joinery.

But don't worry if you don't have a plate joiner. You can build this TV stand

easily with splines and other traditional joinery. Everything you need to know about this is on page 103.

FINISH. One thing I like about the look of this stand is the black trim. But these pieces aren't painted. Instead they're colored with aniline dye, an easy-to-use finish. Since this type of stain may not be familiar to you, some tips for working with it are included on page 102.

OPTIONAL DOORS. As shown in the photo above, the shelf area is open to give you easy access. I've also included the option of adding glass-paneled doors here. If you'd prefer this look, refer to the Designer's Notebook on page 104.

EXPLODED VIEW

OVERALL DIMENSIONS:
$39\frac{1}{2}$W x $26\frac{3}{4}$D x $25\frac{7}{8}$H

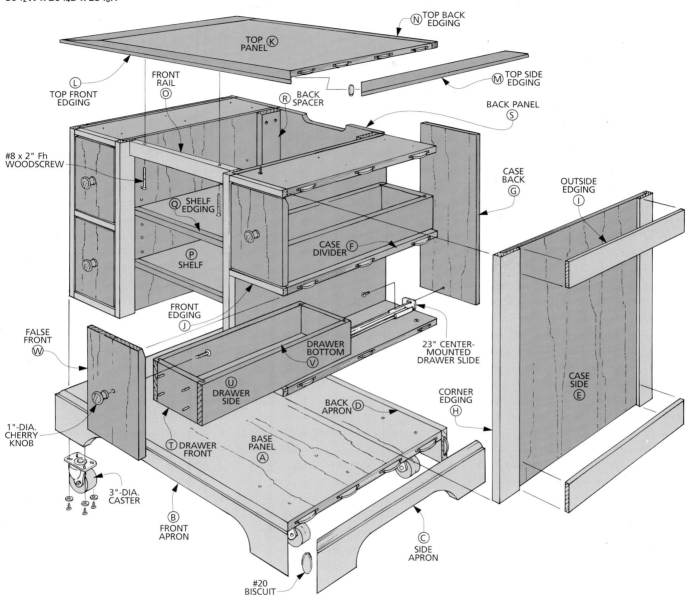

MATERIALS LIST

WOOD

A	Base Panel (1)	$\frac{3}{4}$ ply - $24\frac{1}{2}$ x $36\frac{1}{2}$
B	Front Apron (1)	$\frac{3}{4}$ x $4\frac{3}{8}$ - 38
C	Side Aprons (2)	$\frac{3}{4}$ x $4\frac{3}{8}$ - 26
D	Back Apron (1)	$\frac{3}{4}$ x $4\frac{3}{8}$ - $36\frac{1}{2}$
E	Case Sides (4)	$\frac{1}{2}$ ply - $20\frac{1}{2}$ x $23\frac{3}{4}$
F	Case Dividers (6)	$\frac{3}{4}$ ply - $7\frac{1}{4}$ x $23\frac{3}{4}$
G	Case Backs (2)	$\frac{1}{2}$ ply - $8\frac{1}{4}$ x $20\frac{1}{2}$
H	Corner Edging (6)	$\frac{3}{4}$ x $2\frac{1}{2}$ - $20\frac{1}{2}$
I	Outside Edging (4)	$\frac{1}{4}$ x $2\frac{1}{2}$ - $20\frac{1}{4}$
J	Front Edging (6)	$\frac{3}{4}$ x $2\frac{1}{2}$ - $7\frac{1}{4}$
K	Top Panel (1)	$\frac{3}{4}$ ply - $23\frac{1}{2}$ x $34\frac{1}{2}$

L	Top Front Edging (1)	$\frac{3}{4}$ x $2\frac{1}{2}$ - $39\frac{1}{2}$
M	Top Side Edging (2)	$\frac{3}{4}$ x $2\frac{1}{2}$ - $26\frac{3}{4}$
N	Top Back Edging (1)	$\frac{3}{4}$ x $\frac{3}{4}$ - $34\frac{1}{2}$
O	Front Rail (1)	$\frac{3}{4}$ x $1\frac{1}{2}$ - 19
P	Shelves (2)	$\frac{3}{4}$ ply - $16\frac{7}{8}$ x $19\frac{3}{8}$
Q	Shelf Edging (2)	$\frac{3}{4}$ x $\frac{3}{4}$ - $19\frac{3}{8}$
R	Back Spacers (2)	$\frac{3}{4}$ x 4 - $20\frac{1}{2}$
S	Back Panel (1)	$\frac{1}{2}$ ply - $19\frac{3}{8}$ x $20\frac{3}{8}$
T	Drawer Front/Bk. (8)	$\frac{1}{2}$ x 4 - $6\frac{1}{4}$
U	Drawer Sides (8)	$\frac{1}{2}$ x 4 - $23\frac{3}{8}$
V	Drawer Bottoms (4)	$\frac{1}{2}$ ply - $6\frac{1}{4}$ x $22\frac{7}{8}$
W	False Fronts (4)	$\frac{3}{4}$ x $7\frac{1}{8}$ - 9

HARDWARE SUPPLIES

(24) No. 8 x $1\frac{1}{4}$" Fh woodscrews
(24) No. 8 x 1" Fh woodscrews
(2) No. 8 x 2" Fh woodscrews
(37) No. 20 biscuits
(36) No. 10 biscuits
(4) 3"-dia. swivel casters w/ screws
(4) 23" center-mounted drawer slides
(4) 1"-dia. cherry knobs w/ screws
(8) Spoon-style shelf pins
(4) Magnetic catches w/ strike plates

CUTTING DIAGRAM

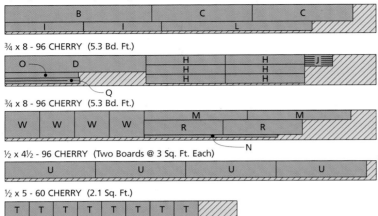

¾ x 7½ - 96 CHERRY (5 Bd. Ft.)

¾ x 8 - 96 CHERRY (5.3 Bd. Ft.)

¾ x 8 - 96 CHERRY (5.3 Bd. Ft.)

½ x 4½ - 96 CHERRY (Two Boards @ 3 Sq. Ft. Each)

½ x 5 - 60 CHERRY (2.1 Sq. Ft.)

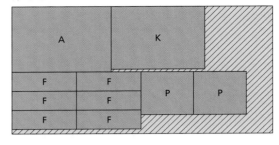

¾" CHERRY PLYWOOD - 48 x 96

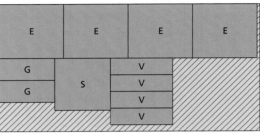

½" CHERRY PLYWOOD - 48 x 96

BASE & DRAWER CASES

As you'll see, this TV stand is built in three main sections: a base, two drawer cases, and a top panel. And since each section is built almost entirely with plate (biscuit) joinery, the construction is fairly quick and straightforward.

Note: There are alternatives for building the Roll-Around TV Stand if you don't own a biscuit joiner. For more on this, see the Joinery article on page 103.

BASE. I started with the base section. It consists of a ¾" plywood base panel (A)

with a solid wood apron that wraps around it to cover the plies on the edges *(Fig. 1)*.

APRONS. After cutting the base panel to finished size, the ¾"-thick aprons are all ripped 4⅜" wide and are crosscut or mitered to fit around the base *(Fig. 1)*. At the front corners, the front aprons (B) and side aprons (C) are each mitered. But the back apron (D) is crosscut to length to fit between the two side aprons. (The length of the back apron matches the length of the base panel, so mine ended up 36½".)

This means the back end of each side apron is cut at 90°, not mitered.

When the aprons have been cut to size, the next thing to do is cut the profile that's centered on the bottom edge of each apron *(Figs. 1a and 1b)*. These cutouts create a "foot" profile on each corner of the base.

To cut these profiles, I laid them out and cut them with a jig saw, staying to the waste side of the line. The curves on the ends can be sanded easily with a drum sander, but it's hard to sand the straight line between them. The solution is to use a router and a straightedge. (For more on how to do this, see the Shop Tip at the bottom of the next page.)

To join the aprons to the base, I laid out and cut slots for No. 20 biscuits. I also put a biscuit in each corner for added strength. Just be sure to position the slots on the miters closer to the inside corner so they don't cut through the front face.

After the glue has dried, there's still one more step before the base is complete. I routed a ½" roundover around the top edge of the base, setting the bit to create a ⅛" shoulder on the top *(Figs. 2 and 2a)*. To do this, you'll have to tip the base up on end.

DRAWER CASES. Now that the base is complete, you can move on to building the two drawer cases *(Fig. 3)*. These are simple plywood boxes with a fixed shelf in the middle, but they're dressed up with hardwood "frames" that are applied to their outside faces.

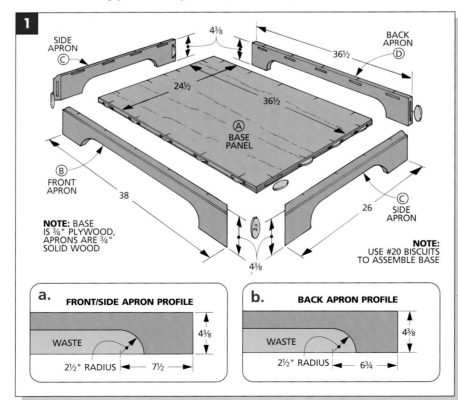

1

SIDE APRON Ⓒ

4⅜

BACK APRON Ⓓ

36½

24½

36½

Ⓐ BASE PANEL

Ⓑ FRONT APRON

38

26

Ⓒ SIDE APRON

NOTE: BASE IS ¾" PLYWOOD, APRONS ARE ¾" SOLID WOOD

4⅜

NOTE: USE #20 BISCUITS TO ASSEMBLE BASE

a. FRONT/SIDE APRON PROFILE

WASTE

4⅜

2½" RADIUS — 7½

b. BACK APRON PROFILE

WASTE

4⅜

2½" RADIUS — 6¾

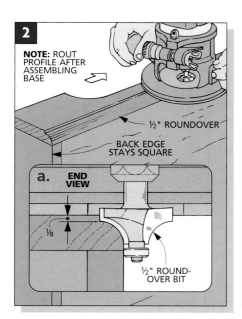

2

NOTE: ROUT PROFILE AFTER ASSEMBLING BASE

½" ROUNDOVER

BACK EDGE STAYS SQUARE

a. END VIEW

⅛

½" ROUND-OVER BIT

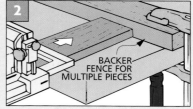

SHOP TIP . . . . *Plate Joinery Tips*

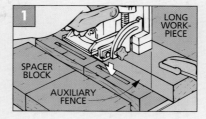

1

SPACER BLOCK

LONG WORK-PIECE

AUXILIARY FENCE

2

BACKER FENCE FOR MULTIPLE PIECES

Plate joinery is quick and easy. Here are a couple of tips to make this process even quicker.

To cut slots near the end of a long piece, use a spacer block next to the workpiece to provide extra support for the tool *(Fig. 1)*.

When you need to cut slots in the edges or ends of multiple pieces, you can save time by clamping down a backer fence to push the pieces against. That way, you don't have to take time to clamp each one separately *(Fig. 2)*.

The case sides (E) are cut to size from ½" plywood. Then the ¾" plywood dividers (F) can be cut to size. But before you assemble these pieces, it's a good idea to label the top and bottom dividers. Then drill countersunk shank holes in their inside faces for attaching the cases to the base and the top (built later) *(Fig. 3a)*.

Like the base, the drawer cases are assembled with biscuits. But because the case sides are only ½" plywood, you'll need to use No. 10 biscuits. Otherwise, the biscuit slots will cut all the way through the plywood panels.

CASE BACKS. In the next step, edging is added around the case sides. But before doing that, I went ahead and cut ½" plywood panels to size to cover the back edges *(Fig. 3)*. Then each case back (G) is simply glued to its case.

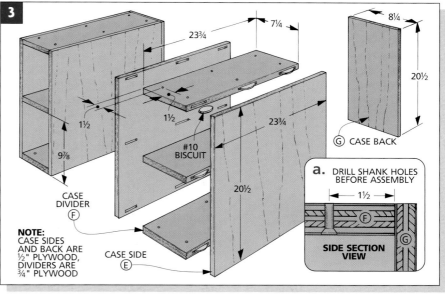

3

7¼

23¾

8¼

20½

G CASE BACK

1½

1½

#10 BISCUIT

23¾

9⅞

20½

CASE DIVIDER
F

NOTE: CASE SIDES AND BACK ARE ½" PLYWOOD, DIVIDERS ARE ¾" PLYWOOD

CASE SIDE
E

a. DRILL SHANK HOLES BEFORE ASSEMBLY

1½

F

G

SIDE SECTION VIEW

SHOP TIP . . . . *Straight Cuts Between Profiles*

After you've cut the profile on each base piece of the Roll-Around TV Stand with a jig saw, you still have to smooth it out. The curves are easy enough. They can be sanded with a drum sander. But how do you clean up the straight portion of the profile?

I use a router and a pattern bit (detail 'a'). (A pattern bit has a bearing above the cutter.)

You'll also need a piece of scrap with a straight edge. Simply clamp the straight edge along the layout line of the profile. Then trim the profile flush (see drawing).

Note: You could also do this on a router table using a flush trim bit. Just make sure the scrap is wide enough that the work-piece doesn't tip while you're routing.

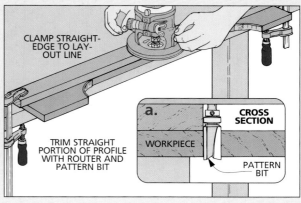

CLAMP STRAIGHT-EDGE TO LAY-OUT LINE

TRIM STRAIGHT PORTION OF PROFILE WITH ROUTER AND PATTERN BIT

a. CROSS SECTION

WORKPIECE

PATTERN BIT

CASE EDGING. The cases are almost complete now. All that's left is to add the hardwood "frame" on the outside faces and cover the plywood edges *(Fig. 4)*. To do this, I started with the L-shaped corner edging (H). It covers the plywood edging on the two front corners and the back outside corner of each case. Plus, it creates the vertical stile of the "frame."

Making the L-shape on the corner edging is a two-step process on the table saw *(Fig. 5)*. With the ³/₄"-thick blanks cut to size, I cut a kerf with the workpiece face down first *(Fig. 5a)*. Then the second pass removes the waste *(Fig. 5b)*. (To hold the workpiece tight against the rip fence, I used a featherboard.)

The corner edging you just made determines the thickness of the two other edging pieces, and you'll want to clamp the corner edging to the case to sneak up on their thicknesses *(Fig. 4a)*.

Note: Don't glue any pieces in place until they are stained black. See the Finishing box on page 102.

First, I completed the "frame" on the outsides of the cases by planing the outside edging (I) to match the corner edging (¹/₄"). Then I cut the pieces to fit between the corner edging *(Fig. 4)*.

The last piece of edging, the front edging (J), is simply cut to cover the edges of the dividers *(Fig. 4a)*.

After staining the workpieces, I glued the trim to the drawer cases and screwed the cases to the base so they were flush with the back edge *(Fig. 4b)*.

TOP, SHELVES, & BACK

With the base and drawer cases built, the last large section to make is the top. Like the base, it's just a plywood panel with solid wood edging.

TOP PANEL. To build the top, I started by cutting the top panel (K) to size from ³/₄" plywood *(Fig. 6)*. Then the front (L) and side edging (M) that will wrap around the panel can be ripped 2¹/₂" wide.

The front and side edging are joined at the front corners with miters, and the sides extend past the back of the top panel ³/₄" *(Fig. 6a)*. This allows for a piece of ³/₄"-wide back edging (N) that's cut to fit between the sides.

Before you use the plate-joiner to attach the edging to the panel, there's a bevel to cut on the bottom edge of the front and side pieces. I angled the blade (about 16°) and set the fence so the edging was ³/₈"-thick on the ends *(Figs. 7 and 7a)*.

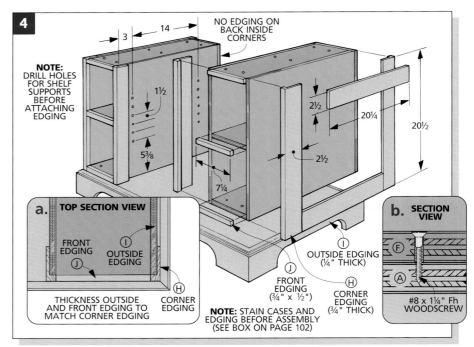

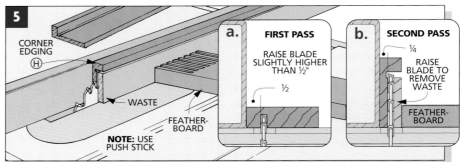

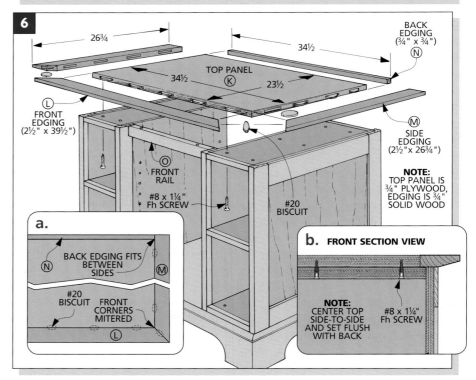

After the bevel is cut, the front and side edging can be attached to the panel with biscuits. Like the base, I also strengthened the miters with biscuits. But when attaching the back edging (N), I simply glued it in place *(Fig. 6)*.

When the glue had completely set up, I screwed the top assembly to the drawer cases. It's flush with the back and centered side-to-side *(Fig. 6b)*.

Next, I worked on the space between the cases, adding a front rail, shelves, and a removable back panel *(Figs. 8 and 9)*.

FRONT RAIL. I started with a front rail (O), which fits between the corner edging (H) on the cases *(Figs. 8 and 8a)*. This $3/4$"-thick piece is cut to size, stained black, and then glued and screwed to the bottom of the top panel flush with the back edge of the corner edging.

SHELVES. This is a good time to cut the $3/4$" plywood shelves (P) and $3/4$"-wide shelf edging (Q) to fit between the case sides *(Fig. 8)*. The shelves aren't as deep as the cases. They butt against the back edge of the corner edging (H) in the front *(Fig. 8a)*. And they stop well short of the back so there's room for the cables and power cords *(Fig. 9)*.

BACK PANEL. With the shelves resting on shelf pins, I began working on the back. Trying to wire TV and audio equipment from the front of a case is a real hassle, so I made the back panel removable. To do this, the back butts against two spacers and is held in place with magnetic catches *(Fig. 9)*.

The back spacers (R) are $3/4$"-thick pieces cut to fit between the top and the base *(Fig. 9)*. Then before screwing them to the cases, I added barrel-style magnetic catches to their back edges, 2" from the ends *(Figs. 9 and 9b)*.

Note: I didn't have a metric drill bit that matched the size of the catches, so I epoxied them into slightly oversized ($9/16$") holes *(Fig. 9b)*.

With the spacers attached, I cut a $1/2$" plywood back panel (S) to fit the opening with a $1/16$" gap around it. Then I made a small cutout at the top and bottom to allow the TV cords to feed in and a power cord to feed out.

Now to attach the back, simply screw the strike plates for the magnetic catches to the inside face of the panel and set the back in place.

Finally, before building the drawers, there's just one more step, mounting the stand on its casters. (Refer to the Technique box on page 101.)

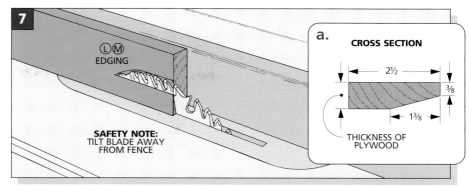

7

L M
EDGING

SAFETY NOTE: TILT BLADE AWAY FROM FENCE

a. CROSS SECTION
2½
3/8
1⅜
THICKNESS OF PLYWOOD

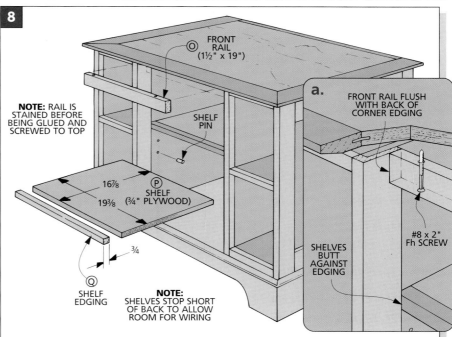

8

O FRONT RAIL (1½" x 19")

NOTE: RAIL IS STAINED BEFORE BEING GLUED AND SCREWED TO TOP

SHELF PIN

16⅞
19⅜
P SHELF ($3/4$" PLYWOOD)

3/4

Q SHELF EDGING

NOTE: SHELVES STOP SHORT OF BACK TO ALLOW ROOM FOR WIRING

a. FRONT RAIL FLUSH WITH BACK OF CORNER EDGING

SHELVES BUTT AGAINST EDGING

#8 x 2" Fh SCREW

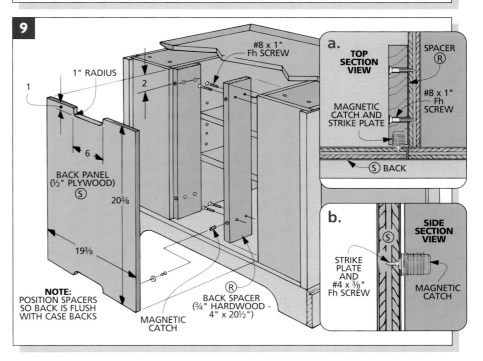

9

1" RADIUS
2
#8 x 1" Fh SCREW

1
6

BACK PANEL ($1/2$" PLYWOOD) S
20⅜
19⅜

NOTE: POSITION SPACERS SO BACK IS FLUSH WITH CASE BACKS

MAGNETIC CATCH

R BACK SPACER ($3/4$" HARDWOOD - 4" x 20½")

a. TOP SECTION VIEW
SPACER R
#8 x 1" Fh SCREW
MAGNETIC CATCH AND STRIKE PLATE
S BACK

b. SIDE SECTION VIEW
S
STRIKE PLATE AND #4 x $3/8$" Fh SCREW
MAGNETIC CATCH

The TV stand has four drawers sized to hold videos, DVDs, CDs, or video games. Each drawer pulls out easily on a slide that mounts on the drawer bottom. This gives them a cleaner look.

DRAWERS

At my house, there's always at least one stack of videos precariously perched on top of the TV. So I designed this stand with four drawers for storing video tapes, CDs, and DVDs. (See the Designer's Notebook below for a way to keep your discs neatly arranged.)

The first thing you notice about the drawers is that their sides are short (see photo above). This makes it easy to get the videos in and out. Also, you don't see any sliding hardware. That's because the drawers ride on center-mounted slides that are hidden underneath each drawer.

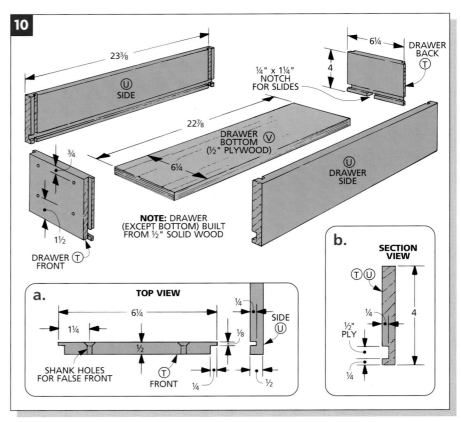

DRAWERS. Each drawer is sized to hold two rows of four to five video tapes, depending on the cases the videos are stored in. I began by cutting the $\frac{1}{2}$"-thick drawer fronts (T), backs (T), and sides (U) to size *(Fig. 10)*. Then to join these pieces, I cut rabbets on the ends of the front and back pieces to leave a $\frac{1}{8}$"-thick tongue. A mating dado is then cut on each end of the sides *(Fig. 10a)*.

Next, I added the drawer bottoms (V). Note that these pieces are cut out of $\frac{1}{2}$"

DESIGNER'S NOTEBOOK

Today's TV stands need space for all types of media. Some simple holders keep them all in order.

CONSTRUCTION NOTES:

■ The drawers on the Roll-Around TV Stand are sized so two rows of VHS cassette boxes will fit neatly inside (see photo above). But the drawers are also the right size for the jewel cases that hold CDs and DVDs.

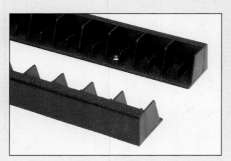

■ One problem with storing CDs in the drawers is that, unless the drawer is close to full, the discs will want to fall over. To keep the discs upright, you may want to purchase and install some plastic CD holders (see photo at left). These two-piece holders simply screw into the bottom of the drawer with one piece on each side. (It's easiest to do this before mounting the sliding hardware on the drawer.) A jewel case fits snugly in each compartment.

■ Similar holders are available to hold audio cassettes and video games. These holders can be found in a number of mail order catalogs (see Sources on page 126).

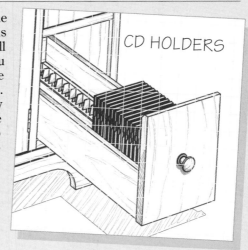

CD HOLDERS

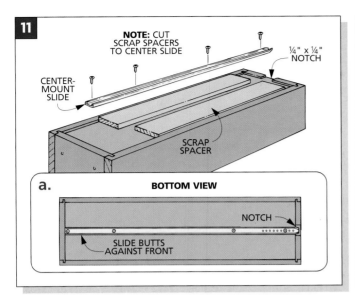

11 NOTE: CUT SCRAP SPACERS TO CENTER SLIDE

¼" x ¼" NOTCH

CENTER-MOUNT SLIDE

SCRAP SPACER

a. BOTTOM VIEW

NOTCH

SLIDE BUTTS AGAINST FRONT

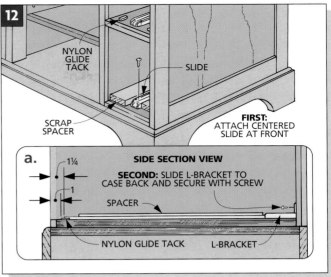

12 NYLON GLIDE TACK

SLIDE

SCRAP SPACER

FIRST: ATTACH CENTERED SLIDE AT FRONT

a. 1¼

SIDE SECTION VIEW

SECOND: SLIDE L-BRACKET TO CASE BACK AND SECURE WITH SCREW

1

SPACER

NYLON GLIDE TACK   L-BRACKET

---

plywood. This is thicker than a typical drawer bottom since you need to screw the drawer slides into these pieces later *(Fig. 11)*. Then I cut grooves in the drawer pieces to hold them *(Fig. 10b)*.

Before assembling the drawers, drill the shank holes for the false fronts that are added later *(Fig. 10a)*.

MOUNT DRAWER. Before adding the false fronts, I mounted the drawers into the cases. There's only one slide for each drawer. So the trick is to mount it so it's parallel to the sides of the case. This is easy to do with the help of some temporary spacers that center the slides automatically *(Figs. 11 and 12)*.

I separated the slides and started with the half that's mounted on the bottom of the drawer *(Fig. 11)*. The first thing to do is cut a small notch on the bottom edge of the drawer back to allow the slide to extend through *(Fig. 11a)*. (I did this with a hand saw and a chisel.)

Next, to keep the slide properly positioned, make two identical spacers that will trap the slide between the drawer sides *(Fig. 11)*. Now butt the slide against the drawer front and screw it down.

To mount the other half of the slide in the case, I cut a second set of spacers *(Fig. 12)*. (The spacers for the drawer and the case will be different sizes.)

Position the slide 1¼" back from the front edge of the case and secure it with a screw in front *(Fig. 12a)*.

At this point, getting a screw into the back of the slide would have been a real hassle. Fortunately, the slide is designed with a sliding L-shaped bracket so adding the screw in back is easy *(Fig. 12a)*. All you do is push the bracket against the back of the case and add another screw.

A center-mount slide can be a little "wobbly." So they come with nylon "glide tacks" to support the sides of the drawer *(Fig. 12)*. The position of the tacks isn't critical. Just push them in place so they won't be visible.

TECHNIQUE . . . . *Shimming Casters*

This Roll-Around TV Stand is designed to roll on casters to make it easier to turn the TV slightly or to gain access to the back of the stand. Mounting the casters is easy *(Fig. 1)*. The trick here is figuring out how much to shim

them so the stand doesn't drag on different surfaces.

Without any shims, the TV stand will roll on a hard surface with about ¼" clearance under the "feet" of the apron (left drawing in *Fig. 2*). But if you have carpet you'll need to

shim the casters down to "lift" the stand so it will roll.

The size of these shims will depend on the thickness of your carpet and the pad under the carpet (middle and right drawing in *Fig. 2*). And unfortunately, this process is one

of trial and error. You'll have to mount the casters and test them on your floor to find out how thick the shims will need to be.

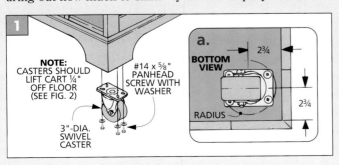

1 NOTE: CASTERS SHOULD LIFT CART ¼" OFF FLOOR (SEE FIG. 2)

#14 x ⅝" PANHEAD SCREW WITH WASHER

a. BOTTOM VIEW

2¾

2¾

RADIUS

3"-DIA. SWIVEL CASTER

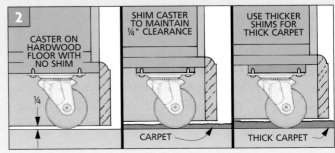

2 CASTER ON HARDWOOD FLOOR WITH NO SHIM

¼

SHIM CASTER TO MAINTAIN ¼" CLEARANCE

CARPET

USE THICKER SHIMS FOR THICK CARPET

THICK CARPET

FALSE FRONT. The last pieces to add are the false drawer fronts (W) *(Fig. 13)*. Typically, the grain on a drawer runs horizontally, but because this drawer is taller than it is wide, I thought it looked better with the grain running vertically. Also, I beveled the top inside edge of each false front to ease the sharp corner.

Once the fronts are cut to size, a 1"-dia. wood knob is centered on each one and screwed in place *(Fig. 13a)*. And finally, screw a false front to each drawer so there is a $\frac{1}{16}$" gap on all sides. ∎

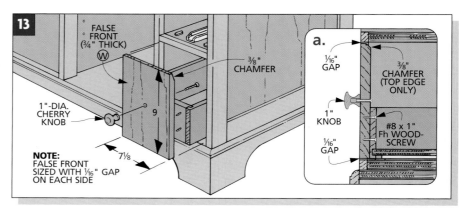

FINISHING . . . . *Using Aniline Dye*

How do you apply a color to a piece of wood without hiding the grain? One answer is aniline dye.

Aniline dye soaks into the wood, so it doesn't cover the grain. In fact it lets the grain shine through.

The dye comes in powder form in a variety of colors. Just mix it with water, then brush it on like a regular stain.

ANILINE DYES

When it came to staining the trim for the TV stand, I decided to used a water-based aniline dye for a couple of reasons. First, this type of dye doesn't fade like oil-based dyes. And since you mix it from a powder, you can adjust the hue by how much powder you add to the water.

I wanted a pronounced contrast between the trim and the cherry panels, so I doubled the concentration to make the dye as black as possible.

RAISED GRAIN. The only drawback to water-based dye is that it tends to raise the wood grain. To get around this, I like to raise the grain with water beforehand, then sand it smooth before applying the dye (see photos above). (If you apply the stain then sand, the dye may end up with an uneven appearance.)

Raise Grain. *First, use a damp sponge to moisten the surface, Then, once it's dry, sand lightly to knock off the "whiskers."*

APPLICATION. Brush on a generous amount of dye, keeping a wet edge. Wipe off any excess when you have covered the workpiece. You can add additional coats to darken the color.

Apply Dye. *Brush on the first coat of dye. If the grain raises again, sand it down lightly before applying the next coat.*

TOP COAT. When the finish dries, it will be a dull color. Don't worry. A couple of top coats will give the stained pieces a nice sheen. (I used an oil-urethane combination for my top coat.)

PRE-ASSEMBLY STAINING

The mix of black trim and cherry panels, along with using solid wood and plywood materials to build the TV stand, required a change in my usual routine for finishing.

First, instead of applying the finish after completing the project, I stained the trim *before* it was glued to the case (first photo at right). Plus, the base had to be stained before adding the drawer cases.

Then to make sure the cherry solid wood and the cherry plywood panels would end up the same color, I also stained the cases before they were assembled.

As a precaution, you don't want to stain any surface that's going to get glued. Otherwise, the glue won't stick. This means you'll need to tape off the "frame" on the sides of the cases (far right photo).

Note: If you find scratches in the black pieces later, you can use a black marker to touch them up.

Dyeing. *The edging pieces for the cases are stained with aniline dye (see above) before they're glued in place.*

Masking. *If you're staining the cherry plywood, tape off the areas where the black trim pieces will be glued in place.*

JOINERY . . . . Biscuit Alternatives

Biscuits are a quick and easy way to join two workpieces. But if you don't have a plate (biscuit) joiner, you can still make the Roll-Around TV Stand — you'll just need to make some modifications when it comes to the joinery. The two methods shown below still allow you to assemble the stand quickly while providing strong joints and easy alignment of pieces.

SPLINES

In most of the places on the stand where biscuits are used, you can substitute a system of slots and splines.

This is pretty straightforward when joining two pieces at a right angle, like the case sides and the dividers *(Fig. 1b)*.

Here, you simply rout a dado across the face of the side panel with a straight bit *(Fig. 2)*. (You could also do this with a dado blade in the table saw.)

Note: I use ¼" hardboard for the splines, but ¼" plywood also works well. Either way, it's a good idea to rout or cut a test piece to check the fit of the spline in the slot before you start work on the pieces for the TV stand.

Then with a slot cutting bit, rout matching slots along the edges of the dividers *(Figs. 3 and 3a)*. Now just cut a spline to fit in each slot.

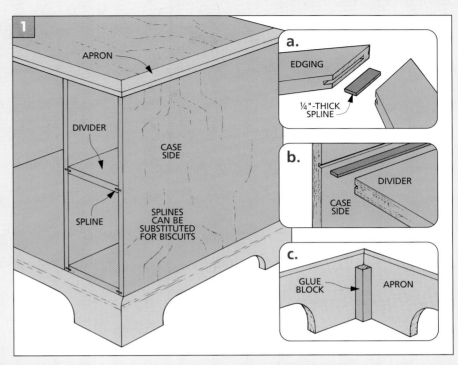

1
APRON
DIVIDER
SPLINE
CASE SIDE
SPLINES CAN BE SUBSTITUTED FOR BISCUITS

a.
EDGING
¼"-THICK SPLINE

b.
DIVIDER
CASE SIDE

c.
GLUE BLOCK
APRON

Note: When cutting the spline, make it slightly narrower than the combined depths of the slots so the spline doesn't bottom out. Otherwise, you'll never get the pieces together.

SPLINED MITERS. When constructing the top for the TV cart, splines can also be used in place of biscuits to join the edging to the top panel *(Fig. 1a)*.

But when it comes to joining the mitered corners of the frame, you won't be able to rout the full width of the workpiece like you did with the dividers. Instead, to make the mitered corner joints, you'll need to rout a stopped groove on the mitered end of each piece *(Fig. 4)*. (Take care to stop your cut short of the outside face.) Then just cut a spline to fit in the grooves *(Fig. 4a)*.

GLUE BLOCKS

The one place where it's not really practical to use splines in place of biscuits is in the two mitered corner joints on the front of the aprons of the stand.

If you were to cut slots on the mitered ends of the aprons, the ends of the slots and the splines would be visible from the top. So here, you can go ahead and simply glue the corners together.

But since you're gluing primarily end grain to end grain, it's still a good idea to reinforce the joint. One way to do this is with a glue block on the back of each corner. This provides more face grain gluing surface *(Fig. 1c)*. Make sure the corner of the block is exactly 90° so it doesn't pull the joint out of square.

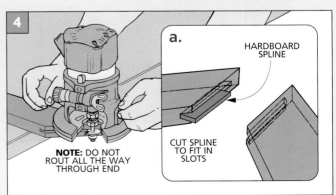

2
STRAIGHT-EDGE
ROUT SLOT FOR SPLINE

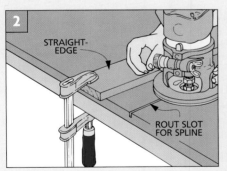

3
DIVIDER
CENTER SLOT ON EDGE OF DIVIDER
a.
END VIEW
SLOT CUTTER BIT

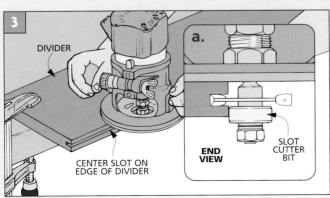

4
a.
HARDBOARD SPLINE
CUT SPLINE TO FIT IN SLOTS
NOTE: DO NOT ROUT ALL THE WAY THROUGH END

DESIGNER'S NOTEBOOK

If you prefer to store your audio and video components behind doors, it's easy to add a pair to the front of the TV stand. Stub tenon and groove joinery makes construction go quickly.

CONSTRUCTION NOTES:

■ The glass-paneled doors are built to fit the opening in the stand with a $^1/_{16}$" gap on each outside edge. After the doors are assembled, $^1/_{32}$" is trimmed off each inside stile to provide clearance between the doors. Start by cutting the door stiles (X) and rails (Y) to size *(Fig. 1)*.

■ The rails and stiles are joined with stub tenons and grooves. So after the door pieces are cut to size, you can cut a $^1/_4$"-wide groove centered on the inside edge of each piece *(Fig. 1a)*. The groove should be $^3/_8$" deep.

■ Now cut a $^3/_8$"-long stub tenon on each end of each rail to fit the groove *(Fig. 1)*.

■ Before assembling the doors, I cut the mortises for the hinges *(Fig. 1)*. I did this on my table saw. Start by laying out the locations of the mortises. Then attach an auxiliary fence to the miter gauge to support the workpiece. Make several passes over a dado blade set $^1/_8$" above the saw table to cut the 2"-wide mortises.

■ Once the mortises are cut, the doors can be glued up. Check carefully that the assemblies stay square and don't rack.

GLASS-PANELED
DOORS

■ The glass panels fit into rabbets in the back of each door. I used a $^3/_8$" rabbet bit set just deep enough to remove the top lip of the groove (refer to *Fig. 17* on page 122). This leaves a $^1/_2$"-deep rabbet to hold the glass and some glass stop. (After you finish with the router, you'll need to square up the corners with a chisel, since the bit won't reach into them.)

■ Now cut the glass stop (Z), miter the ends, and use brads to hold the stop in place *(Fig. 2a)*. See the Shop Tip on page 91 for a safe way to cut these small pieces.

■ Next, drill a hole centered on the width of the inside stile of each door and mount a 1" cherry knob *(Fig. 1)*.

■ Then the hinges can be attached and the doors hung on the cabinet.

■ Lastly, I attached a couple of double ball catches to the cabinet and inside the doors *(Fig. 2)*.

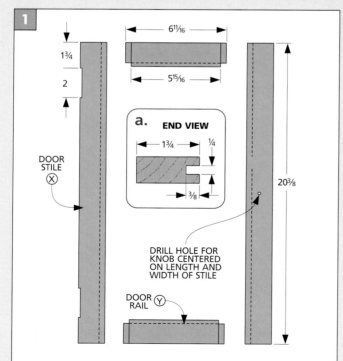

MATERIALS LIST

NEW PARTS

X	Door Stiles (4)	$^3/_4$ x 1$^3/_4$ - 20$^1/_2$
Y	Door Rails (4)	$^3/_4$ x 1$^3/_4$ - 6$^{11}/_{16}$
Z	Glass Stop	$^1/_4$ x $^1/_4$ - 120 rgh.

HARDWARE SUPPLIES
(2 pair) 1$^3/_8$" x 2" brass butt hinges
(2) 1"-dia. cherry knobs w/ screws
(2) 1$^{11}/_{16}$" brass double ball catches
(2 pcs.) $^1/_8$" glass, 6$^5/_8$" x 17$^9/_{16}$"

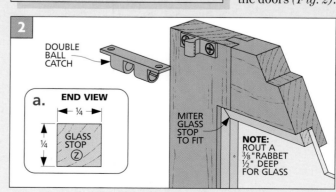

Tambour CD Case

This project has a number of pieces that are identical or that must line up precisely. A couple of simple jigs and a template provide the precision you need to make everything come together perfectly.

For a while I had been wanting to make a project that uses a tambour — but not the typical "bread box" with horizontal slats that slide up. I wanted to make a vertical slat tambour that opened to the sides. This case for compact discs gave me the perfect opportunity to give it a try.

INNER CASE. This project is actually a case within a case. The inner case is constructed first. It's just a box with dividers to hold and separate the plastic CD boxes. I made the case to hold 28 of these boxes.

TAMBOURS. The most interesting part of this project is the tambour doors on the outer case. Each tambour door is made

up of 29 slats, each $\frac{1}{2}$" wide. When the doors are closed, the CDs are protected and hidden from view.

There's nothing tricky about making these doors; they're just wooden slats held together with a piece of canvas. (The Technique article on page 113 has more about making tambours.)

The tricky part was routing perfectly matched grooves in the top and bottom of the outer case for the tambour doors to ride in. To simplify this, I used a template and a guide bushing on the router.

Then, to shape the top and bottom pieces so they matched the groove, I used the template again. But this time I

used it with a rub arm on the router table. The results are perfectly matched pieces.

WOOD AND FINISH. To set the tambour doors apart from the case, I made them from contrasting wood. The doors are made out of walnut (same as the dividers) while the inner case, top, and bottom are made from red oak.

Once the case was constructed, but before the tambours were installed, I applied two coats of tung oil finish, sanding lightly between coats.

OPEN FRONT. For a case that's quick and easy to build, see the Designer's Notebook on page 112 for an open-front case built without the tambour.

EXPLODED VIEW

OVERALL DIMENSIONS:
18½W x 7½D x 10⅝H

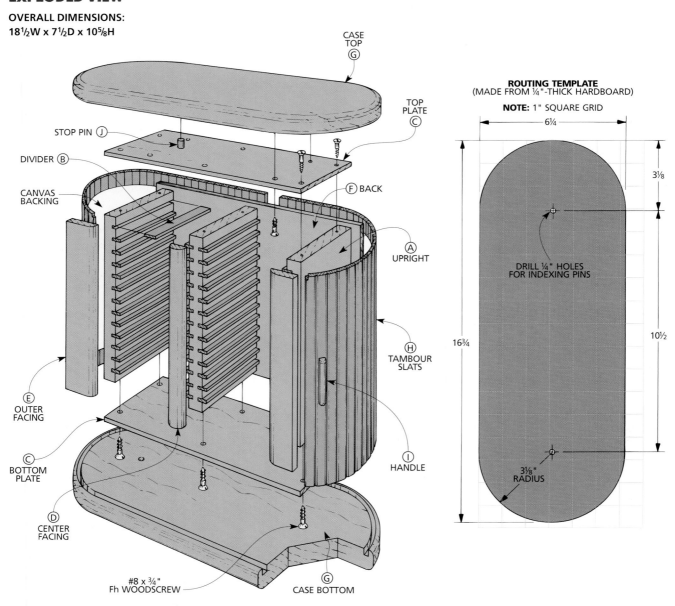

CASE TOP Ⓖ

TOP PLATE Ⓒ

STOP PIN Ⓙ

DIVIDER Ⓑ

CANVAS BACKING

Ⓕ BACK

Ⓐ UPRIGHT

Ⓗ TAMBOUR SLATS

Ⓔ OUTER FACING

Ⓒ BOTTOM PLATE

Ⓓ CENTER FACING

Ⓘ HANDLE

#8 x ¾" Fh WOODSCREW

CASE BOTTOM Ⓖ

ROUTING TEMPLATE
(MADE FROM ¼"-THICK HARDBOARD)

NOTE: 1" SQUARE GRID

6¼

3⅛

16¾

10½

DRILL ¼" HOLES FOR INDEXING PINS

3⅛" RADIUS

MATERIALS LIST

WOOD
A	Uprights (3)	¾ x 4¾ - 9 rough
B	Dividers (52)	⅛ x ½ - 4¹¹⁄₁₆
C	Top/Btm. Plates (2)	¼ x 4¾ - 12¼
D	Center Facing (1)	⅜ x ¾ - 9⅛
E	Outer Facings (2)	⅜ x 1¾ - 9⅛
F	Back (1)	¼ ply - 9⅛ x 13¼
G	Case Top/Btm. (2)	¾ x 7½ - 19 rough
H	Tambour Slats (58)	³⁄₁₆ x ½ - 9⁹⁄₁₆
I	Handles (2)	¼ x ¼ - 2
J	Stop Pins (2)	¼ dowel x ⅜

HARDWARE SUPPLIES
(16) No. 8 x ¾" Fh woodscrews
(1 pc.) Medium weight artist's canvas

CUTTING DIAGRAM

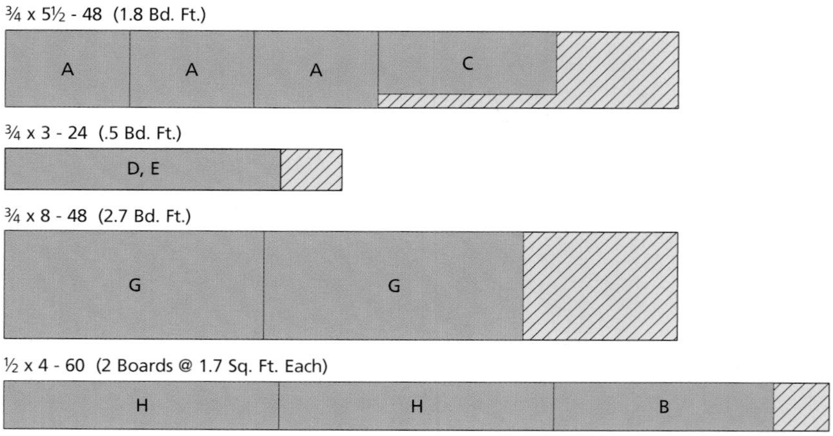

¾ x 5½ - 48 (1.8 Bd. Ft.)

| A | A | A | C | |

¾ x 3 - 24 (.5 Bd. Ft.)

| D, E | |

¾ x 8 - 48 (2.7 Bd. Ft.)

| G | G | |

½ x 4 - 60 (2 Boards @ 1.7 Sq. Ft. Each)

| H | H | B | |

UPRIGHTS

The CD case is built from the inside out. So the first pieces to work on are the three uprights that form the compartments of the inner case.

UPRIGHTS. To make the uprights (A), start by cutting three $3/4$"-thick blanks to a width of $4^3/4$" *(Fig. 1)*. Then trim these pieces to a rough length of 9".

After the upright pieces have been cut to their rough length, the next step is to cut a series of matching kerfs in all three pieces for the dividers to fit into. (The CD jewel cases slide on and are supported by the dividers.)

I cut kerfs equal to the width of the saw blade (about $1/8$"). The right and left uprights are kerfed on their inside faces only. But the center upright is kerfed on both sides *(Fig. 1)*.

INDEXING JIG. All told, you'll need to cut 52 kerfs to hold the dividers. Instead of taking the time to lay out each kerf, the quickest way to cut them is to use a simple indexing jig, like the one shown in the Shop Jig box below.

Besides being quicker, this jig keeps all of the kerfs aligned between the uprights. If the kerfs don't align, the CD boxes will sit at an angle or might not even slide into the case at all.

After the kerfs were cut, I trimmed the uprights to finished length. To do this, cut the pieces so the space between each outside kerf and the end of the upright is $1/2$" *(Fig. 1a)*. Also, make sure each upright has thirteen kerfs. (In my case, the uprights measured $8^5/8$" long.)

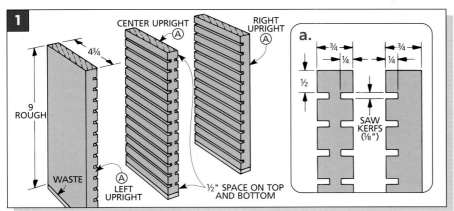

SHOP JIG .... Indexing Jig

Cutting a series of uniformly-spaced kerfs is quick and automatic with this simple indexing jig.

The jig clamps to my table saw's miter gauge. It's similar to a box joint jig, but on box joints the distance between the slots is the same as the width of the slots. For the uprights in the CD case, the distance between the kerfs has to be a uniform $1/2$", but the kerfs are only $1/8$" wide.

AUXILIARY FENCE. To make the jig, start by clamping a $2^1/2$"-wide piece of $3/4$" stock to your miter gauge *(Fig. 1)*.

Then raise the saw blade to the depth of the kerfs to be cut in the uprights ($1/4$"). Turn on the saw and make a pass to cut a notch in the fence.

KEY. Now, unclamp the fence and glue an indexing key into the notch *(Fig. 1a)*.

After the glue dries, use a chisel to pare $1/16$" off the top of the key. This ensures that when the workpiece is placed over the key, it will rest flat on the surface of the saw, not on top of the key.

SECOND NOTCH. Now clamp the fence to the miter gauge again so the distance

between the blade and the key equals the desired distance between the kerfs ($1/2$" for the CD case). Then make another pass over the blade *(Fig. 1)*.

USING THE JIG. Now you're ready to start cutting. For the first pass, keep the workpiece flat on the table, with one end against the key *(Fig. 2)*.

For the next pass, place the newly cut kerf over the key and run the workpiece over the blade again *(Fig. 3)*. Then just repeat this sequence to cut a series of kerfs along the full length of each upright.

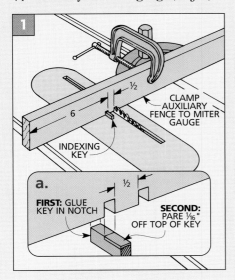

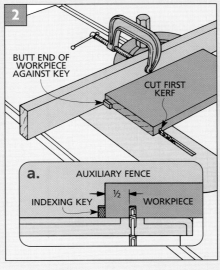

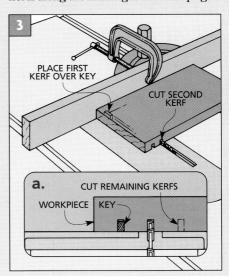

Typically when ripping thin stock, I use a thin push stick to guide the piece past the blade (*Fig. 1*). But when cutting the tambours, I noticed a problem with this technique.

As the push stick moves the workpiece through the cut, the unsupported side of the blank will sometimes split off just before the cut is completed. This leaves a little splinter of wood on the top corner of the blank (*Fig. 1a*).

If you're making a series of thin strips (such as for the tambour slats), that splinter can keep the workpiece from going tight against the fence on the next pass. (Or from sitting flat on a jointer table if you're jointing the blank between passes.)

Though the splinter can be trimmed off with a pocketknife or chisel, I've come up with a solution that prevents the splinter in the first place.

I use a push block made from an 11"-long piece of 2x4 (*Fig. 2*). Cut out or glue on a 1/4" "heel" on the bottom of the block. This pushes both the workpiece and the blank through the blade, eliminating the little splinter.

By adding a heel on top of the block too, you can turn the block over and keep working when the first heel gets torn up.

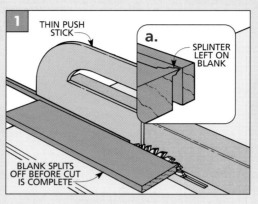
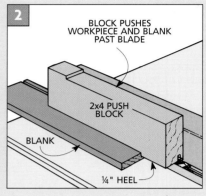

DIVIDERS

After the uprights are kerfed and cut to finished length, the next step is to make the dividers that fit into the kerfs to support the CD boxes.

Making the dividers (B) is a two-step procedure. First, 1/2"-thick stock is ripped into thin strips. Then the strips are cut to their finished length.

DIVIDER STRIPS. To make the divider strips, I started by resawing two blanks to 1/2" thickness. Next, I cut the blanks into 4" wide by 16"-long pieces.

Then these pieces are ripped into thin strips (*Fig. 2*). You'll end up with some extra dividers, which will be handy should one break or chip out.

Since I didn't want the saw marks to show on the strips, I cut them a little thicker than the kerf and then sanded them to get a snug fit.

Note: To get the cleanest cut, I used a wide push block to rip the eleven strips off each blank. (For more on this push block, see the Shop Tip above.)

CUT TO LENGTH. The next thing to do is to cut all the dividers to the same length. To do this, I clamped a stop block to an auxiliary fence on the miter gauge (*Fig. 3*). The stop block is positioned so the dividers will be 1/16" shorter than the width of the uprights to allow for expansion and contraction.

GLUING DIVIDERS. Once the dividers are cut, the next step is to glue them in the kerfs. Put a drop of glue in each kerf, near the front edge of the divider. (But don't spread the glue in the kerf.) Then set the upright on edge and push the dividers down against the work surface to get them flush with the front edge of each upright (*Fig. 4*).

TOP & BOTTOM PLATES

After all of the dividers are glued in place, a top and bottom plate are needed to tie the uprights together.

Determining the width of the top and bottom plates (C) is easy enough. They fit flush with the front and back edges of the uprights — so they're the same width as the uprights (4 3/4").

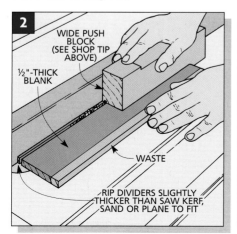
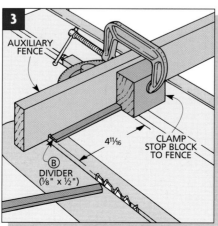
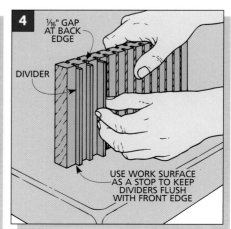

However, determining the length of the plates requires a bit more work. That's because the uprights need to be spaced so a CD jewel case (which is $4^7/8$" wide) will fit between them — with a $1/8$" space along the sides.

SPACERS. To get this spacing, I made four 5" x 5" spacers from $1/2$"-thick scrap and inserted them where the CD cases will go *(Fig. 5)*. Then all I had to do was to measure across the outside edges of the end uprights to get the length of the plates ($12^1/4$", in my case).

CUT PLATES TO SIZE. After determining the size, cut the top and bottom plates (C) out of $1/4$"-thick stock *(Fig. 5)*.

ATTACH THE PLATES. Next, drill countersunk shank holes in the top and bottom plates for the woodscrews that will mount them to the uprights *(Fig. 5)*.

Before screwing the plates in place, drill four more countersunk screw holes at the four corners of the top plate on the inside face *(Fig. 5a)*. These holes will be used later to attach the outer case top.

FACINGS & BACK

After the plates are glued and screwed on, I made three facing pieces to cover the ends of the kerfs on the uprights. (The two outer facings also hide the inside of the tambours when the case is open.)

All three facing strips are cut from one blank that starts out $2^1/2$" wide and 20" long *(Fig. 6)*. First, round over three edges of the blank.

Cutting off the facing pieces is now a three-step process *(Fig. 7)*. (Before doing this, I cut the blank into two 10" pieces to make it easier to work with.)

The first step is to trim the center facing (D) off one edge *(Step 1 in Fig. 8)*. The second step is to cut the outer facings (E) to a finished width of $1^3/4$" *(Step 2 in Fig. 8)*. The final step is to resaw the outside facings to a thickness of $3/8$" *(Step 3)*.

Before gluing the facing pieces in place, trim them so they're flush with the top and bottom of the inner case ($9^1/8$") *(Fig. 9)*. Then glue the center facing (D) to the front edge of the middle upright. And glue an outer facing (E) to each outer upright *(Fig. 9a)*.

BACK. All that's left to complete the inner case is to add the $1/4$" plywood back (F). The top and bottom of the back are flush with the top and bottom of the case, but the sides extend $1/2$" beyond both uprights. This helps hide the tambour backing. Then glue the back (F) in place.

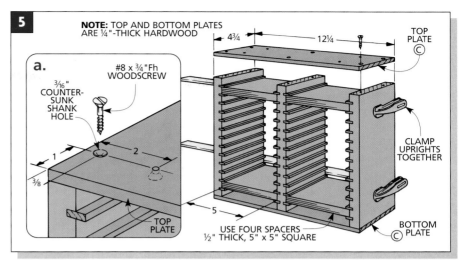

5
NOTE: TOP AND BOTTOM PLATES ARE $1/4$"-THICK HARDWOOD

TOP PLATE C

a.
$3/16$" COUNTERSUNK SHANK HOLE

#8 x $3/4$"Fh WOODSCREW

$4^3/4$ $12^1/4$

1   2

$3/8$

TOP PLATE

CLAMP UPRIGHTS TOGETHER

5

USE FOUR SPACERS $1/2$" THICK, 5" x 5" SQUARE

BOTTOM PLATE C

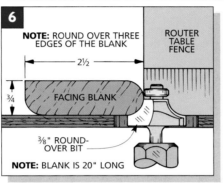

6
NOTE: ROUND OVER THREE EDGES OF THE BLANK

ROUTER TABLE FENCE

$2^1/2$

$3/4$ FACING BLANK

$3/8$" ROUND-OVER BIT

NOTE: BLANK IS 20" LONG

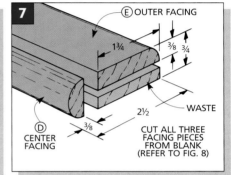

7
E OUTER FACING

$1^3/4$ $3/8$ $3/4$

WASTE

D CENTER FACING

$3/8$ $2^1/2$

CUT ALL THREE FACING PIECES FROM BLANK (REFER TO FIG. 8)

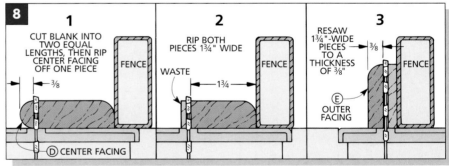

8
1
CUT BLANK INTO TWO EQUAL LENGTHS, THEN RIP CENTER FACING OFF ONE PIECE

$3/8$ FENCE

D CENTER FACING

2
RIP BOTH PIECES $1^3/4$" WIDE

WASTE $1^3/4$ FENCE

3
RESAW $1^3/4$"-WIDE PIECES TO A THICKNESS OF $3/8$"

$3/8$ FENCE

E OUTER FACING

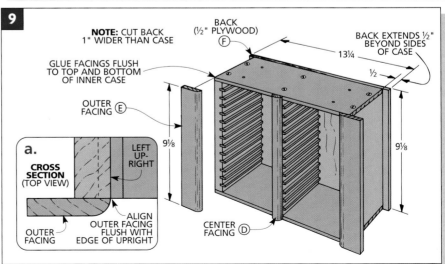

9
NOTE: CUT BACK 1" WIDER THAN CASE

BACK ($1/2$" PLYWOOD) F

BACK EXTENDS $1/2$" BEYOND SIDES OF CASE

GLUE FACINGS FLUSH TO TOP AND BOTTOM OF INNER CASE

$13^1/4$ $1/2$

OUTER FACING E

$9^1/8$

$9^1/8$

a.
CROSS SECTION (TOP VIEW)

LEFT UPRIGHT

OUTER FACING

ALIGN OUTER FACING FLUSH WITH EDGE OF UPRIGHT

CENTER FACING D

CASE TOP & BOTTOM

In order for the tambour to slide properly it has to run between two grooved pieces. But making these grooved pieces identical can be a problem.

The solution is to use a template. The template lets you rout identical grooves, and it also helps you make the case top and bottom the same size.

TEMPLATE. First, lay out the template (*Fig. 10* and the Routing Template on page 106). Then cut it to rough size and sand it smooth (*Fig. 11*).

BLANKS. The next step is to glue up a couple of 8" x 19" blanks for the case top and bottom (G) (*Fig. 12*).

To keep from getting mixed up, mark the inside front edge of both blanks, and both sides of the template (*Fig. 12*). Now center the template on one blank and clamp it down.

INDEXING HOLES. A couple of indexing pins keep the template in place when routing. Mark their locations and drill holes through the template and ¹/₂" into the blank (*Fig. 12*). And don't worry about these holes. They'll be hidden by the inner case later.

To locate the holes on the other blank, flip the template over and use the first holes as a drilling guide (*Fig. 12*).

INDEXING PINS. Once the holes are drilled, put a ¹/₄" dowel pin in each hole and trim the pins flush with the top of the template.

ROUT GROOVES. With the template in place on a blank, the groove can be routed. To do this, just mount a ¹/₄" straight bit in the router and a ⁷/₁₆" guide bushing to the router base. Then, with the bit adjusted to cut a ¹/₄"-deep groove, start routing on the back edge of the template (*Fig. 13*).

Once a groove is routed in each blank, the next step is to cut the blanks to shape. To lay out the shape, I made a small pencil guide from posterboard and ran it along the template (*Fig. 14*). Then remove the template and cut ¹/₈" outside the line.

RUB ARM. To trim the pieces to their finished shape, again I used the template but this time with the router table and a rub arm clamped to the fence (*Fig. 15*).

The rub arm is clamped to the router table fence above a ¹/₄" straight bit mounted in the router (*Fig. 15a*). Then, adjust the height of the arm so it touches the template and the bit trims only ¹/₁₆" off the blank (*Fig. 15*).

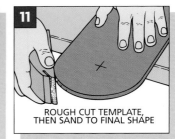

10 LAY OUT TEMPLATE PATTERN ON ¹/₄"-THICK HARDBOARD
PATTERN ON PAGE 106

11 ROUGH CUT TEMPLATE, THEN SAND TO FINAL SHAPE

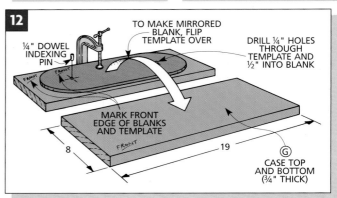

12 ¹/₄" DOWEL INDEXING PIN — TO MAKE MIRRORED BLANK, FLIP TEMPLATE OVER — DRILL ¹/₄" HOLES THROUGH TEMPLATE AND ¹/₂" INTO BLANK — MARK FRONT EDGE OF BLANKS AND TEMPLATE — 8 — 19 — FRONT — G — CASE TOP AND BOTTOM (³/₄" THICK)

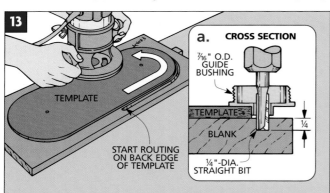

13 TEMPLATE — START ROUTING ON BACK EDGE OF TEMPLATE
a. CROSS SECTION — ⁷/₁₆" O.D. GUIDE BUSHING — TEMPLATE — BLANK — ¹/₄" — ¹/₄"-DIA. STRAIGHT BIT

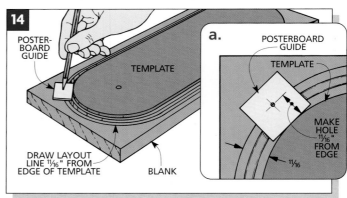

14 POSTER-BOARD GUIDE — TEMPLATE — DRAW LAYOUT LINE ¹¹/₁₆" FROM EDGE OF TEMPLATE — BLANK
a. POSTERBOARD GUIDE — TEMPLATE — MAKE HOLE ¹¹/₁₆" FROM EDGE — ¹¹/₁₆"

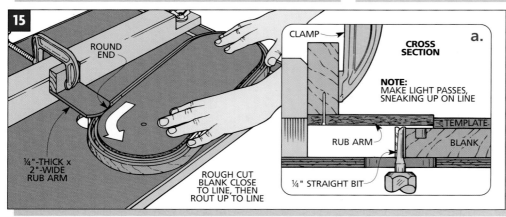

15 ROUND END — ¹/₄"-THICK x 2"-WIDE RUB ARM — ROUGH CUT BLANK CLOSE TO LINE, THEN ROUT UP TO LINE
a. CLAMP — CROSS SECTION — NOTE: MAKE LIGHT PASSES, SNEAKING UP ON LINE — TEMPLATE — RUB ARM — BLANK — ¹/₄" STRAIGHT BIT

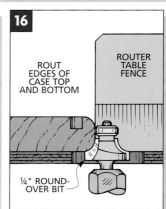

16 ROUT EDGES OF CASE TOP AND BOTTOM — ROUTER TABLE FENCE — ¹/₄" ROUND-OVER BIT

Now, make several passes, moving the fence away from the bit slightly between each pass until the workpiece is cut to the pencil line.

To complete the top and bottom, I rounded over both edges *(Fig. 16)*.

TAMBOUR SLATS

The tambour doors on the case are simply slats glued to a piece of canvas *(Fig. 17)*. But, the thought of cutting and routing all 58 tambour slats (H) is intimidating.

THREE-STEP PROCESS. Making the slats is a three-step process. (For more, see the Technique article on page 113.)

Basically, the edges of a larger blank are rounded over. Then a slat is trimmed off the edge *(Fig. 17)*. Then simply start the process all over again.

CUT TO LENGTH. Once you've ripped nine strips from each blank, cut each strip to length ($9^9/_{16}$") to make a couple of tambour slats (H) *(Fig. 17a)*.

FINAL ASSEMBLY

Once I completed the tambours I added handles and door stops before gluing and screwing the case together.

HANDLES. The handles (I) are simply a couple of $1/_4$" x $1/_4$" pieces *(Fig. 18)*. I cut

each piece 2" long and rounded over the front edges and ends with a file. Next, center the pulls on the length and width of the second slat of each door. Then, glue them in place.

STOPS. Next, to keep the doors from opening or closing too far, I added a stop pin (J) in the front and back of the top groove *(Fig. 19)*. These stops are $3/_8$"-long pieces of $1/_4$" dowel glued into holes centered on the length of the case.

One problem is that the front pin will prevent the doors from closing together tightly. So chisel or file a $1/_8$"-wide notch in the top front edge of the first slat of both tambours *(Fig. 19a)*.

ASSEMBLY. After the tambours are notched, it's time to assemble the inner case with the doors, top, and bottom.

To get the pieces aligned, mark a light line centered on the length of the bottom *(Fig. 19)*. Then, position the inner case so the center upright is centered on the line, and the front of the inner case is $1^1/_8$" from the inside of the groove *(Fig. 20)*.

FINISH. Before attaching the top to the inner case, I finished all of the pieces with two coats of tung oil.

SCREW ON THE TOP. The last step is to screw the top to the inner case. (The top is not glued so it can be removed.)

Start by centering the top on the inner case. Now, using the holes you drilled earlier as a guide, mark and drill four pilot holes for the screws. Then to complete the case, put the tambours in the grooves and trap them as you screw the top in position *(Fig. 21)*. ∎

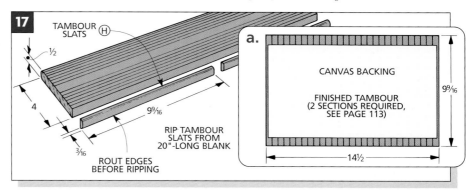

17 TAMBOUR SLATS (H)
$1/_2$
4
$9^9/_{16}$
$3/_{16}$
RIP TAMBOUR SLATS FROM 20"-LONG BLANK
ROUT EDGES BEFORE RIPPING

a. CANVAS BACKING
FINISHED TAMBOUR (2 SECTIONS REQUIRED, SEE PAGE 113)
$9^9/_{16}$
$14^1/_2$

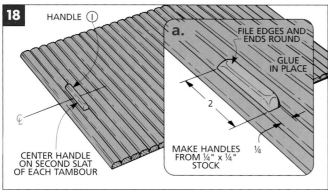

18 HANDLE (I)
a. FILE EDGES AND ENDS ROUND
GLUE IN PLACE
2
$1/_4$
MAKE HANDLES FROM $1/_4$" x $1/_4$" STOCK
CENTER HANDLE ON SECOND SLAT OF EACH TAMBOUR

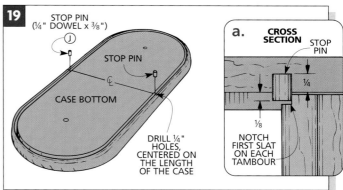

19 STOP PIN ($1/_4$" DOWEL x $3/_8$")
(J)
STOP PIN
CASE BOTTOM
DRILL $1/_4$" HOLES, CENTERED ON THE LENGTH OF THE CASE

a. CROSS SECTION
STOP PIN
$1/_4$
$1/_8$
NOTCH FIRST SLAT ON EACH TAMBOUR

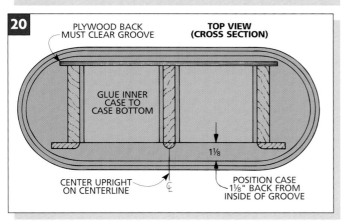

20 PLYWOOD BACK MUST CLEAR GROOVE
TOP VIEW (CROSS SECTION)
GLUE INNER CASE TO CASE BOTTOM
$1^1/_8$
CENTER UPRIGHT ON CENTERLINE
POSITION CASE $1^1/_8$" BACK FROM INSIDE OF GROOVE

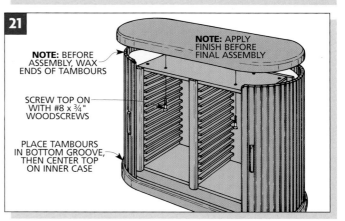

21 NOTE: APPLY FINISH BEFORE FINAL ASSEMBLY
NOTE: BEFORE ASSEMBLY, WAX ENDS OF TAMBOURS
SCREW TOP ON WITH #8 x $3/_4$" WOODSCREWS
PLACE TAMBOURS IN BOTTOM GROOVE, THEN CENTER TOP ON INNER CASE

DESIGNER'S NOTEBOOK

The open-front design of this case means your discs are always right at your fingertips. The inner case is the same and, since there's no tambour to make, it's quicker to build.

CONSTRUCTION NOTES:

■ The inner case is the same as for the Tambour CD Case, except the outer facings (E) are only ³/₄" wide. Then an outer case is built around it. Start by cutting the side panels (K) to size *(Fig. 1)*.

■ Now round over the three long outside edges of each side panel *(Fig. 1)*.

■ Next, cut to size a top and bottom (G) for the outer case *(Fig. 1)*.

■ After laying out a curve on the front edge of the top *(Fig. 1)*, I fastened it to the bottom using carpet tape. Then I cut both to rough shape at the same time and sanded up to the layout line.

■ Now rout ¹/₈" roundovers around both faces of the top and bottom *(Fig. 1)*.

■ Next, drill and counterbore screw holes in the case top *(Figs. 1a and 2)*. Square up the counterbores with a chisel to accept plugs that are added later *(Fig. 2)*. (Identically-placed screw holes in the case bottom are simply countersunk.)

■ To assemble the case, start by gluing the side panels to the inner case so they extend ¹/₄" behind the uprights *(Fig. 2)*. (This forms a rabbet for the case back.)

Then center the assembly side-to-side on the case bottom with the case bottom extending ¹/₈" past the rear edges of the side panels and screw it in place.

■ To secure the case top, screw it to the side panels and the top plate *(Fig. 2)*.

■ Cut square plugs (L) to fit the counterbores *(Fig. 1a)*. Make sure you cut them so the face grain faces up, then sand ¹/₁₆" chamfers around them.

■ Finally, cut a back (F) from ¹/₄" plywood to fit the opening in the back of the case and glue it in place *(Fig. 1)*.

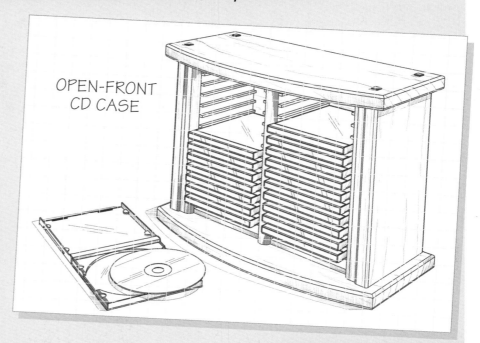

OPEN-FRONT CD CASE

MATERIALS LIST

CHANGED PARTS

E	Outer Facings (2)	³/₈ x ³/₄ - 9¹/₈
F	Back (1)	¹/₄ ply - 9¹/₈ x 12¹/₄
G	Case Top/Btm. (2)	³/₄ x 7³/₈ - 15

NEW PARTS

K	Side Panels (2)	³/₄ x 5¹/₂ - 9¹/₈
L	Plugs (4)	⁷/₁₆ x ³/₈ - ³/₈

HARDWARE SUPPLIES

(8) No. 8 x 1¹/₂" Fh woodscrews
Note: Do not need artist's canvas or parts H, I, J

1

OUTER FACING (³/₈" HARDWOOD - ³/₄" x 9¹/₈")
E

6

CASE TOP (³/₄" HARDWOOD) G

15

7³/₈

¹/₈" ROUND-OVERS

a.

SIDE SECTION
PLUG (⁷/₁₆" HARDWOOD - ³/₈" x ³/₈")
L

³/₈

⁵/₈

#8 x 1¹/₂" Fh WOOD-SCREW

SIDE PANEL K

9¹/₈

¹/₈" ROUND-OVERS

G CASE BOTTOM

F BACK (¹/₄" PLYWOOD - 12¹/₄" x 9¹/₈")

5¹/₂

2

#8 x 1¹/₂" Fh WOOD-SCREW

1

1

³/₈

DRILL ³/₈"-DIA. COUNTERBORES, THEN SQUARE UP WITH CHISEL

SIDES EXTEND ¹/₄" PAST BACK EDGES OF UPRIGHTS

BACK

TECHNIQUE ...... *Making Tambours*

There's nothing magical about a tambour door. It's just a sliding door that's flexible. This flexibility allows the tambour to slide in a curved track.

The way to make a tambour flexible is to join a series of individual slats with some sort of flexible hinge. The most common method of hinging these slats is to glue them to a fabric backing.

SLATS

When I make a tambour, I rip the tambour slats off the edge of a board. This allows me to rout the profile on the edges of the slat before it's cut off the board.

The thickness of the blank should equal the width of the slats. (I wanted the slats 1/2" wide for the CD case, so I started with a 1/2"-thick board.)

Note: To save some time, I make the blank a little more than twice as long as the slats. Then two slats can be cut to length from each strip.

ROUT THE EDGES. Once you have a board the correct thickness, the first step in making the slats is to round over all four edges of the blank *(Step 1)*.

CUT TO THICKNESS. Now just rip a slat from each edge of the stock *(Step 2)*.

After the slats have been cut off, there will probably be some saw marks on the edges of the blank. A pass over the jointer or with a plane will clean these up. Then repeat the process of routing, cutting, and jointing until you have enough slats.

Note: There are bound to be some warped, twisted, or unattractive slats, so I cut 20% more than I need.

GLUING UP THE TAMBOURS

Now it's time to glue the fabric backing to the slats. The tricky part here is getting the slats to fit together tightly. The secret is to use a jig to hold the slats flat. The jig is made of two hold-down bars and two end blocks screwed to a plywood base.

ASSEMBLY. Screw one hold-down bar (rabbet facing down), to the plywood. Then screw an end block perpendicular to the hold-down bar *(Step 3)*.

To start, slide one end of the tambour slats (face down) under the hold-down and screw a second hold-down over the other ends of the slats *(Steps 4 and 5)*.

Then push the tambour slats against the end block tightly so the glue won't seep through. Now, screw down the remaining end block *(Step 5)*.

FABRIC. The next step is to glue on the fabric backing. The material I normally use for backing is a light to medium-weight artist's canvas. This can be found at art supply stores.

Note: You can dye the fabric to match the color of the wood, but the fabric may shrink. So dye it before you cut it to size.

Cut the fabric to fit between the hold-downs and long enough to cover the slats. Then use a brush to apply an even coating of glue to the back of the tambour slats.

Finally, press the fabric in place and use a short piece of dowel to roll out any wrinkles in the backing *(Step 6)*.

BREAKING THE TAMBOUR. Once the tambour is dry, you'll probably find that some glue has seeped between the slats. For this reason the back of the tambour needs to be "broken." To do this, gently bend the tambour back at the cracks.

FINISHING. All that's left is to apply the finish. I usually use a wipe-on finish such as tung or Danish oil.

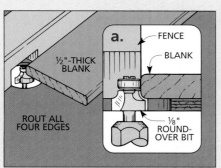

1 To make the 1/2"-wide tambour slats, start by routing a 1/8" roundover on all four edges of a 1/2"-thick blank.

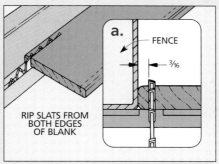

2 Rip the slats to thickness from both edges of the blank. Then plane off the saw marks and repeat the procedure.

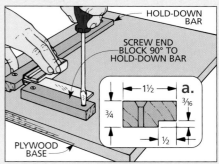

3 Now make a gluing jig. Start by screwing an end block and a rabbetted hold-down bar 90° to each other.

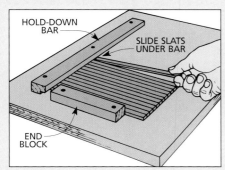

4 With routed edges face down, place one end of the slat under the bar. Keep adding slats until they're all in place.

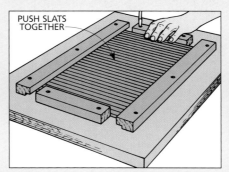

5 Screw the other hold-down bar in place. Push the slats tight against the end block and screw the other end block down.

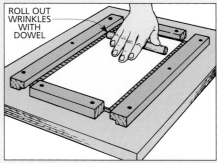

6 Cut the canvas backing material so it fits between the hold-downs. Apply glue to the slats and press the fabric in place.

Entertainment Center

Doors only have to do two things: open and close. Unless there's a TV behind them. Then it's nice if they open and slide out of the way. That's what makes this project attractive and functional.

Sliding doors are the key to making this cabinet work. The whole idea is to open the doors in front of the TV and slide them back into the cabinet so they're not left hanging open. This may sound like it would be complicated. But with a special set of adjustable sliding door hardware, it's easy.

This hardware is a two-part hinge system. One part is a concealed hinge that fits into a hole in the back of the door frame. The other part is a sliding track that's screwed inside the cabinet. Then the two parts just snap together.

The best thing about this hardware is that it's adjustable in three directions.

If the doors don't line up perfectly the first time, no problem. You can still get them to look right — just by turning a screw. It works so well, you shouldn't have to move the hinges at all.

SIZE. The Entertainment Center is rather large, since it's designed to hold a 27" TV. It's also quite deep in order to accommodate the big hump on the back of most regular TVs. By using plywood for the panels, I kept the construction simple and the cost down.

Since stereo equipment doesn't need as much depth in the cabinet, it's in a shallower compartment than the TV. This creates a hidden chamber behind the

stereo compartment — an ideal place to corral all the dangling wires.

DUAL-PURPOSE JIG. Building this project requires two full sheets of ³⁄₄" plywood, plus a sheet of ¹⁄₄" plywood. Since sheets of plywood are awkward to handle, I built a simple jig that guides a circular saw for cutting the plywood pieces to size. I also used the same jig to guide a router to cut the grooves that join all the plywood pieces together. (Refer to the Shop Jig box on page 117.)

DRAWERS. The doors below the TV conceal a storage area. If you'd prefer drawers here, refer to the Designer's Notebook on page 123.

EXPLODED VIEW

OVERALL DIMENSIONS:
55¹/₈W x 24¹/₄D x 49¹/₂H

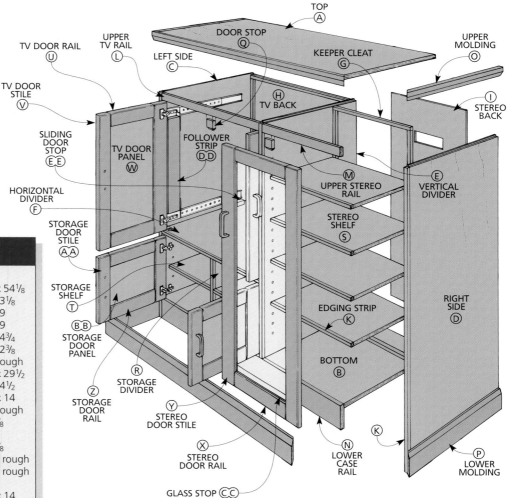

MATERIALS LIST

CASE
A	Top (1)	¾ ply - 23¾ x 54¹/₈
B	Bottom (1)	¾ ply - 23 x 53¹/₈
C	Left Side (1)	¾ ply - 23 x 49
D	Right Side (1)	¾ ply - 23 x 49
E	Vertical Divider (1)	¾ ply - 23 x 44¾
F	Hrzntl. Divider (1)	¾ ply - 23 x 32³/₈
G	Keeper Cleats	¾ x ¾ - 384 rough
H	TV Back (1)	¼ ply - 31⁷/₈ x 29½
I	Stereo Back (1)	¼ ply - 20 x 44½
J	Storage Back (1)	¼ ply - 31⁷/₈ x 14
K	Edging Strips	¾ x ¾ - 300 rough
L	Upper TV Rail (1)	¾ x 1½ - 31⁷/₈
M	Upr. Stereo Rail (1)	¾ x 1½ - 20
N	Lower Case Rail (1)	¾ x 4½ - 52⁵/₈
O	Upper Molding	½ x 1½ - 108 rough
P	Lower Molding	½ x 3¾ - 108 rough
Q	Door Stops (2)	¾ x 2 - 2
R	Storage Divider (1)	¾ x 16¾ x 14

SHELVES
S	Stereo Shelves (4)	¾ ply - 15¾ x 19⁷/₈
T	Storage Shelves (2)	¾ ply - 15¾ x 15⁷/₁₆

DOORS
U	TV Door Rails (4)	¾ x 2⁵/₈ x 11³/₁₆
V	TV Door Stiles (4)	¾ x 2⁵/₈ x 28
W	TV Door Panels (2)	¼ ply - 11¹/₈ x 23¹/₈
X	Stereo Dr. Rails (2)	¾ - 2⁵/₈ x 15¼
Y	Stereo Dr. Stiles (2)	¾ x 2⁵/₈ - 42¾
Z	Storage Dr. Rails (4)	¾ x 2⁵/₈ - 11³/₁₆
AA	Stor. Dr. Stiles (4)	¾ x 2⁵/₈ - 14
BB	Stor. Dr. Panels (2)	¼ ply - 11¹/₈ x 9¹/₈
CC	Glass Stops	¼ x ³/₈ - 120 rough
DD	Follower Strips (4)	¾ x 3 - 23 rough
EE	Sliding Dr. Stops (2)	¾ x ¾ - 1

HARDWARE SUPPLIES
(46) No. 6 x ⁵/₈" Fh woodscrews
(30) ½" brads
(48) 1¼" finish nails
(6) Self-closing concealed hinges w/ screws
(2 pr.) Sliding door hardware w/ screws
(1) ⅛"-thick glass, 15¹/₈" x 37⁷/₈"
(5) 3¾" door pulls
(24) Spoon-style shelf pins

CUTTING DIAGRAM

ALSO NEEDED: TWO 4x8 SHEETS ¾" PLYWOOD, PLUS ONE 4x8 SHEET ¼" PLYWOOD

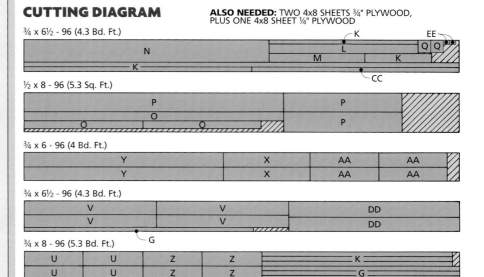

¾ x 6½ - 96 (4.3 Bd. Ft.)

½ x 8 - 96 (5.3 Sq. Ft.)

¾ x 6 - 96 (4 Bd. Ft.)

¾ x 6½ - 96 (4.3 Bd. Ft.)

¾ x 8 - 96 (5.3 Bd. Ft.)

PLYWOOD CASE

The Entertainment Center consists of three main groups of parts — the plywood case, adjustable shelves, and doors.

The case and shelves are built from two 4x8 sheets of ¾"-thick plywood (good on two sides). All the pieces are held together with tongue and dado joints.

Keeping all the parts straight can be a little confusing. So, to get organized, I started by cutting all the case pieces to finished size. Then I cut the joints.

CUTTING THE PLYWOOD

Trying to control a full sheet of plywood while pushing it through a cut on the table saw is just asking for trouble. So instead, I used a shop-made edge guide to cut all the pieces from the two sheets of plywood. (Instructions for making the edge guide can be found in the Shop Jig box on the opposite page.)

FIRST SHEET. In order to get all the parts from two sheets of ¾" plywood, I followed a particular cutting sequence. First, I cross-cut one of the sheets to produce a piece the finished length (54⅛") of the case top (A) *(Figs. 1 and 2)*. Set aside the

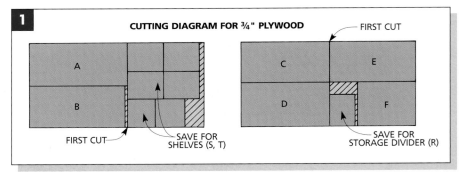

1 CUTTING DIAGRAM FOR ¾" PLYWOOD

short half of this piece to be used later for the plywood shelves *(Fig. 1)*.

Now rip the long half of the sheet to finished width, producing the case top (A) *(Fig. 2)*. Rip the other piece to finished width (¾" narrower), then cut it to finished length for the case bottom (B).

SECOND SHEET. Next, crosscut the second sheet of plywood to produce a piece 49" long for the case sides *(Figs. 1 and 2)*. (Set aside the shorter cut-off piece for right now.) Then rip the piece to produce identically sized pieces for the left side (C) and right side (D) *(Fig. 2)*.

Without changing the position of the table saw fence, rip the remaining plywood piece to produce two pieces the same width as the sides *(Fig. 2)*. Then cut

these two pieces to finished length to produce the vertical divider (E) and the horizontal divider (F) *(Fig. 2)*. Set aside the small piece that's left to be used later for the storage divider (R) *(Fig. 1)*.

Lastly, I drilled a 2½"-dia. hole in the vertical divider to allow wires from the TV to pass through *(Fig. 2)*.

Note: It helps to label all the pieces along with the top, front, and inside of each piece so you can keep track of them during the joinery and assembly stages.

CUTTING THE JOINTS

When all the case parts have been cut to finished size, work can begin on the tongue and dado joinery.

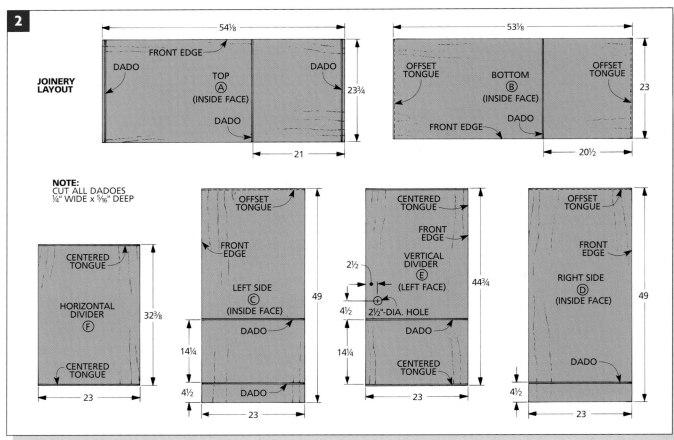

MEASURE AND MARK. Again, to keep everything organized, I marked the position of each tongue and dado on the plywood before actually cutting the joints *(Figs. 2 and 3)*. Once that was done, I began cutting the dadoes.

ROUT DADOES. I used a ¼" straight bit in the router to cut all the dadoes. But rather than try to balance the workpiece on my router table, I held the router in my hands and guided it with a straightedge. Here again, I used my shop-built edge guide (see the Shop Jig box below).

ROUT TONGUES. Next, I used a rabbet bit to rout the ¾"-wide rabbets that form the tongues. Note that some tongues are offset. These are formed by routing a rabbet on one edge of the workpiece *(Fig. 4)*. In other places, the tongue is centered on the thickness of the workpiece. These are formed by routing a rabbet on two sides of the workpiece *(Fig. 5)*.

Note: It's best to start by routing a test tongue on a scrap piece of ¾" plywood. This way you can sneak up on the depth of the rabbet to produce a tongue that fits the dado.

First I routed the offset tongues on both ends of the case bottom (B) and the top end of each case side (C, D) *(Figs. 2, 3a, and 3d)*. Then adjust the bit to cut a centered tongue on each end of the dividers (E, F) *(Figs. 2, 3b, and 3c)*.

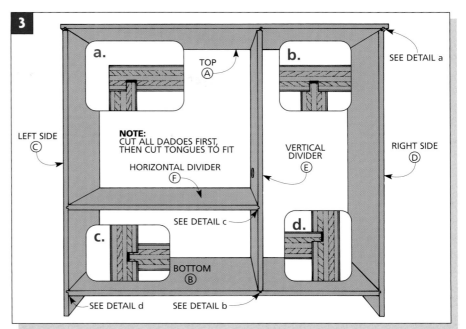

3

a.

TOP Ⓐ

b.

SEE DETAIL a

LEFT SIDE Ⓒ

NOTE: CUT ALL DADOES FIRST, THEN CUT TONGUES TO FIT

VERTICAL DIVIDER Ⓔ

RIGHT SIDE Ⓓ

HORIZONTAL DIVIDER Ⓕ

SEE DETAIL c

c.

d.

BOTTOM Ⓑ

SEE DETAIL d   SEE DETAIL b

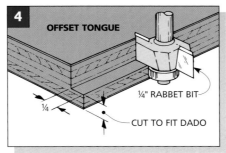

4 OFFSET TONGUE

¼" RABBET BIT

¼

CUT TO FIT DADO

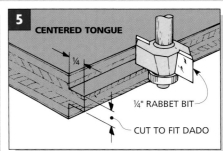

5 CENTERED TONGUE

¼

¼" RABBET BIT

CUT TO FIT DADO

This shop-made edge guide makes using a circular saw more accurate. Plus it can be used to guide either a circular saw or a router (see photos at right).

The secret lies in the way the jig is built. It's made from a base of hardboard that's screwed to a narrow piece of plywood (see drawing). (I made the jig 48" long for cross-cutting a sheet of plywood.)

Start with a wide enough base so the edge guide will fit both your circular saw and your router (see drawing).

First, cut off the right edge of the base by running the circular saw along the right edge of the fence. Then, do the same thing on the other side of the jig with a straight bit in the router. (Rout from left to right.)

To use the jig, just line up the edge of the base on your intended cut line and clamp the jig in place. Now run the tool along the fence.

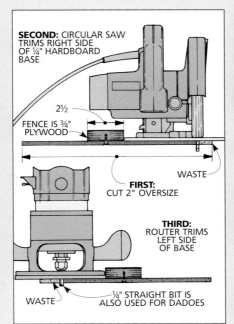

SECOND: CIRCULAR SAW TRIMS RIGHT SIDE OF ¼" HARDBOARD BASE

2½

FENCE IS ¾" PLYWOOD

WASTE

FIRST: CUT 2" OVERSIZE

THIRD: ROUTER TRIMS LEFT SIDE OF BASE

WASTE

¼" STRAIGHT BIT IS ALSO USED FOR DADOES

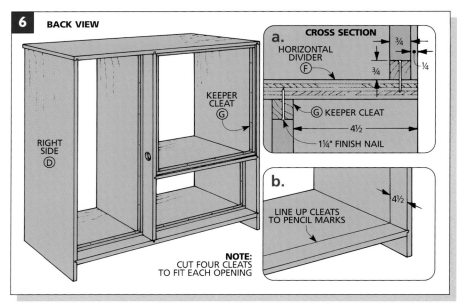

6 BACK VIEW

a. CROSS SECTION

HORIZONTAL DIVIDER (F)

¾

¾

¼

G KEEPER CLEAT

4½

1¼" FINISH NAIL

KEEPER CLEAT (G)

RIGHT SIDE (D)

b.

4½

LINE UP CLEATS TO PENCIL MARKS

NOTE: CUT FOUR CLEATS TO FIT EACH OPENING

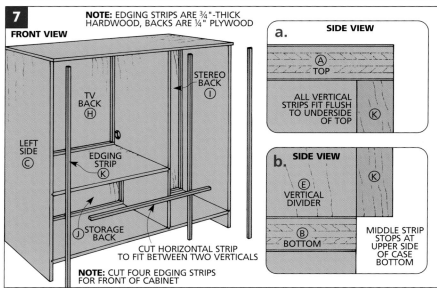

7

NOTE: EDGING STRIPS ARE ¾"-THICK HARDWOOD, BACKS ARE ¼" PLYWOOD

FRONT VIEW

a. SIDE VIEW

A TOP

ALL VERTICAL STRIPS FIT FLUSH TO UNDERSIDE OF TOP

K

STEREO BACK (I)

TV BACK (H)

LEFT SIDE (C)

EDGING STRIP (K)

STORAGE BACK (J)

CUT HORIZONTAL STRIP TO FIT BETWEEN TWO VERTICALS

NOTE: CUT FOUR EDGING STRIPS FOR FRONT OF CABINET

b. SIDE VIEW

K

E VERTICAL DIVIDER

B BOTTOM

MIDDLE STRIP STOPS AT UPPER SIDE OF CASE BOTTOM

CLEATS, BACKS, & EDGING STRIPS

Once you've cut the joints on the plywood parts, the case can be assembled. But first I dry-assembled the parts to check that the case would be square and that the joints fit well.

Note: Keep all the corners flush at the back. The front edge of the top (A) should overhang the side panels by ¾".

When you're satisfied with the fit, glue and clamp the parts together. (See the Shop Tip below for some help doing this.)

KEEPER CLEATS. After the case is glued up, measure the openings for the three plywood backs *(Fig. 6)*. Then cut four keeper cleats (G) for each of the openings to hold the backs in place *(Fig. 6a)*.

Note: The ¼" plywood TV back (H) is mounted flush to the outside of the case *(Fig. 6a)*. So nail these cleats ¼" in from the back edges. But note that the stereo back (I) and storage back (J) are inset 4½" *(Figs. 6a and 6b)*.

BACKS. Now the three ¼" plywood backs (H, I, J) can be cut to fit. But don't screw them to the cleats just yet — you'll need to remove them later to cut openings for the TV and stereo wires.

EDGING STRIPS. Next I turned my attention to the front of the cabinet. The first step here is to cover the exposed edges of the plywood sides and dividers with hardwood edging strips (K) *(Fig. 7)*.

To do this, first rip four strips of ¾"-thick stock to match the thickness of the plywood parts. Two of the strips are cut to length to fit the edges of the case sides *(Fig. 7a)*. Another is cut to match the length of the vertical divider *(Fig. 7b)*.

SHOP TIP .... *Clamping Large Assemblies*

With large cabinets, a clamp won't always reach where you want it.

So try using short nails to temporarily pull the pieces together. Angle the nails so they won't poke through the side *(Fig. 1)*.

And to cross one clamp over another, use a pair of 2x4s that extend beyond the workpiece *(Fig. 2)*.

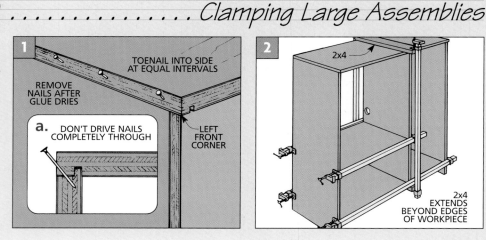

1 TOENAIL INTO SIDE AT EQUAL INTERVALS

REMOVE NAILS AFTER GLUE DRIES

a. DON'T DRIVE NAILS COMPLETELY THROUGH

LEFT FRONT CORNER

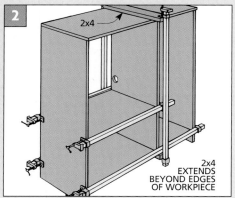

2 2x4

2x4 EXTENDS BEYOND EDGES OF WORKPIECE

For the horizontal divider, sneak up on the length of the strip until it fits between the side and the vertical divider *(Fig. 7)*.

RAILS & MOLDING STRIPS

The remaining plywood edges on the case top and bottom aren't covered with edging strips, but with a molding strip (along the top), and a rail (across the bottom) *(Figs. 9 and 10)*.

UPPER RAILS. I made the front rails for the case from ³⁄₄"-thick oak. The upper rail is actually two pieces — the upper TV rail (L) on the left, and the upper stereo rail (M) on the right *(Fig. 8)*.

Start by cutting both pieces 1¹⁄₂" wide, and to length to fit their openings. Then glue and clamp them in place.

LOWER RAIL. Next, the lower case rail (N) is cut to size *(Fig. 8)*. This covers the plywood edges on the bottom, and keeps the cabinet from sagging.

CUT MOLDING. Once the lower rail is glued in place, the upper molding (O) and lower molding (P) can be added around the top and bottom of the case *(Figs. 9 and 10)*. After cutting the pieces to width and rough length, I cut a 20° bevel on each strip to add a decorative look (see the Shop Tip above right).

ATTACH MOLDING. When all the sections of molding have been beveled, you can miter them to finished length and glue them in place.

There's a trick to getting the molding strips to fit around the cabinet with a minimum of gap at the mitered corners. The trick involves starting with the front (the longest) strip of molding.

First, cut a 45° miter on one end of the strip. Then measure the case to determine the finished length. Now miter the other end of the strip so the distance from short point to short point of the miters equals this length.

With the front strip cut the correct length, temporarily clamp it in place while you measure for the side strips. These strips are mitered on the front edge first, then cut to length with a 90° cross-cut on the back edge.

When all the molding strips have been cut to fit the cabinet, they can be glued and clamped in place.

DOOR STOPS. After the rails and molding strips have been glued onto the case, door stops (Q) can be cut and attached to the upper rail. There's one stop for the TV doors, and one stop for the stereo door. (The storage doors are stopped by the storage divider that's installed later.)

Start with a blank cut to finished width and rough length to be used for both stops. Then cut a ¹⁄₄"-wide rabbet on the

SHOP TIP
Zero-Clearance Insert

A zero-clearance insert prevents the narrow edge of the molding from tipping into the table saw opening. A push stick keeps your hand away from the blade.

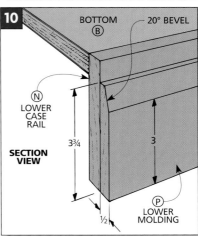

lower edge *(Fig. 8a)*. The rabbet stops the doors so they're inset ¹⁄₄" from the front of the cabinet.

After the stops are cut to size, you can soften the corners by cutting chamfers on the lower ends of each stop *(Fig. 8a)*. Then glue the stops into place on the back edge of each upper rail *(Fig. 9)*.

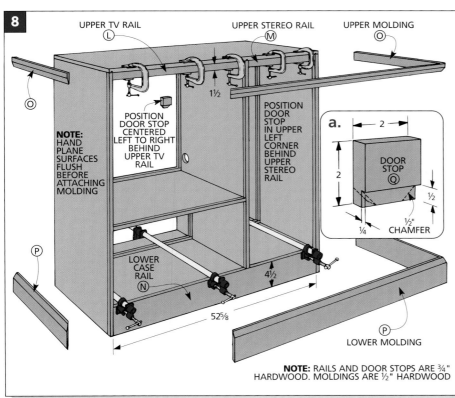

8

UPPER TV RAIL
(L)

UPPER STEREO RAIL
(M)

UPPER MOLDING
(O)

(O)

1½

POSITION DOOR STOP CENTERED LEFT TO RIGHT BEHIND UPPER TV RAIL

POSITION DOOR STOP IN UPPER LEFT CORNER BEHIND UPPER STEREO RAIL

NOTE: HAND PLANE SURFACES FLUSH BEFORE ATTACHING MOLDING

a.

2

2

DOOR STOP (Q)

¹⁄₄

CHAMFER

½

½"

(P)

LOWER CASE RAIL (N)

4½

52⁵⁄₈

(P)

LOWER MOLDING

NOTE: RAILS AND DOOR STOPS ARE ³⁄₄" HARDWOOD. MOLDINGS ARE ½" HARDWOOD

9

SECTION VIEW

½

¹⁄₈" ROUNDOVER

(A) TOP

³⁄₄

1½

UPPER MOLDING (O)

DOOR STOP (Q)

20° BEVEL

UPPER RAIL

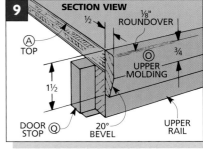

10

BOTTOM (B)

20° BEVEL

(N) LOWER CASE RAIL

3¾

3

SECTION VIEW

½

(P) LOWER MOLDING

STORAGE DIVIDER & SHELVES

When the outside of the case is completed, you can use the left-over plywood to build the parts that go inside.

DIVIDER. The first piece is a divider (R) for the storage compartment. The height (length) is easy to figure — it's the same as the height of the compartment *(Fig. 11)*. But the depth takes a little figuring. First measure from the front edge of the cleat that holds the plywood back in place, to the front edge of the edging strip on the horizontal divider *(Fig. 11)*.

Then subtract 1³/₄" from this measurement to allow for the edging strip

that's attached later and for the doors. (In my case, the dividers are 16³/₄" wide.)

EDGING STRIPS. Next, glue an edging strip (K) to the front of the divider. I cut this a little longer than needed, then trimmed it after it was glued in place. (See the Shop Tip on the opposite page.)

Now the divider can be centered in the storage compartment and screwed in place from the top and bottom *(Fig. 11)*.

SHELVES. Next, cut four stereo shelves (S) and two storage shelves (T) to fit in their compartments *(Fig. 12)*.

The first thing to do here is to rip the plywood into three equal-width pieces (in my case 15³/₄") *(Fig. 12)*.

Then cut the shelves for each compartment to length so they're ¹/₈" shorter than the compartment is wide *(Fig. 12)*. Now glue an edging strip on the front edge of each shelf.

MARKING TEMPLATE. To locate the positions of the holes for the shelf support pins, I used a template.

To make a template, first cut a piece of hardboard to a width of 6" *(Fig. 13)*. Then cut the template to length to fit inside the stereo opening. Now, drill a series of ¹/₄" holes the full length of the template.

Note: Position the holes 2¹/₂" from the back edge of the template *(Fig. 13)*. Then, always keep this edge to the rear

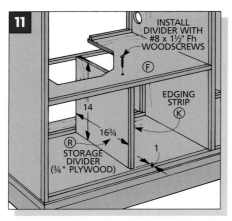

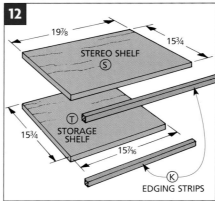

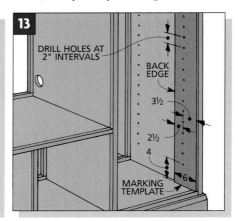

SHOP JIG .... *Shelf Pin Jig*

Each of the shelves in the Entertainment Center is supported by four shelf pins. To "lock" the shelves in place, I routed shallow recesses on the bottom of each one to fit over the pins (see photo).

By using a hardboard template, I was able to make the recesses align perfectly with the holes for the shelf pins.

I held the template in the cabinet, making sure the back edge was against the back cleat. Then I transferred the location of the holes in the cabinet to the template *(Fig. 1)*.

Now, cut a ⁵/₈"-wide notch in the template centered on each of the marks *(Fig. 1a)*. This notch accepts a ⁵/₈" guide bushing for the router.

ROUTING NOTCHES. To rout the recesses in the shelves, clamp the template onto a shelf with the back edges flush *(Fig. 2)*.

Mount a ⁵/₈" guide bushing in the router base and ¹/₂" straight bit in the router. Then rout a recess for each shelf pin by sliding the bushing into each notch *(Fig. 2a)*.

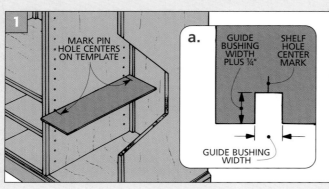

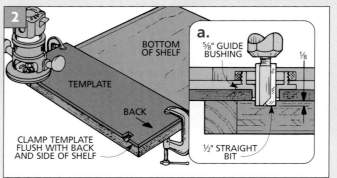

14

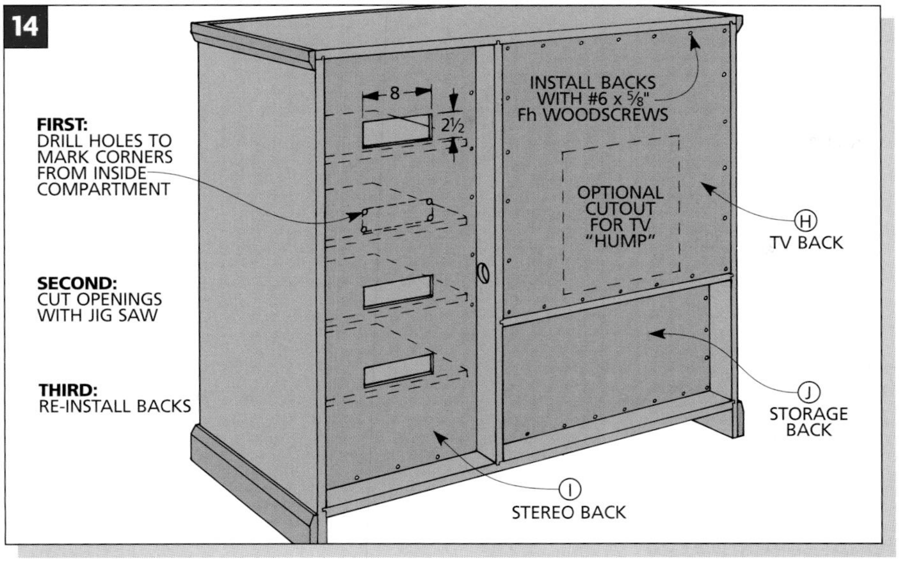

FIRST:
DRILL HOLES TO MARK CORNERS FROM INSIDE COMPARTMENT
SECOND:
CUT OPENINGS WITH JIG SAW
THIRD:
RE-INSTALL BACKS
8
2½
INSTALL BACKS WITH #6 x ⅝" Fh WOODSCREWS
OPTIONAL CUTOUT FOR TV "HUMP"
H
TV BACK
J
STORAGE BACK
I
STEREO BACK

of the cabinet when marking the holes. This positions the pins an equal distance from the front and back of each shelf when they're finally installed.

To drill the holes in the storage compartment, just cut the template shorter.

BACKS

One of my favorite features of this Entertainment Center is the "wire management" area concealed behind the stereo compartment. It hides all the wires that look like spaghetti coming out of the back of the electronic components.

To get to the components, you have to cut slots in the plywood back *(Fig. 14)*. But first, position the shelves in the stereo compartment to fit your equipment.

STEREO OPENINGS. Mark the position of all the slots from inside the stereo compartment. I did this by first drilling a small starter hole to indicate the corners of each slot. Then I removed the back and used a jig saw to complete the openings.

TV OPENING. If the television you'll be placing in the cabinet has a deep "hump" on the back, you may need to cut an opening in the TV back to allow the doors to close in front of the TV *(Fig. 14)*.

Then screw all the backs in place.

DOORS

The most challenging part about this project is building the doors. The doors are inset ¼" from the front edge of the cabinet, with an equal (⅛") space around each door. Rather than build the doors to allow for the ⅛" space, I think it's easier to build them to fit inside the cabinet tightly. Then the ⅛" space is created all around by trimming the doors after they've been assembled.

RAILS AND STILES. First I cut two rails (U, X, Z) and two stiles (V, Y, AA) for each door frame. Rip these to a uniform width from ¾"-thick stock *(Fig. 15)*.

Then cut all the stiles to finished length so they fit the height of each door opening exactly *(Fig. 15)*. Next, set the stiles in the cabinet and cut the rails to fit between them, adding ½" to allow for ¼"-long tongues on the ends of each rail (refer to *Fig. 16* on page 122).

SHOP TIP

Trimming Edging Strips

Rather than trying to cut an edging strip to exact length, I cut the strip a little long and trim the ends flush with the sides of the shelf after the glue has dried.

To do this, I use a spacer to provide a surface to run the shelf against (see drawing).

Once the first end is trimmed, flip the shelf over. Then, without moving the fence or the spacer, trim off the opposite end.

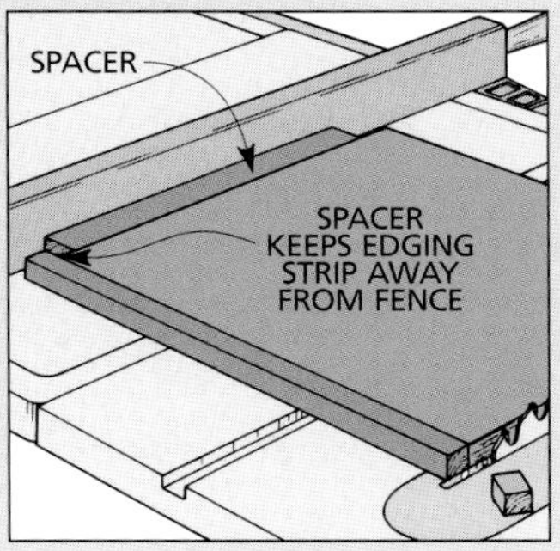

SPACER
SPACER KEEPS EDGING STRIP AWAY FROM FENCE

15

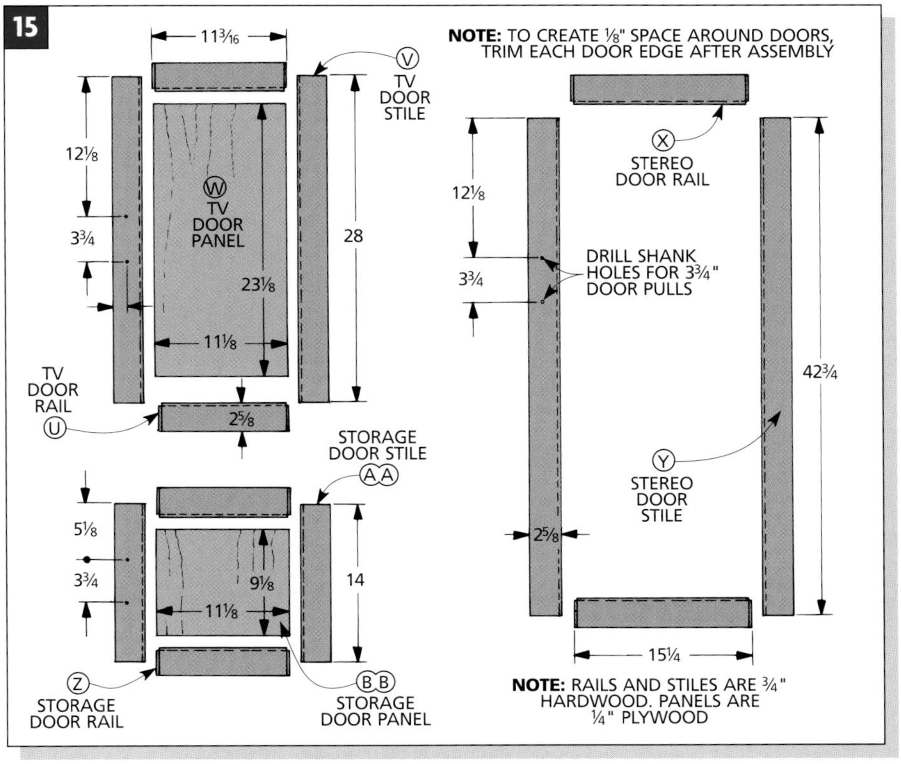

NOTE: TO CREATE ⅛" SPACE AROUND DOORS, TRIM EACH DOOR EDGE AFTER ASSEMBLY
11³⁄₁₆
V
TV DOOR STILE
12⅛
3¾
W
TV DOOR PANEL
28
23⅛
11⅛
TV DOOR RAIL
U
2⅝
STORAGE DOOR STILE
AA
5⅛
3¾
9⅛
11⅛
14
Z
STORAGE DOOR RAIL
BB
STORAGE DOOR PANEL
X
STEREO DOOR RAIL
12⅛
3¾
DRILL SHANK HOLES FOR 3¾" DOOR PULLS
42¾
Y
STEREO DOOR STILE
2⅝
15¼
NOTE: RAILS AND STILES ARE ¾" HARDWOOD. PANELS ARE ¼" PLYWOOD

GROOVES. All the doors have a panel that fits in a groove centered on the inside edge of the frame *(Fig. 16)*. On the stereo door the panel is a $1/8$"-thick piece of smoked glass. On the other doors it's a piece of $1/4$" plywood.

I used the table saw to cut the groove for a snug fit with the $1/4$" plywood.

Note: The plywood I used for door panels had a lower grade back — not too attractive when the doors are open. So I covered the inside of each door panel with a matching (oak) veneer before assembly. Then cut the grooves to fit the thickness of the plywood plus the veneer.

TONGUES. When the grooves have been cut in the frame pieces, cut $1/4$"-long tongues on the ends of the rails to fit in the grooves on the stiles *(Fig. 16)*.

ROUNDOVERS. Before assembling the doors, I routed a roundover on the inside edge of each rail and stile *(Fig. 16)*. (The outside edges are rounded over *after* the doors are cut to fit the openings.)

To highlight the joints between the stiles and rails, I created a shadow line by rounding over the shoulder at each end of each rail *(Fig. 16)*. You'll need to remove the bearing from the roundover bit to do this (see the Shop Tip at right).

PANELS. Now the frames can be dry-assembled to check the fit and for square.

While the frame is assembled, measure for the panels (W, BB) that fit inside the frames. To do this, add $3/8$" to the inside dimensions of the frames. This allows for two $1/4$"-deep grooves, with a $1/16$" gap all around to make assembling the doors easier.

Once the panels are cut to size, the doors can be assembled with the panels glued inside the frames.

CUT TO FIT. Now $1/8$" can be trimmed off the outside edge of each door to create a uniform space.

Note: To create $1/8$" space between the double doors, I trimmed $1/16$" off the mating (inside) stiles. This slight difference in the width of the inside and outside stiles won't be noticeable.

INSTALL THE GLASS. Before installing the glass panel in the stereo door, I routed a rabbet around the back inside edge of the frame. To do this, I used a $1/4$" rabbeting bit to to remove just the inside lip of the groove *(Fig. 17)*.

I installed the glass with stops glued in the rabbets behind the glass. The glass stops (CC) are pieces of $1/4$"-thick hardwood cut to a width of $3/8$" *(Fig. 17a)*.

DOOR INSTALLATION. The hinges I used for the Entertainment Center are concealed, so there's nothing showing on the outside of the cabinet. The details for installing these hinges and hanging the doors are in the Hardware article beginning on page 124. ◼

for installing these hinges and hanging the doors are in the Hardware article beginning on page 124.

SHOP TIP
Routing Under a Tongue

On a workpiece with a tongue, the router bit bearing prevents the cutters from reaching the piece.

So I remove the bearing, then run the workpiece along an auxiliary router table fence — it acts just like a bearing (see drawing).

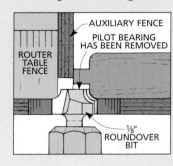

AUXILIARY FENCE

PILOT BEARING HAS BEEN REMOVED

ROUTER TABLE FENCE

$1/8$" ROUNDOVER BIT

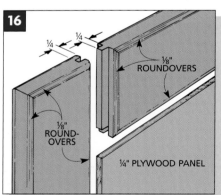

16

$1/4$

$1/4$

$1/8$" ROUNDOVERS

$1/8$" ROUND-OVERS

$1/4$" PLYWOOD PANEL

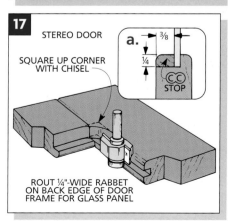

17

STEREO DOOR

a.

$3/8$

$1/4$

CC STOP

SQUARE UP CORNER WITH CHISEL

ROUT $1/4$"-WIDE RABBET ON BACK EDGE OF DOOR FRAME FOR GLASS PANEL

DESIGNER'S NOTEBOOK

The straight lines and beveled trim of the Entertainment Center are reminiscent of the Mission style. A change of pulls completes the look. And adding drawers make the storage even more accessible.

CONSTRUCTION NOTES:

■ The first change involves the keeper cleats for the storage area. The cleats are positioned $17^3/4$" from the front edge of the plywood case *(Fig. 2)*. This makes the storage divider (R) $17^3/4$" wide as well.

■ To build the drawers, cut the sides (FF), fronts (GG), and backs (GG) to size from $1/2$"-thick stock *(Fig. 1)*.

■ The locking rabbet joint is made by cutting a dado $1/4$" wide and $1/4$" deep across each end of the sides *(Fig. 1a)*. Then cut a rabbet on each end of each front and back to leave a tongue to fit the dado in the sides.

■ Next, cut a groove $1/4$" from the bottom edge of each drawer piece to accept a piece of $1/4$" plywood.

■ To find the size of the drawer bottoms, just dry-assemble a drawer and measure the interior. Then add $1/2$" to each measurement to allow for the grooves, and cut a plywood drawer bottom (HH) to this size for each drawer.

■ Now you can glue each drawer together around a bottom.

■ Each drawer receives a $3/4$"-thick false front (II). These are cut to size to allow for a $1/16$" gap around each drawer *(Fig. 1)*.

■ Before attaching the false fronts, mount the drawer glides in the cabinet *(Fig. 2)*. Then attach the drawers to the glides.

■ To position the false fronts, put a strip of carpet tape on the front of the drawer. Then use pennies as spacers to set a $1/16$" gap around the front. When the false front is positioned, press it against the drawer, then pull the drawer out and screw the false front in place.

■ Finally, attach the Mission-style pulls and handles to the drawers and also to the TV and stereo compartment doors.

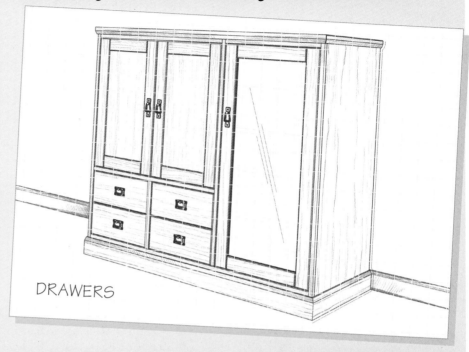

DRAWERS

MATERIALS LIST

CHANGED PART		
R Storage Divider (1)	$3/4$ ply - $17^3/4$ x 14	
NEW PARTS		
FF Drawer Sides (8)	$1/2$ x $6^1/2$ - 17	
GG Drawer Ft./Bk. (8)	$1/2$ x $6^1/2$ - $14^1/16$	
HH Drawer Bottoms (4)	$1/4$ ply - $16^7/16$ x 14	
II Drwr. False Fts. (4)	$3/4$ x $6^{13}/16$ - $15^5/16$	
Note: Don't need parts T, Z, AA, BB.		

HARDWARE SUPPLIES
(16) No. 8 x 1" Fh woodscrews
(4 pr.) 16" full-extension drawer glides
(4) $1^1/8$" Mission-style drawer pulls w/ screws
(3) $2^3/8$" Mission-style door pulls w/ screws
(16) Spoon-style shelf pins
(2) Self-closing concealed hinges w/ screws
Note: $3^3/4$" door pulls not needed

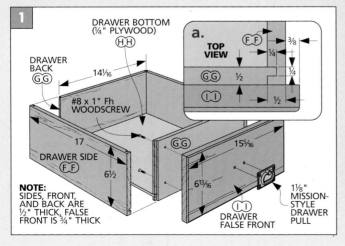

1

DRAWER BOTTOM ($1/4$" PLYWOOD) (HH)

DRAWER BACK (GG)

$14^1/16$

#8 x 1" Fh WOODSCREW

17

DRAWER SIDE (FF)

$6^1/2$

(GG)

$15^5/16$

$6^{13}/16$

(II)

DRAWER FALSE FRONT

$1^1/8$" MISSION-STYLE DRAWER PULL

NOTE: SIDES, FRONT, AND BACK ARE $1/2$" THICK, FALSE FRONT IS $3/4$" THICK

a. TOP VIEW

(FF) $3/8$

$1/4$

(GG) $1/2$ $1/4$

(II) $1/2$

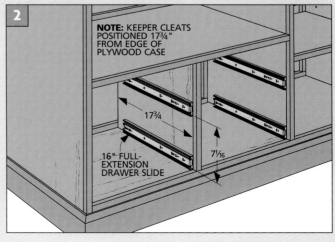

2

NOTE: KEEPER CLEATS POSITIONED $17^3/4$" FROM EDGE OF PLYWOOD CASE

$17^3/4$

16" FULL-EXTENSION DRAWER SLIDE

$7^1/16$

HARDWARE .... *Concealed Hinges*

What's the most difficult part of mounting doors in a cabinet? I think it's getting the hinges positioned correctly. If you're a little off, the door will fit crooked in the opening. If you're a long ways off, the door may not close at all.

The beauty of the concealed hinges on the Entertainment Center is how easy they are to mount and adjust. It's simply a matter of drilling holes and screwing the hinges in place.

ADJUSTABLE. But the best part comes after the doors are mounted. The hinges are adjustable — in three directions. By turning one of three screws, the door can be shifted 1/8" out or in, left or right, up or down. So if you're a little off at first, you can leave the hinges in place and make up for it with the adjusting screws.

DESIGN. What makes this hardware so easy to use is its two-part design. The actual hinge has a round cup that fits into a hole drilled in the door. Then a separate mounting plate fits on the cabinet.

When the two parts are mounted to the door and cabinet, hanging the door is simple. All you have to do is slide the hinge (on the door) onto the plate (in the cabinet). Then tighten a screw.

OTHER FEATURES. Another feature I like about these hinges is that they fit completely inside the cabinet, so you can't see the hardware from the outside.

Both types of hinges I used are self-closing. You just pivot the door about halfway then let go — the door will close itself the rest of the way.

SOURCES. The hinges shown here are available from many home centers or from mail order sources (see page 126). They are sometimes referred to as "European hinges." Detailed instructions for mounting the hardware are usually included. But the steps below show you what is involved.

SWINGING DOOR

A concealed hinge consists of two parts. The actual hinge attaches to the door with a small cup on one end that fits into a shallow hole in the door stile *(Fig. 1)*. At the other end, an arm extends out and slides into a mounting plate attached to the cabinet (see photo at right).

For the door to hang properly, the only trick is to get both parts of the hinge to align when the door is placed in the opening. There's an easy way to do this.

DOOR FRAME. Begin with the door half of the hinge. First, drill a 1 3/8"-dia. (35mm) hole in the door stile *(Fig. 1)*. Position each hole the same distance from the ends of the door stile (in my case, 2").

Also, keep the edge of each hole the same distance from the edge of the stile (1/8").

Then press a hinge cup into the hole and mark the location of both mounting screws. After the holes are drilled, screw the hinges to the door frame.

CABINET. The mounting plate on the other end of the hinge is simply attached to the cabinet with three screws. To drill the screw holes, I made a template that positions the holes so the center of mounting plate aligns with the center of the hinge cup *(Fig. 2)*.

Drill the hole pattern *(Fig. 2a)*, and add a cleat on the front edge to position the template on the front of the cabinet.

Concealed Hinge. *This hinge has two parts that separate for easy mounting. The cup fits into a hole in the door. Then the mounting plate is screwed to the cabinet. The two parts then snap together.*

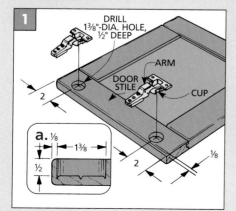

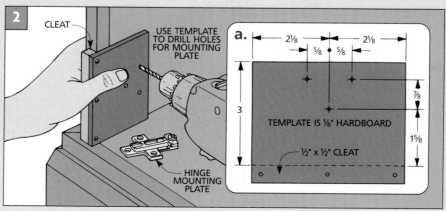

HINGED SLIDING DOOR

The hardware for a hinged sliding door is installed in almost the same way as the swinging door hinge explained on the opposite page. But, to allow it to slide inside the cabinet, the mounting plate is attached to a sliding roller mechanism. The roller unit (which acts much like a typical drawer slide) is then attached inside the cabinet.

The door is installed with two sliding roller mechanisms, one towards the top of the door and another one parallel to it at the bottom. To keep the door sliding smoothly into the cabinet, the upper and lower slides are connected by a wood follower strip *(Fig. 4)*.

INSTALL HINGE CUP. To mount the hardware, begin the same as for the swinging door *(Fig. 3)*. Locate the holes for each cup an equal distance from the end of the stile, and an equal distance from the outside edge. This second distance determines the gap between the door frame and the cabinet.

ATTACH SLIDES. After the hinge cups are installed, temporarily push the mounting plates (with roller slides

attached) onto the arms that extend from the hinge *(Fig. 4)*. Now cut a follower strip (DD) to tie the upper and lower slides together, and screw it to the mounting plates with woodscrews.

INSTALL SLIDES. Once the follower strips are in place, remove the slide assembly from each door so the slides can be mounted inside the cabinet.

To keep the roller slides aligned with the hinge cups on the door, they must be positioned properly in the cabinet. To make this easier, I use a spacer strip to hold the slides in place temporarily while screwing them to the cabinet *(Fig. 5)*.

GUIDE ROLLER. To keep the door sliding smoothly into the cabinet, a guide roller is screwed to the front edge of the cabinet shelf *(Fig. 6* and photo at right). As the door is opened, it pivots around this roller. Then, as the door slides inside, the roller keeps the door from slapping against the TV.

Now the hinges can be reattached to the mounting plates *(Fig. 7)*. Then final adjustments can be made to position the door in the opening.

Sliding Door Hardware. *A guide roller and sliding mechanism guide the TV doors back into the case.*

DOOR STOP. The first adjustment is to limit the distance the door can travel into the cabinet. A small stop block (EE) glued to the cabinet shelf will stop the door from sliding completely into the opening *(Fig. 5)*. This keeps the door pulls from hitting the front edge of the cabinet.

Finally, adjust the door for an equal gap all around. These adjustments are made by turning the screws in the two hinge parts *(Fig. 7)*.

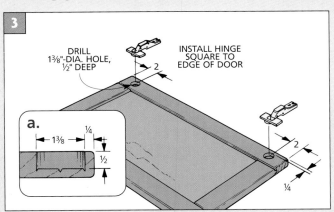

3
DRILL 1⅜"-DIA. HOLE, ½" DEEP
INSTALL HINGE SQUARE TO EDGE OF DOOR
2
2
¼
¼
a.
1⅜
¼
½

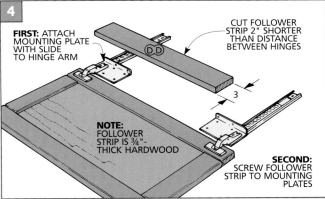

4
FIRST: ATTACH MOUNTING PLATE WITH SLIDE TO HINGE ARM
DD
CUT FOLLOWER STRIP 2" SHORTER THAN DISTANCE BETWEEN HINGES
3
NOTE: FOLLOWER STRIP IS ¾"-THICK HARDWOOD
SECOND: SCREW FOLLOWER STRIP TO MOUNTING PLATES

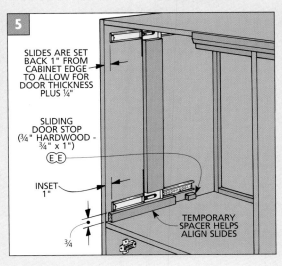

5
SLIDES ARE SET BACK 1" FROM CABINET EDGE TO ALLOW FOR DOOR THICKNESS PLUS ¼"
SLIDING DOOR STOP (¾" HARDWOOD - ¾" x 1")
EE
INSET 1"
¾
TEMPORARY SPACER HELPS ALIGN SLIDES

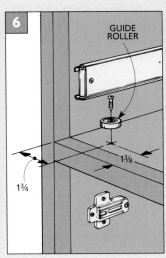

6
GUIDE ROLLER
1⅜
1¾

7
SIDE-TO-SIDE ADJUSTMENT
SLIDE HINGES INTO MOUNTING PLATES AND ADJUST DOOR TO FIT OPENING
IN-OUT ADJUSTMENT
UP-DOWN ADJUSTMENT

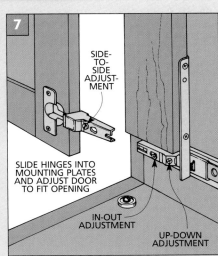

One of the first things we take into consideration when designing projects at *Woodsmith* is whether the hardware is affordable and easy to find.

You'll be able to find most of the hardware and supplies for the projects in this book at your local hardware store or home center. Sometimes, though, you may have to order hardware through the mail. If that's the case, we've tried to find reputable sources with toll-free phone numbers and web sites (see the Mail Order Sources box at right).

Note: We *strongly* recommend that you have all of your hardware and supplies in hand *before* you begin building any projects in this book. It can be discouraging to start a project and then find out that your hardware doesn't fit or is no longer available.

MAIL ORDER SOURCES

Some of the most important "tools" you can have in your shop are your mail order catalogs. The ones listed below are filled with special hardware, tools, finishes, lumber, and supplies that can't be found at a local hardware store or home centers. You should be able to find many of the supplies for the projects in this book in one or more of these catalogs. Many even offer online ordering.

Note: The information below was current when this book was printed. August Home Publishing does not guarantee these products will be available nor endorse any specific mail order company, catalog, or product.

THE WOODSMITH STORE

10320 Hickman Road
Clive, IA 50325
800-835-5084
www.woodsmithstore.com
Our own retail store with tools, jigs, router bits, books, and finishing supplies. Our hardware inventory includes concealed hinges, casters, catches, knobs, and fasteners. We don't have a catalog, but we do send out items mail order.

LEE VALLEY TOOLS LTD.

P.O. Box 1780
Oggensburg, NY 13669-6780
800-871-8158
www.leevalley.com
Several catalogs actually, with tools and hardware. In the tool and hardware catalog you'll find spoon-style shelf pins, a good variety of router bits, flocking, knobs, lazy Susan turntables, and CD holders.

ROCKLER WOODWORKING & HARDWARE

4365 Willow Drive
Medina, MN 55340
800-279-4441
www.rockler.com
A very good hardware catalog, including hinges, catches, casters, threaded inserts, Confirmat screws and connector bolts. Accessories include spindles, a variety of pulls, wood plugs, and zero-clearance inserts. You'll also find drawer guides, sliding door hardware, T-molding, CD holders, Roto-Hinges, full-extension drawer glides, and Mission-style hardware.

WOODWORKER'S SUPPLY

1108 North Glenn Rd.
Casper, WY 82601
800-645-9292
www.woodworker.com
A complete catalog packed with hardware supplies, power tools and accessories, figure-8 fasteners, finishing supplies and glues, Confirmat screws, connector bolts and more.

WOODCRAFT

560 Airport Industrial Park
P.O. Box 1686
Parkersburg, WV 26102-1686
800-225-1153
www.woodcraft.com
Almost everything you'd need, from layout to hardware to finishing supplies. A good selection of hinges, router bits, door and drawer hardware, and tools. You'll also find full-extension drawer glides and Mission-style hardware.

CONSTANTINES

1040 E. Oakland Park Blvd.
Ft. Lauderdale, FL 33334
800-443-9667
www.constantines.com
One of the original woodworking mail order catalogs. Find checkers, brass hinges, pulls, spring catches, threaded inserts, thumb screws, flocking, knobs, casters, magnetic catches, lazy Susan turntables, CD holders, figure-8 fasteners, wood plugs, shelf pins, self-adhesive felt dots, plus sliding door and drawer hardware. You'll also find a good selection of dowels and finishing supplies.

INDEX

AUGUST HOME
PUBLISHING COMPANY

President & Publisher: Donald B. Peschke
Executive Editor: Douglas L. Hicks
Project Manager: Craig L. Ruegsegger
Creative Director: Ted Kralicek
Art Director: Doug Flint
Senior Graphic Designers: Robin Friend, Chris Glowacki
Assistant Editor: Joel Hess
Editorial Intern: Cindy Thurmond
Graphic Designers: Jonathan Eike, Vu Nguyen

Designer's Notebook Illustrator: Chris Glowacki
Photographer: Crayola England
Electronic Production: Douglas M. Lidster
Production: Troy Clark, Minniette Johnson
Project Designers: Chris Fitch, Ryan Mimick, Ken Munkel, Kent Welsh
Project Builders: Steve Curtis, Steve Johnson
Magazine Editors: Terry Strohman, Tim Robertson
Contributing Editors: Vincent S. Ancona, Jon Garbison, Brian McCallum,
Bryan Nelson
Magazine Art Directors: Todd Lambirth, Cary Christensen
Contributing Illustrators: Harlan Clark, Mark Higdon, David Kreyling,
Erich Lage, Roger Reiland, Kurt Schultz, Cinda Shambaugh, Dirk Ver Steeg

Corporate V.P., Finance: Mary Scheve
Controller: Robin Hutchinson
Production Director: George Chmielarz
Project Supplies: Bob Baker
New Media Manager: Gordon Gaippe

For subscription information about
Woodsmith and *ShopNotes* magazines, please write:
August Home Publishing Co.
2200 Grand Ave.
Des Moines, IA 50312
800-333-5075
www.augusthome.com/customwoodworking

Oxmoor House®

Oxmoor House, Inc.
Book Division of Southern Progress Corporation
P.O. Box 2463, Birmingham, Alabama 35201

ISBN: 0-8487-2687-1
Printed in the United States of America

To order additional publications, call 1-800-765-6400.
For more books to enrich your life, visit **oxmoorhouse.com**